Search Engine Marketing

DATE			

About the Authors

Andreas Ramos develops and manages web marketing strategies for clients such as MIT and Aveda. He is a co-founder of and technical advisor to a number of Silicon Valley startups. He wrote one of the first books on web design in 1996. Andreas has worked at SGI, SUN Microsystems, and Brio, has a master's degree from the Universität Heidelberg, Germany, and speaks four languages. Andreas lives in Palo Alto, California. Visit him at www.Andreas.com.

Stephanie Ann Cota is an expert in e-commerce business and online marketing. Author of leading books, Stephanie works to educate and teach clients and students worldwide. Stephanie has conducted seminars on topics such as web analytics, integrated marketing, search engine optimization (SEO), online business models, and customer relationship management (CRM). Stephanie also runs The CCG Group, LLC, a search marketing agency in Palo Alto. Stephanie is a member of the Web Analytics Association and served on their Educational Certification Committee in partnership with the University of British Columbia. Stephanie holds a B.A. in Digital Media Art & Design as well as an E-Commerce Business Management Certificate from San Jose State University. Visit her at www.StephanieCota.com.

In 2005, Andreas Ramos and Stephanie Cota co-founded Position2, a VC-funded SEO/PPC company in Silicon Valley that grew to 65 staff employees. Andreas and Stephanie developed the company's strategies and processes.

In 2008, Stephanie and Andreas set up The CCG Group, Inc. to focus on analytics-driven marketing for clients. They are an Omniture Partner and a certified agency with Google, Yahoo!, Microsoft, and Facebook. Visit them at www.The-CCG-Group.com

Search Engine Marketing

Andreas Ramos

Stephanie Cota

New York Chicago San Francisco Lisbon
London Madrid Mexico City Milan New Delhi
San Juan Seoul Singapore Sydney Toronto

The **McGraw·Hill** Companies

Library of Congress Cataloging-in-Publication Data

Ramos, Andreas.
  Search engine marketing / Andreas Ramos, Stephanie Cota.
    p. cm.
  Includes index.
  ISBN 978-0-07-159733-3 (alk. paper)
  1. Internet marketing. 2. Web search engines. 3. Communication in marketing.
  4. Internet advertising. 5. Electronic commerce. I. Cota, Stephanie. II. Title.
  HF5415.1265.R357 2009
  658.8'72—dc22

                                                                        2008041748

McGraw-Hill books are available at special quantity discounts to use as premiums and sales promotions, or for use in corporate training programs. To contact a special sales representative, please visit the Contact Us page at www.mhprofessional.com.

Search Engine Marketing

1 2 3 4 5 6 7 8 9 0   FGR FGR   0 1 9 8

ISBN   978-0-07-159733-3
MHID   0-07-159733-6

Sponsoring Editor	Roger Stewart
Editorial Supervisor	Patty Mon
Project Manager	Harleen Chopra, International Typesetting and Composition
Acquisitions Coordinator	Carly Stapleton
Copy Editor	Bart Reed
Proofreader	Naomi Lynch
Indexer	Broccoli Information Management
Production Supervisor	Jean Bodeaux
Composition	International Typesetting and Composition
Illustration	International Typesetting and Composition
Art Director, Cover	Jeff Weeks
Cover Designer	Pattie Lee

We use Koi-Planet.com, a fictitious website, as an example. Koi-Planet.com sells koromo koi, a type of goldfish. Laura is a fictitious customer. We don't sell koi. We don't even own any koi. Just four goldfish.

In loving memory of Cassandra Sim

Contents at a Glance

Contents

Foreword

This is not the first book to explain web analytics, and it's certainly not the first book to cover search marketing, but it is the first book to bring analytics, online marketing, and traditional offline marketing together with a focus on using data to drive decision-making.

All too often I have seen people approach web analytics as an afterthought. Campaigns are created, an SEO strategy is implemented, keywords are bought, and eventually someone decides they need data so they implement analytics. After clicking around in reports, they give up because the reports didn't tell them how the site could be improved. Worse yet, the marketing efforts are not measured at all within the site because no planning was made for them.

An interesting analogy would be exploring the wilderness. We live in an age where you can hike through the woods for 8 hours, pull out your GPS, and it tells you exactly where you are. Marketers assume analytics works the same way: Pop open the screen and there you have it—dials and graphs and charts that tell you stuff.

Unfortunately, web analytics is much more like an old-fashioned map and compass. Like a compass, web analytics is not accurate, but it is directional. Like a map, it's sometimes hard to read, but if you pay attention to the way the terrain is changing and keep checking against the map, you can stay on course. Neither is going to help you much if you hike for 80 hours and only then glance at the map.

Before you set out, you need to know where you're going. You'll notice this book starts with a detailed breakdown of KPIs and only then gets into the specifics of how to use those to measure your online and offline campaigns. This approach is the single most important factor in planning an effective strategy. KPIs are *how you know you're on target with the business goals.* Web analytics is *how you make corrections if you're not on target.*

Using KPIs to measure and improve your business is the single most important decision you can make, and it has far-reaching consequences for all your marketing. Everything becomes quantifiable—whether PPC, SEO, or offline activity. Everyone can understand what drives your business because they can see the goals clearly and know how their activity moves a KPI. You're no longer lost in the woods.

—John Marshall
CTO, MarketMotive.com
Founder and ex-CEO of ClickTracks Analytics

Acknowledgments

We thank the following people for valuable suggestions and discussions (listed alphabetically): Craig DeNoce, Howard Dernehl, Adam Gordon, Eurydice Katzenjammer, Bruce Linn, Marilynn McGlynn, Bob Platkin, Richard Sachs, Rick Schaefer, Monie TenBroeck, and Jing Yan. Special thanks to Maggie Xin Guan, who knows Baidu.

The KPI chapter includes invaluable contributions from Roslyn Layton, MBA, who collaborates with us on marketing metrics and financial analytics, and Seann Birkelund, VP of Business Development at Education.com. We also thank Rajiv Parikh, MBA (Harvard) and CEO at Position2, along with the people in marketing, sales, and finance at Cisco, Microsoft, Yahoo!, Omniture, MIT, Unica, VendorRate, Aveda, GamesCampus, and other companies who discussed ideas, answered questions, and reviewed sections of this chapter.

We'd also like to thank the following people who've been open with information: Yuchun Lee, CEO of Unica; Kevin Cavanaugh, Vice President of Technology at Unica; Akin Arikan, Senior Segment Manager for Internet Marketing at Unica; Christopher Parkin, Senior Director, Product and Solutions Marketing at Omniture; Wendy Wedlake, Account Executive at Omniture; John Squire, Chief Strategy Officer at CoreMetrics; John Marshall, CTO of MarketMotive.com; Avinash Kaushik, Analytics Evangelist at Google; Shari Thurow, author of *Search Engine Visibility;* and our agency support teams at Google (RG, EH, LW, MD, JA, LH, GF), Yahoo! (MC and DC), and Microsoft (TR and NM).

This project was also made possible by a great team at McGraw-Hill: Roger Stewart, sponsoring editor, and Carly Stapleton, acquisitions coordinator.

Introduction

This book shows you how to use analytics to track, optimize, and manage results in both online and offline marketing campaigns according to your business goals. With the expansion of Google's advertising services into radio, TV, newspapers, and PDAs, you can use analytics to manage your multichannel marketing and sales campaigns. Analytics, SEO, and PPC are not technical issues. These are business issues. We show you how to use these tools to increase your leads and sales.

Audience

This book is for VPs, directors, and managers in both online and offline marketing and sales. The book is also for those who manage a website, use SEO, or manage PPC campaigns.

Why We Wrote This Book

In our previous books, we didn't tell the best secrets. We know nearly all the authors of the top SEM books; they don't tell everything either. They hold back their best secrets.

No more. We've decided to tell all. Everything is here for you. Strategies and techniques we've developed over the years, all the good stuff, and, yes, lots of Google secrets. This is a click-and-tell book. We spill the beans. Sing like a bird. Open the kimono. Pull back the curtains on the wizard.

Why are we doing this? We've learned it's okay to tell our clients everything. They want to know what's going on, so they trust us to help them manage their business.

So by telling everything, we can help

- **VPs and directors of sales and marketing**   With the move to digital media, major changes are happening. By learning how digital media works, people in sales and marketing can improve their profitability, grow their companies, and advance their careers.

- **Other SEO/PPC companies**   Many SEO/PPC companies don't have access to agency support teams. This book helps them improve their services.

- **The little companies**   We manage services for large corporations, but we also work with a few small companies: Andreas manages SEM for his three brothers (two lawyers and a shop owner); Stephanie manages the SEM for her mom (a bookkeeper). Our small customers do better because they get our Silicon Valley skills. There are millions of small companies in Europe, the United States, China, India, and South America. They can't afford the top agencies. However, our book lets the small shops compete against the big corps.

We want to take SEO and PPC out of the technical box and bring it to the top-line business level where it belongs. For many years, SEO, PPC, and analytics were managed by technical people. They understood technology but they didn't know business. Maybe they heard about ROI, but they didn't know about cost-per-lead, cost-per-acquisition, or breakeven points. This problem happens at Google itself; Google AdWords reports technical data, but has very little business reporting. Why? Because AdWords was built by engineers, not people in business or marketing.

By framing SEM as a business issue with a focus on business goals, we show you how to make multichannel SEM work for you.

For extra material, including links, case studies, and updates, visit our book's website at Insider-SEM.com. We welcome your feedback and comments. If you spot an error, please let us know so we can correct it for other readers.

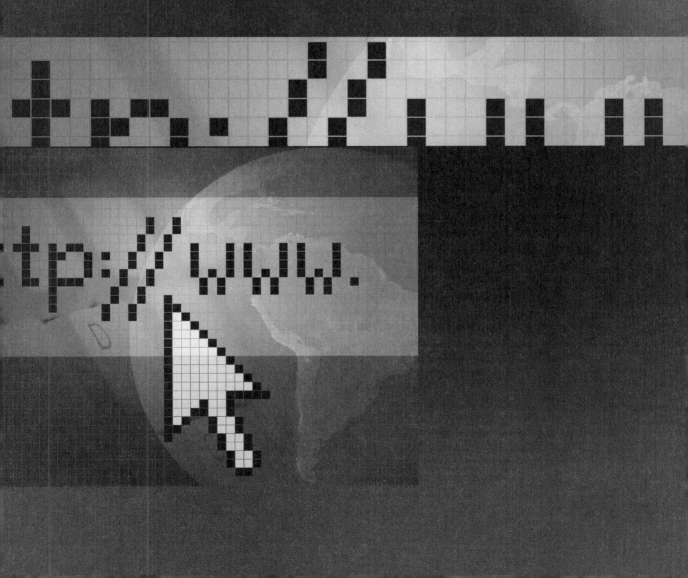

Chapter 1
Integrated Marketing

In this book, we will show that offline and online media are converging into digitized media. The ability of analytics to track and manage digitized marketing is turning traditional and online marketing into sales-performance marketing.

Just as you can track the results in paid search (pay-per-click or PPC), you can use analytics to track search engine optimization (SEO), PPC, link building, and bulk e-mail. And just like you can track PPC, you can use analytics to track marketing campaigns in other media, such as radio, TV, newspaper ads, printed coupons, direct mail, and so on. The customer response to all these forms of marketing can be captured by digital tools, which allow you to compare and manage those media.

We will also show you how to manage those campaign by using key performance indicators (KPIs). With a few simple numbers, you can compare campaigns against each other; you can drop the unprofitable campaigns, and you can increase the ones that produce profits.

Digitized media give the consumer a high degree of choice, which creates thousands of channels. Digital tools also allow the marketer to create and manage thousands of campaigns, each tailored and personalized to those channels.

Digitization of marketing presents opportunities for marketers. With analytics for better decision-making, marketers can grow a company's sales. They can also use analytics to prove their work. This moves the emphasis from branding-based marketing to performance-based marketing—namely, sales-based marketing. This means marketers can demand additional compensation such as bonus and commissions, similar to sales people.

What We Can Learn from Offline Marketing

Many of the basic ideas in marketing were developed by offline marketers. Marketing started in newspapers in the 1800s. In the twentieth-century, radio and TV were added. Marketers used direct marketing, database marketing, profiling, clustering, and segmentation. They qualified prospects and leads to make sales. For example, supermarkets developed inventory and sales tracking systems. At first, coupons were recorded by hand. As supermarkets computerized in the 70s and 80s, information was gathered at the point of purchase by an electronic device that read a coded ticket on the product. This recorded the product SKU, price, and amount. If customers used a loyalty card or credit card, the supermarket assigned a unique identifier to each customer. They learned customer preferences and built a large pool of data to extrapolate buying patterns. Supermarkets also used this data to print store receipts with coupon offers to sell related products, to repeat sales, or to sell new items. The data was also used for marketing decisions in advertising dollars, advertisement placement, inventory count, amount of shelf space, pricing, order placement, and product delivery. By combining scanner data with consumer interviews, supermarkets could calculate customer lifetime value (LTV).

In contrast, web marketing, which started with the dot-coms in the mid-90s, was often done by young computer people without experience in traditional marketing. In furious (and often destructive) evolution, web designers and web marketers tried many new things, such as banner ads, bulk e-mail, portals, advertising in search engines, and so on. Phases and fads were often measured in months. At the time, traditional marketing and web marketing didn't seem related because the underlying technologies were so different.

In the last few years, offline and online marketing have begun to converge. Tools from online marketing are being applied to offline marketing. Ideas and processes from offline marketing are being added to online marketing. With analytics, we can now track marketing down to the individual customer and sale, which means marketing is turning into sales. Digitized marketing is changing the nature of marketing.

In the 1960s, a U.S. advertiser could show four TV ads on two nights to reach 90% of the U.S. audience. Advertisers quickly learned they could show a TV commercial simultaneously on the three networks, so no matter where the viewer turned, they had to see the commercial. Every consumer had to pass through this *TV road block*.

To get the same 90% reach of the 1960s, it now takes 85 TV ads. There are now thousands of cable TV channels, newspapers, radio stations, billboards, and other ad formats, plus some ten billion pages on the Web.

Digitization changes both sides of a media:

- Digital technology offers consumers countless choices, so they consume media in literally thousands of forms. For example, when music is digitized, it can be heard on MP3 or iPod players. They can create their personal radio stations at Pandora.com. By digitizing news and using an RSS reader, they can easily scan dozens of newspapers each day. The Web allows them to visit companies anonymously, which puts them in charge of the media. Because there are thousands of free alternatives, media channels can't charge the customers (they can always find it free elsewhere). So the only way to monetize media is through advertising.

- On the other side of the coin, marketers can use digital tools to manage ad campaigns into those myriad channels. Digital tools allow segmentation, so markets can target specific audiences. Campaign management tools let the marketer create ads and manage dozens of placements. These tools also contain rules that trigger on certain conditions, which means marketing goes from a few campaigns per year to literally thousands of campaigns simultaneously.

The biggest benefit of digital media delivery is in advertising. Most media earn their money by displaying advertising. The bulk of newspaper and magazine revenues is based on advertising, not subscriptions. TV and radio are based entirely on advertising. By improving the ability to display advertising, the media channels can either earn more money or simply stay in business.

Web marketing itself is evolving. Several years ago, SEO and PPC were the main issues in search marketing. Tracking was done with web stats packages that simply read the server log files to report the total number of visitors, number of viewed pages, time-on-page, and other basic data. PPC was trackable because Google included simple reporting tools. SEO for the most part was untrackable, and many assumed it was a form of public relations (PR).

Today, this model has flipped around. Analytics is now the main issue. Digital media send data to the analytics. This includes PPC (Yahoo!, Google, Microsoft), SEO, banner ads, bulk e-mail, and so on. The traditional media (radio, TV, and print) have been digitized and added into the data stream. All of these marketing channels feed data into analytics.

Analytics is used to study and manage these channels. The various digital campaigns feed data into the analytics tool. Analytics can show and compare the results of a campaign: where the converting traffic came from, how much it cost per lead, how much it cost per sale, the value per visitor, and so on. Because analytics can compare campaigns, analytics is turning into a business tool to manage channels on the basis of your business goals and results. We use analytics to answer two questions: What is going on? What can we do about it? You decrease (or shut down) the campaigns that don't perform. You increase the campaigns that produce profits.

Google's Role in the Digitization of Analog Media

The most significant driver of this revolution in digital marketing has been Google. Although other companies invented PPC and analytics, Google popularized these tools. Google AdWords was easy to use and it worked better than the other services, so hundreds of thousands of advertisers used it for their campaigns. The tool allowed advertisers to pay only if someone clicked on the ad, and the tool reported the cost-per-click down to the penny. As a result, advertisers learned to manage campaigns by the numbers. They learned marketing could be trackable.

By 2007, Google reached the limits of PPC. With close to 90% market share, there isn't much more growth for Google in online marketing. So Google began to expand into other media markets. They developed tools similar to AdWords that let you place advertising in AM/FM radio. You select a radio station in a city, you upload a sound clip, you place a bid, and your ad plays on AM radio. With Google's bulk purchase of radio ad minutes, you can place ads on the radio for as little as $2.14 per ad play.

Through Google, you can also place ads in TV. This includes hundreds of video channels, such as CNN, MSNBC, and Animal Planet. You upload a video clip, select the markets, place the bids, and your ad campaign is on TV. Google is also going after the newspaper market. Through Google's tools, you can place ads in hundreds of newspapers, including *The New York Times* and newspapers in smaller cities. Google is also rolling out tools for advertising on mobile devices, such as cell phones and PDAs. These new tools will change the old media.

Google has also added an analytics package to help advertisers study and manage the results. Marketing now wants more tools. They want to go further into the data. This includes enterprise-level analytics, automated marketing rules, business intelligence, data mining, predictive modeling, and so on. Other companies offer these advanced tools.

The Limits of Traditional Media in a Fragmented Marketing World

Analog media were unable to track sales with certainty. Radio, TV, and newspapers used polls, such as Nielsen rating services, to establish statistical models about their audience. By calling people or using viewer diaries, they could establish that on Monday afternoon, Channel 4 had 10,000 viewers. But this produced only aggregate numbers. The connection of views to sales couldn't be tracked. Traditional medias had to guess at the viewer's intent.

TV stations didn't know if the show was being watched. They had no idea if the TVs were turned on or if people were sitting in front of them. Radio could broadcast music, but they didn't know if people were listening at all. Newspapers could only track the sales and subscriptions. They knew they printed 100,000 copies and they knew 80,000 were delivered to homes and another 20,000 were sold at newsstands. But they had no idea if anyone actually read these. The same problem existed for magazines, mail order, and billboards.

The best they could do was track sales by using coupons. An advertiser places a coupon in a newspaper and by Tuesday, they know 5000 coupons were redeemed. That's about all they can know. Another 10,000 people could have clipped out the coupon, but never came to the store. Another 20,000 people could be interested, but also didn't come to the store. The advertiser can only track coupons that are redeemed. They can't track other information that could improve the campaign.

Using Unique URLs and Tracking Codes

To track traditional media such as radio or TV with digital tools, you send the visitor to a web page. In your radio or TV ad, you include a unique URL that is easy to remember and relevant to the campaign. Visitors go to their laptops or PDAs and use web browsers to reach the URL. At that web page, analytics and other tracking tools can record the visits, actions, conversions, and so on.

If your URL is difficult to spell or remember, you can register several URLs that are easier to spell. Use the names of seasons or months (such as KoiSummer.com or KoiJuly.com) or cities and states (KoiAtlanta.com). You can use these for various campaigns. You can also use unique URLs for each media. To track the results from TV and radio, send the TV views to KoiSummer.com and the radio listeners to KoiJuly.com.

You can use unique URLs with newspaper classified ads, TV commercials, radio commercials, billboards, direct mail, magazine coupons, bumper stickers, and so on. Any form of advertising can display a URL. You can even use unique URLs on the Goodyear blimp and track the visits and sales at the website.

An additional step is to use *301-redirects,* which redirect the visitor from a URL to another website. If you don't want to build several websites, you can set up the unique URLs and use 301-redirects (a few lines of code at the server) to send the visitors to your main website.

The Buying Cycle and the Moment of Purchase

The goal of marketing is to focus advertising at the active target audience to reach them at the moment they decide to buy. This reduces the cost of advertising and increases the likelihood of success. Digital marketing allows the advertiser to reach the consumer at the moment the consumer decides to buy.

Let's look at the steps involved in buying. When someone buys a product, they go through a process known as the *buying cycle,* which has four phases: awareness, research, comparison, and purchase. In general, consumers first become aware of a need or desire. They then research the market and compare the products. They finally select what they want and purchase the product. (Depending on the researcher and market, this is also called the marketing cycle, purchase cycle, sales cycle, purchase path, buying funnel, and similar concepts, and these have three to seven phases.)

For example, Laura is looking at her yard, and she would like a pond with fish. She thinks off and on about this for a few days. This is the *awareness-of-need phase.* Laura begins to ask friends and family about fish ponds. She slowly realizes that she needs a fish pond with a filter and pump. She learns about fish and finds that large Japanese fish called koi would be best. She talks with coworkers and neighbors. She begins to use the Web and search engines. She is in the *research phase.* Finally, after several weeks, she has narrowed it down to the general type of pump and the breed of koi. Immersible or external pump? Asagi or koromo koi? She *compares the products.* Finally, she knows what she wants (it fits her yard, her needs, her budget, and her tastes) and Laura turns to the Web to find a vendor who can deliver what she wants. This is the *purchase phase.*

In the awareness, research, and comparison phases, Laura isn't ready to buy. She is learning about the products. She is looking for information. She will ignore ads and "buy now" pages. In the purchase phase, Laura has decided what she wants. She knows the make, model, and features. She also knows the price. She won't pay attention to other products. She is looking for a vendor who can reliably deliver her selection.

The length of the buying cycle depends on the product or service. For low-cost consumer products, this may be a few days. For large purchases, this can take a month or so. For industrial equipment, this can take six months or more. For real estate, this can take six years or more.

Interview: Bob Platkin, Director of Marketing

Bob Platkin is perhaps best known to the American public for having repositioned two major brands in the 1980s. He turned A.1. Steak Sauce into a condiment for hamburgers. He also developed the marketing strategy for the famous Grey Poupon mustard TV commercials, where two wealthy men in a Rolls-Royce "pass the Grey Poupon." Bob has held senior marketing positions at Nabisco/Heublein (A.1. Steak Sauce, Grey Poupon mustard, Smirnoff), Stanley Works, Colt Firearms, the American Can Co. (Northern Tissue), and Ted Bates Advertising (Colgate-Palmolive). Bob founded Urbina Design, an electric appliance company, and continues to consult with companies in marketing strategies.

Q: What was the story behind Grey Poupon? Why did you take that approach?

A: Grey Poupon mustard was a sleepy niche item on the gourmet shelves at supermarkets. They advertised in the three leading high-end gourmet magazines. It was sold as an ingredient for gourmet recipes. The product had a nice 5%–10% growth every year.

We found we had 90% distribution in supermarkets but only reached 30% of households. My strategy was to sell Grey Poupon mustard for sandwiches and hot dogs. This was very bold. They had an extremely profitable product, but I was telling them to mass-market it.

We relaunched the product as a condiment. Don't talk about white wine. Don't show French recipes. We made it into an everyday spread for sandwiches. We even did ads with "haute dogs." To get the public familiar with it, we put it in airline in-flight meals. Grey Poupon took off at about 20% annual growth and didn't stop growing for a decade.

Q: How did you grow A.1. Steak Sauce?

A: We forced distribution through advertising to create a demand for A.1. Steak Sauce. Normally, you don't force distribution through advertising. A company would first get their product distributed and then do advertising to sell the product, not the other way around.

We put coupons in the Sunday papers. By creating demand, supermarkets had to stock it. By tracking each coupon's unique ID, we could calculate the marketing costs. We used the data to tune the numbers to reflect reality. We didn't have computers. We didn't even have spreadsheets. This was all done by hand with pocket calculators.

To keep things manageable, we started in one city. After two months, we had revenue. We used the profits to expand to the next city. We also used our data to calculate customer lifetime value. We compared customers who bought a second time to those who only bought it once. By knowing the volume of repeat business, we could sell the product to stores in the next city. We used data to continuously improve our process and grow big in a very short time.

A.1. Steak Sauce had been known as a steak sauce, so we repositioned it for hamburgers. People put it on hamburgers and felt like, "Hey, I'm eating steak!"

Another company was Stanley Tools. Stanley tools were sold in Wal-Mart. Every Monday morning, Wal-Mart gave large spreadsheets to the executives, including myself. I would analyze why a product didn't do well in a region. On the converse, products that did sell well were quickly replenished. We looked at the variables, isolated the leading causes, and tried to solve those. We used Wal-Mart Retail Link, which was their analytics and sales performance tool. It used SKU numbers and checkout scanner data.

Q: What is the difference between marketing then and now?

A: Back then, if you had the money, you were king. By creating *TV road blocks* (i.e., buying up all of the ads on prime time, which forced everyone to see your ad and also kept your competitors out of the picture), the retailers had to stock you!

Google is like the TV road blocks of the 1980s. By being at the top of just three search engines (Google, Yahoo!, and Microsoft), you get access to over 98% of your market.

Back in the 80s, supermarkets and retailers were formidable barriers to entry. To sell your product, you had to get into the supermarkets. Google obliterated them. Anyone can set up a website, run an online campaign in Google, and be in business.

What's even better is when you show up in the unpaid results. When people are looking for information and they find you in the unpaid listings, they will consider your site to be authoritative.

You can also buy keywords, banner ads, video, and so on to create repetition. If you dominate the paid advertising space in your market or industry, you can spend the majority of your budget to get a good market that is ready to purchase. This expands your customer base, making you yet bigger.

Q: Can you give us some tips about marketing?

A: The share of advertising matched the share of the market. If you had enough money, you could buy your market share. If your ad budget was 40% of the overall market's ad budget, you'd end up with 40% of the market. Madison Avenue gave you money to blow, and it worked! Great advertisers could take an everyday product and quickly turn it in a million-dollar success. Most of your advertising went to positioning.

We figured out the unique selling point (USP). The USP is the features and benefits that distinguish a company. For example, your research found that the three most important factors for your product were flavor, texture, and price. Now if your competitor was advertising on flavor, you couldn't advertise on flavor because your money would end up supporting your competitor. It would be better for you to advertise on texture.

Another thing: If you advertise on flavor, then your product must support the advertising. If you say your product is crispier than the others, then it must be crispier and appear crispier. If it's not, the public will reject your campaign.

A company can have a single message for a product. Advertisers can create the image for the product. For example, Volvo created the concept of safety. With a huge propaganda campaign and countless repetition, they make safety seem like a real issue. People buy Volvo because the car is "safe." Volvo owns this market now.

Repetition is important. After three or four times, a person remembers an ad. This is why the marketers threw large budgets at the product's positioning.

Don't spread yourself too thin. Control the message at a micro level to dominate niches until you are a share leader in one market channel and use the profits to dominate the next marketing channel. Bootstrap until you have substantial profits, then go for mass market.

Integrated Marketing: The New Approach

Integrated marketing is the use of two or more marketing channels to sell a product or service. The same message is sent via multiple marketing channels, such as web, radio, TV, and postal mail. By using several channels, you widen the exposure of a company's brand or product.

With integrated marketing, you create a product message that is both consistent with and relevant to the target customer. You can produce campaigns with unified messaging for TV, radio, Web, and newspaper print ads. The keywords, the unique selling proposition (USP), the messaging, the look, the sound, and the customer can all be unified into a broad ad campaign that works in multiple channels.

Today, a marketing team can use software from Unica or Omniture to launch and manage literally thousands of campaigns. By switching to digital technology, we can begin to track data. Thus the field of analytics came into play. At first, there were simple web stats packages that allowed the IT team to manage websites by raw aggregate numbers. They tracked visits, page views, and similar, to see if they had to add more capacity. Marketing and sales took over the websites, and they needed tools to track sales. As a result, the first business analytics tools were created. In the last year, analytics has undergone rapid evolution. The ability to track websites and PPC can be expanded into other digital campaigns.

The ability of analytics to track results is being extended into these media. With unique URLs, PURLs, and tracking URLs, you can now track sales, cost-per-action (CPA), and return on investment (ROI) in radio, TV, and print just as in PPC. Soon, the consumption of nearly all media will be IP-based. This allows tracking of distribution and consumption. This also allows campaign results to be compared against each other.

The goal for marketers is to optimize the customer's experience. This means giving your customer what they want, when they want it, in the media form they want it in. This is the way for businesses to open the pocketbooks of their customers.

Digital marketing strategies may include the following tools:

- **Analytics**   Software to track and analyze the results of marketing campaigns. It allows segmentation and profiling of customers. Companies include Omniture, Unica, Coremetrics, and Google Analytics.

- **PPC (pay-per-click or paid search)**   Ad services by the major search engines that let you place ads on the search results pages.

- **Multivariate testing (MTV)**   Software that allows you to create and test permutations of your web pages to find the version that performs best. MVT is offered by companies such as Offermatica and Optimost.

- **Targeted messaging**   Using databases, analytics, behavioral targeting, and customer profiles to send targeted messages.

- **Business intelligence (BI)**   Software that collects and presents the company's sales and financial activity.

- **CRM**   Software to track customers, such as Salesforce and Sugar CRM

Marketing can be digitized. This means it can be quantified and rationalized. New advertising, enabled by digitization and digital tools (analytics, multivariate testing, and so on), allows *integrated marketing* across multiple channels.

Previously a small marketing team could only carry out and manage several dozen ad campaigns. Now they can execute and manage several hundred campaigns simultaneously. The tools can collect and analyze massive amounts of data in multiple dimensions. You use analytics to study the data. You use KPIs to guide your efforts. Digitized marketing can be tracked, so marketing is evolving into sales. Marketing channels are now turning into sales channels. With the ability to compare the various channels and by knowing the KPIs, a company can test channels to find the ones that produce profits. Once they know which ones work, they can turn up the volume by focusing more of their budget on the top-performing channels.

In online marketing, due to advancements in web analytics and BI technologies, we know about our visitors. We know where they come from (approximate or specific location as well as any referring sites or search engines such as Google), what they are looking for by the keywords they type in, what they show interest in, and so on. We can add to a Claritas demographic profile which tells us about our market's lifestyle and behaviors.

Because digital technology allows tracking, Directors, VPs, SVPs, and CMOs are expected to show and describe the results of their marketing efforts. They have to boil down many scenarios with many outcomes into clear wins and present this to upper management. *Sales-marketing* is about generating as well as increasing revenue for your company. Think about how to tell those stories around your big wins as well as incremental wins.

There are a couple of ways to increase revenue. You can market to your target audience or you can find new market opportunities. A number of tools enable this.

To reach customers in a highly fragmented world, marketers must learn how to deliver their messages across many channels. For example, a company selling koi fish can advertise through e-mail lists, radio, web banners, SEO, and paid search (PPC). This will generate the traffic to your business.

Applying an end-to-end strategic approach, coupled with business processing rules, to your prospects focuses your traffic to deliver meaningful and well-qualified prospects, leads, and customers. This method is also referred to as *strategic marketing*. Through this, you deliver value to your prospects and customers.

Because the majority of a business's prospects prefer to visit the business's website first before engaging in any purchases, it is critical to apply web analytics to help them solve for their needs. Furthermore, analytics can be applied to your current customer database or CRM system to identify new market opportunities and to sell more products and services to customers based on what they may need.

As a business marketer, it is your responsibility to develop a data mining and segmentation strategy. This helps your teams divide up the customer base into smaller, understandable categories. From this, your teams should be launching new campaigns based on the method of listening to and processing the messages your customers are sending. This cycle repeats over and over in a continuous fashion to improve the sales-marketing process.

The advertiser displays a message at the audience through multiple marketing channels. These channels can include search engines, radio, TV, and newspapers. Each of these channels points the viewer to a unique URL. The URLs have tracking code so the analytics can capture data on origin, location, keywords, and so on. Analytics tools can use rules to manage decisions. The rules can use visitor ID, such as IP address, cookies, e-mail login ID, or loyalty card ID. For example, if the visitor came via TV, a video can be offered. Visitors who use their cell phones to visit the unique URL can be shown content that is formatted for mobile devices.

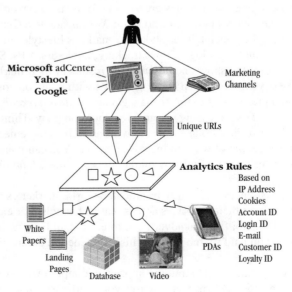

Manage Integrated Marketing with Enterprise Marketing Management (EMM)

Automated marketing is known as *enterprise marketing management (EMM)*. This is also called marketing resource management (MRM) and marketing operations management (MOM). EMM uses various tools to manage marketing strategies and tactics. This can include analytics, campaign management, automated reports, dashboards, lead management, event-driven marketing, predictive modeling, and more.

EMM is used in marketing to reduce costs, increase productivity, and grow revenue. Companies can identify and act on customer activities. Marketers can collaborate across teams and with their external agencies to launch and manage complex marketing campaigns. EMM includes:

- Analytics to understand and anticipate customer behavior

- Event-detection to track and respond to customers

- Campaign management to carry out timely, consistent communications with customers

- Lead management to track leads

- Marketing resource management (MRM) to manage budgets, creative production, marketing content, and other resources

Generally implemented as an integrated solution, EMM reduces time-to-market through automation, improves customer targeting through analytics, and proves the profit value of marketing through closed-loop measurement and reporting. Two vendors with integrated marketing solutions are Unica and Omniture.

Unica and Omniture

Unica and Omniture, both have analytics tools with automated decision-making, but they approach the market from different directions and they offer different solutions:

- Unica starts from offline marketing, so their tools are based on the needs of multichannel marketing. Unica includes analytics, segmentation, propensity scoring, lifetime value prediction, predictive modeling, resource management, automated decision-making, dashboards, and tracking. Unica has the most complete EMM solution on the market. Forrester Research ranks Unica as the clear market leader in EMM, both in terms of execution and completeness of vision. It also has the strongest offering and strategy of any EMM vendor. Unica's platform is Affinium NetInsight.

- Omniture approaches the market from web marketing, so it is focused on analytics tools. It includes tools to automatically manage PPC, multivariate testing, data warehousing, and behavioral targeting. Omniture is evolving from analytics to business optimization software. It can measure customer trends, enable appropriate analysis for the various levels of users in a company, automate processes, and optimize the customer experience. Omniture's analytics software is known as Omniture SiteCatalyst.

Both of these companies offer extensive support and service, including consulting services.

Seven Tips from Unica

Here are seven tips for integrated marketing from Unica.

Set up your online segmentation strategy based on visitor usage and activity. In this case, the audience is divided up into four segments: couch potatoes (they don't participate in blogs or other user activities), readers, critics, and content creators. As shown next, you can compare these groups to find which one produces the most value by engagement, conversions, and revenue.

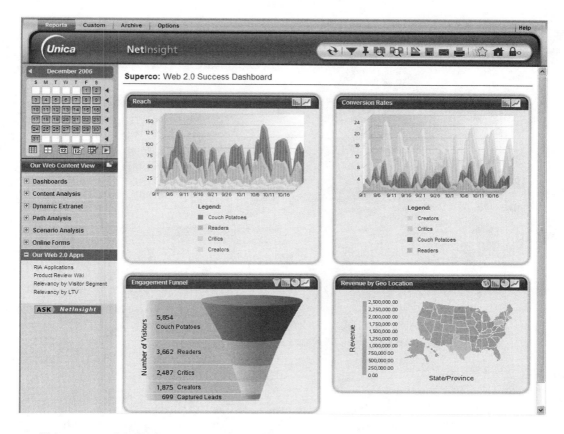

Using your sales database, you can identify new market opportunities across medium and high-value lifetime visitors. You can explore the results from keywords, referrers, locations, and content segmentation, as shown next.

Remember, customers are not defined by clicks alone. Look for groups of customers and try to find additional similar customers.

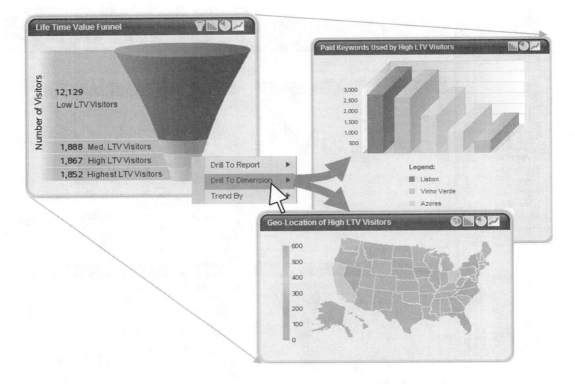

Use event triggers to manage bids and campaigns. You can set up rules to trigger campaigns based on visitor actions, as shown next. If they abandon the shopping cart, send them a tailored offer. If they buy, send them an up-sell offer or additional services. Make offers that are relevant or valuable to your customer.

Use cross-channel campaigns to reach customers, as shown next. For example, a visitor comes to your website and browses the pages for bicycles. Do you show them additional ads for bicycles? You find that they

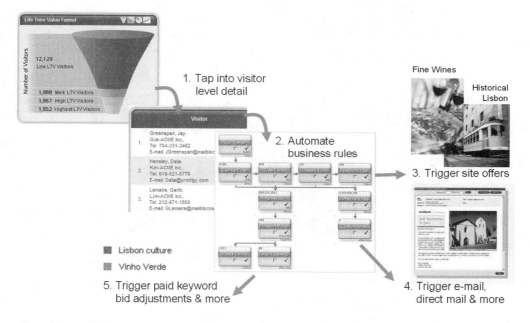

clipped out a newspaper coupon and came to the store and bought a kayak. You use the data from one channel in another channel; you now show the visitor online ads for kayak accessories, including paddles, vests, and so on.

Look at why your customers go away, as shown next. Often, site optimizers experiment with different layouts, colors, call-to-actions, messaging, and so on. But sometimes, you'll find these site optimization experiments won't keep customers. Customers buy because they find something is useful and valuable. Offer them highly targeted and relevant retention offers. Turn your marketing campaigns into a service for your customer by matching your offer to what your customer is interested in.

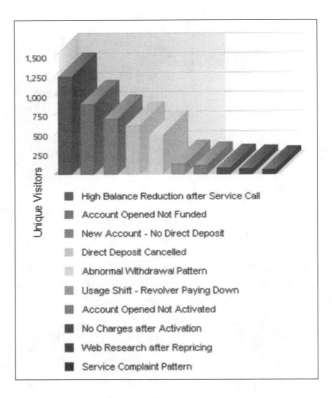

Use site map overlays. These show you where the customers are clicking. As you can see next, Unica and Omniture's site overlay shows you the profitability of the links so you can restructure your website to maximize profits.

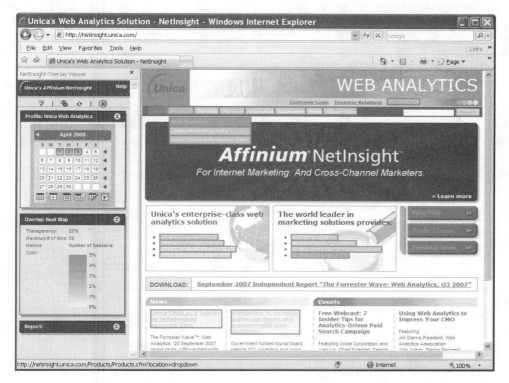

Use the reporting tools to create questions about your data, as shown next. You can use predefined questions or create your own. Once your question is built, views and reports are created on the fly for analysis and decision-making.

Interview: Yuchun Lee, CEO of Unica

Yuchun Lee cofounded Unica in 1992. Over 600 companies use Unica for their EMM. Yuchun Lee holds degrees in electrical engineering and computer science from MIT and an MBA from Babson College. Mr. Lee is the CEO of Unica.

Q: What is integrated marketing? How do you define it?

A: Integrated marketing is a process by which all communications and marketing programs delivered to a customer or prospect are relevant and consistent. This applies whether the communications are offline or online, inbound or outbound.

Online marketing channels include any e-marketing campaigns or programs, from search engine optimization (SEO), pay-per-click, affiliate, e-mail, banner, to the latest web-related channels for webinar, blog, RSS, podcast, and Internet TV. Offline marketing channels are traditional print (newspaper, magazine), mail order, public relations, industry analyst relations, billboard, radio, and television.

Unica's enterprise marketing management (EMM) technology delivers a complete platform for integrated marketing. It is uniquely based on a system of record for marketing, which you can think of as institutional memory for the marketing organization. The system of record brings together marketing assets, such as creatives, reports, budgets, and business definitions (for example, customer segments and best practices) so that marketers can manage their creation and usage, rapidly assemble them to execute different programs, and measure performance. This free flow of accurate, up-to-date information speeds marketing execution, reduces mistakes, boosts productivity through automation and reuse, and enables faster, better decisions.

EMM helps companies manage their marketing campaigns, programs, and activities across time and across channels. In that respect, all those pieces work together to help marketers better address the needs of the customer through whatever channel the customer wants, ensuring sensitivity to customer preferences and consistency of message delivery. This is what integrated marketing and EMM are all about.

Q: Can you give a few examples of EMM? How does the customer experience this? How does it work for the company?

A: Marketing is more complex than any other part of an enterprise in terms of the different kinds of processes it requires. If you have 1000 sales people in a company, they're pretty much doing the same thing. If you have 50 marketers, they are doing 200 different things. The key thing to understand is that EMM enables the automation of dozens and dozens of different marketing processes, which taken holistically add up to what we call "enterprise marketing management."

Let's talk about some of the things EMM solves. From an analytics perspective, we have customers, such as Lands' End, who use our technology to automate their direct mailings. Lands' End has hundreds of versions of their catalogs. Depending on who you are, you get a special version that is designed to appeal to your interests. Our technology helps them manage the mailings of those catalogs and to assess the effectiveness of their catalog versions and targeting strategies. An online example is Monster.com, who automates the execution of over 1,000,000 targeted e-mails per day based on job seeker preferences and behavior.

Another example is to look at the different marketing processes and tools that marketers manage: signage, local advertising, store openings, events, etc. All of these activities have multiple moving parts. Customers use our software to define and store information about these activities so that every time they open a new store, it's the same process, including the same approval process and workflow. If you look at a company like Lowe's, which has regular Sunday newspaper inserts, they need to determine which products get promoted, their placement within the insert, the graphics and the approval for those graphics, the prices, and so on. This can involve several hundred people working in different countries. They use Unica software to help streamline and coordinate these complex processes. By and large, EMM helps companies solve their mission-critical problems in marketing, and that's what it's all about.

Q: What is integrated analytics? How do you define it?

A: Analytics are a key part of integrated marketing. If you look at the core marketing processes, they consist of analysis of customers and data, planning of marketing budgets and resources, production and design, including message development, execution of programs and campaigns, and measurement of results. So there are five steps: analysis, planning, production, execution and measurement. Analytics is a vital step in these marketing processes. Integrated analytics, in our view, spans time and channels. It allows marketers to analyze customers in a holistic fashion, synchronizing data about their lifestyle and their preferences, the permissions they've given, their purchase and interaction history. Truly integrated analytics enables companies to develop and deliver marketing messages that are so timely and relevant they feel like a valued service to their customers.

Q: How does Unica deal with a company's existing analytics tool? Is it a layer on top of the analytics?

A: It depends on the type of analytics tool and the company's situation. Unica offers a wide range of capabilities , including reporting, web analytics, predictive modeling, event detection, and real-time analytics for delivering personalized offers during web and call center interactions. While many companies often have existing capabilities in some of these areas, they are often isolated, complex applications that are not fully integrated into their marketing operations. Unica can help in two ways. In some instances, we integrate with existing capabilities. For example, we have many customers that use SAS to build predictive models. These models can be used within our overall marketing automation solution to help segment and optimize campaigns. In other situations, companies find that their legacy analytics capabilities are too complex and costly to maintain and integrate. As a result, we see companies adopting our analytics capabilities because of their ease of use, functional capabilities, and integration within our EMM suite.

Q: Google Analytics is free. What's the business case for graduating to a larger package? The CEO wants to know why she should spend good money for another tool.

A: Anytime you can get something for free, it's probably worth considering. Google Analytics is a standalone application that provides basic reporting, but it lacks segmentation and integration capabilities. We believe that site analytics delivers significantly more business insights when you are able to integrate all your critical online and back office data. You are also able to act more effectively on these insights when your web analytics solution is part of an integrated marketing platform.

Q: At what size can a company start to apply EMM? At how many customers or what level of revenue does it become appropriate?

A: We find that companies with at least $30 million in annual revenue have the business need and marketing budget to invest in EMM. We do see smaller web-centric companies investing in our site analytics solution because of the mission-critical nature of their sites. But in general our range of companies is from $30 million to the largest companies in the world. If you look around the U.S., there are about 25,000 companies in that range. Globally it's about 50,000 companies to be very conservative. It's a pretty big market.

Q: What's the ideal size of the team?

A: We often see teams of about 50 to 100 people in the marketing organization, but we have some customers effectively leveraging our EMM capabilities with teams as small as five or six people. Smaller teams tend to focus on our marketing automation capabilities while larger teams also gain significant benefit from our collaboration and workflow management capabilities.

Q: What about Web 2.0? Analytics was based on the Web 1.0 model and tracking of page-by-page click activity. But Web 2.0 sites are actually an application, not a website. Is it a mistake to apply Web 1.0 analytics to Web 2.0? Do we need an entirely new approach to Web 2.0 sites?

A: There's a common tactical issue that companies must address in web analytics around page tagging vs. event tagging for Web 2.0 content. Event tagging is technically straightforward in most analytics tools, but marketers do need to determine what events should be captured for analysis. There is a tendency to "just capture everything," but too many client-side analytics events can impact a user's experience on your site, which negates one of the big reasons people are deploying Web 2.0 interface technologies.

The bigger issue we see with Web 2.0 is a change in paradigm around how consumers interact with a company. Media fragmentation has made it increasingly challenging for marketers to get their messages across. Then there is the networking effect that happens in the Web 2.0 world. It's the social network that's influencing people and their perception of companies and brands. Power has shifted to the consumer, and their individual experiences of your brand—both positive and negative—can easily echo across the Web. This viral effect is something that marketers also seek to leverage with compelling and innovative viral campaign strategies. These changing paradigms impact what you need to measure and place a premium on understanding your customer's experience of your company both directly and indirectly.

Q: One of the problems with Web 2.0 is the lack of a clear business model, which means a lack of clear KPIs. How would you address this?

A: Business models and appropriate metrics are still evolving around Web 2.0. But remember, any time you spend marketing money, you can establish performance objectives or you can treat it as more of a branding activity. A lot of marketers would tell you that marketing cannot be measured. I personally don't believe that's true. I think that you can often find proxies to assess your marketing efforts. We are seeing the world move more toward *measurable marketing*. I think Web 2.0 media and its linkage to web analytics as a technology is the perfect example of why people want to measure usage and apply metrics that range from engagement to more specific ROI models where appropriate. I can tell you that Web 2.0 media is much more measurable than television, but not nearly measurable enough when compared to other types of marketing campaigns, such as keyword search, paid search, and organic search. It depends on how your company defines measurement and how strongly the CFO wants exact numbers from the CMO. Ten years from now—or sooner—CMOs are going to have to justify marketing spend across all channels and media types.

Q: In the event of a recession, what would you recommend to Web 2.0 sites?

A: One strategy would be to do more with what you have. Another is to invest in technology that offers a strong measurable ROI. Let me give you an example. In the last recession there was a major retailer who had 26 projects. After the first year, only two projects got funded. Our project was one of them because it had measurable ROI. If you spend $1 you will get $5 back.

Q: Where do you think cross-channel analytics vs. web analytics is going in the next few years?

A: I believe that web analytics as a standalone market will eventually disappear. As a result, I think there are three trajectories for web analytics technologies going forward. One trajectory is for web analytics to be an integral part of an e-commerce platform where people are opening up online stores. The second is for web analytics to be absorbed into the more general category of business intelligence using analytics to interpret business data, not just for the website but for the business as a whole. The third trajectory is for web analytics to be part of a marketing suite because a website is a very integral part of the marketing organization in many industries. Our view is that web analytics as a technology needs to be an integral part of EMM. We think web analytics will be a key component of cross-channel analytics and we are seeing clear signs from marketing buyers who believe this, too.

Q: Why is cross-channel marketing important today?

A: The Internet has affected the way a company communicates with the customer and has facilitated a shift of power to the customer. To be effective as a marketer, there are two things you have to do. You have to be relevant to the customer, and you have to be consistent across channels. If you don't have an integrated cross-channel marketing framework, you can't accomplish this.

Q: The Web gave us online marketing, which has been a new form of marketing for the last ten years. EMM and cross-channel marketing merge online marketing and offline marketing. Will the Web become "just another media"?

A: Think of the Web as another channel. If you look at handheld devices or e-mail, they each have their own pluses and minuses. As an effective marketer, one has to figure out how to deliver messages to buyers effectively and consistently across these channels. It's a mistake to view the Web as something so special that it should be a siloed part of a company or something that you don't integrate with the rest of your interaction channels. Shopping, purchase, fulfillment, and service activity occur across a mix of channels and in different patterns depending on the customer. Effective marketing must operate holistically across channels to fulfill its promise of delivering timely and relevant messages and experiences.

Q: Asia and Europe are far ahead of the U.S. in cell phone use. They've moved from desktop computers to cell phones. They shop on their cell phones; they pay for services with their cell phones; they read books on their cell phones. With Apple's iPhone and the Google phone, we may finally get advanced cell phone services in the U.S. This allows geo-based marketing, plus in-store offers. Where are the opportunities for analytics on mobile devices?

A: I think there is a tremendous potential there. I think overall in Asia and Europe we are barely scratching the surface when it comes to providing a robust channel for communications between the company and the consumer. The Internet and mobile phone infrastructures are on a five- to ten-year convergence course. These two infrastructures will converge, and one will carry the other's traffic so there will be no difference between them.

Once that happens, the phone becomes a very interesting channel for marketers and individuals. Not only can it enable instant messaging and e-mail, it also offers an Internet browser. Plus, it's also a geographically enabled device. But, unlike a computer, which can be shared, is not always on, and is often stationary, a mobile phone is personal. It's almost always carried by someone and is often active 24/7.

It's a very special channel that marketers can take advantage of, but because it's so personal, it makes the right type of marketing even more challenging. You can't just spam everybody who has a phone. We advise companies to think of marketing as a service. With accurate targeting, you can deliver timely and relevant messages to your customers. This turns marketing into a valued service.

Q: What top three tips and tricks do you recommend for companies looking to deploy this?

A: First, I wouldn't try to buy the whole thing at once. This is a very complex set of technologies that requires thought on which areas to apply first. I would advise working with a vendor like Unica who has lots of experience helping customers formulate a roadmap to adopt this technology. That's number one.

Second, pick a vendor that has the holistic view of marketing. Too often we see companies trying to apply very short-term solutions to complex, long-term problems. That will only add more complexity down the road. Think holistically about marketing.

Third, check references. Talk to companies who are doing this successfully and get the inside scoop. There are few vendors who are delivering the goods.

Conclusion

Both Google AdWords and the various analytics tools show marketing can be managed as a trackable activity. With the broad acceptance of the Web by consumers and unique URLs, the power of online marketing's digital tracking can be used with traditional marketing.

Digitized marketing creates new abilities: tracking the customers, offering the customers what they really want, better reports for marketers, tools for automated distribution of campaigns across multiple channels, and tools for event-triggered campaigns.

Traditional marketing and online marketing are merging into one. Several years ago, it appeared online marketing would remain a small segment of marketing. That has changed. Online marketing will become part of general marketing. Marketing is a trillion-dollar industry in the U.S. and makes up the largest discretionary budget within companies. The combination of both online and offline marketing opens the door to many new tools and services in marketing.

In writing this book, we talked with senior people at Cisco, Omniture, Unica, Google, Yahoo!, Microsoft, Education.com, Aveda, 24-Hour Fitness, and many other companies. All of them felt these new tools will evolve rapidly in the next few years. This industry has only just begun.

In this book, we will cover:

- **KPIs** Digitized marketing allows you to manage your campaigns. You use key performance indicators (KPIs), which are the key numbers. We will show you how to define your KPIs for maximum profitability and use KPIs to manage your campaigns and channels.

- **Analytics**   An overview of analytics, along with a hands-on guide to using Google Analytics.

- **SEO**   Search engine optimization (SEO) helps you to make sure your website is findable by your audience when they are searching for you in search engines. We will show you how to use analytics and KPIs to manage your SEO.

- **PPC**   Use pay-per-click (PPC) to place advertising in search engines, radio, TV, and newspapers. We will also show you how to use analytics and KPIs to manage your PPC campaigns.

Chapter 2
KPIs

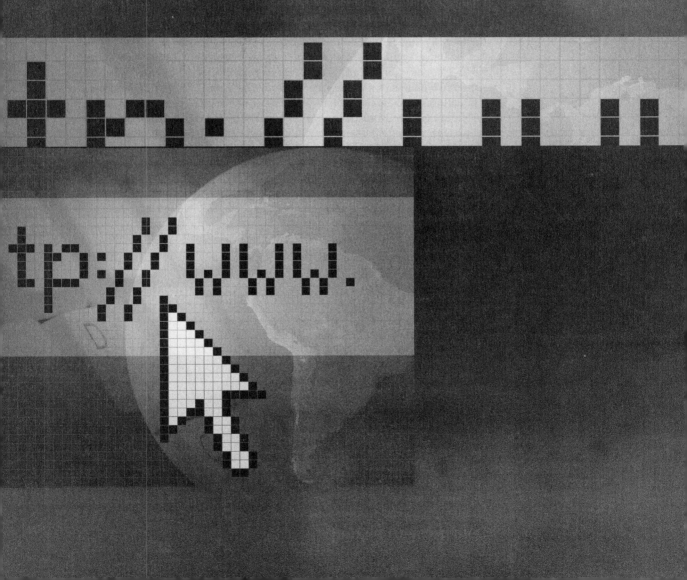

Key performance indicators (KPIs) are the metrics that guide and measure your progress toward your business goals. KPIs support both the strategy and tactics for your business decisions. By knowing your KPIs, you'll know how to manage your marketing campaigns for maximum profitability.

The most important KPIs for your business are average order value (AOV), customer lifetime value (CLV), project rate of return (PRR), cost-per-action (CPA), cost-per-lead (CPL), and close rate (CR). These numbers quantify your goals and provide guidelines for your marketing efforts.

Business is also a social activity. For your projects to be successful, you need cooperation and collaboration with your team. To win support for your project, you need to be able to show the value of marketing in a simple and powerful way. Communicating information is just as important as gathering and analyzing data. By clearly stating the KPIs, you can tell the story you need to grow your business as well as your career.

There is often a conflict between the finance and marketing departments. The two camps don't speak each other's language. Marketing sees the accountants as bean counters who don't understand that it takes money to make money, and finance thinks marketing is a black hole with no connection to the bottom line. With a set of simple metrics, both sides can understand each other. You don't need more than third-grade math to calculate these numbers.

A KPI-Driven Business Process

KPIs inform and guide the business process. They give you a rational method, based on objective data and results, for making business decisions. You first set your goals and then you establish how to measure the progress toward those goals. Thus, you will be able to answer the questions *What is working?* and *What needs to be changed?* The following process will help you make the most of KPIs:

1. Define your tactical goals. This comes down to a simple goal: *You want to get more* _____. This may be leads, sales, subscriptions, downloads, views of a video, and so on.

2. Establish the target KPIs. By knowing the KPIs, you'll know how much you can spend and still make a profit.

3. Launch your marketing campaigns in SEO, PPC, radio, TV, print, and so on. Use the target KPIs to set the budgets.

4. Measure the actual KPIs. Collect the results and see the actual KPIs for each campaign.

5. Optimize your marketing channels. Improve the successful campaigns and reduce or close the unsuccessful campaigns.

6. Communicate the results to your team, including coworkers and upper management.

Let's look at each of these in greater detail.

Define Your Goals

The tactical goals for your project generally come down to a simple goal: *You want more* _____. This may be leads for services, product sales, newsletter subscriptions, PDF downloads, views of a video, and so on.

Calculate Your KPIs

You need to establish the maximum amount you can pay for a customer and still be profitable. We'll describe this in general terms, explain each of the KPIs along with their formulas, give you a worksheet with the formulas, and then demonstrate this with an example. First, an overview of the KPIs:

- Find the average order value (AOV). Divide the total revenue for the period by the number of orders to get the average value for an order. Some customers may buy a single item; other customers buy several items at different prices. Use these to find the average value of an order.

- Find the customer lifetime value (CLV). Multiply the AOV by the average customer's number of annual purchases and length of customer lifetime (usually, several years) to get the CLV. This is how much the customer is worth to you in revenue.

- The question is then how much you're willing to spend to acquire that customer (in other words, how much you invest to get a certain amount of revenue). In many companies, your finance team tells you that you must achieve a certain return in order to get the funding for your project. For example, for every dollar you spend, you should get four dollars in revenue. Use the PRR to calculate this.

- Find your close rate (CR), which is the number of leads you need to get customers. If you need 100 leads to get 20 customers, that is a 20% CR.

- Multiply the CPA by the CR to get the target CPL. This tells you how much you can spend to get a lead.

Let's look at each of these KPIs in detail.

Average Order Value

Average order value (AOV) is the average value (in dollars, Euros, and so on) of your orders. This is the total value of an order, not the price of each item in the order.

This assumes the items in a sale are generally in the same price range. It can produce misleading numbers if the order basket has items that differ by several orders of magnitude. If a sale includes a $500,000 house and a bird bath, the average value isn't $250,000. If your orders include items with a wide range in price, you may need to develop KPIs for different amounts of sales.

To find the AOV, divide your revenues by the number of orders. Pick a time frame (such as last month, last 60 days, last quarter) that is representative, and look in your records for the amount of revenue and the number of orders.

$_____ Total Revenue / _____ Number of Orders = $_____ Average Order Value (AOV)

We use revenues, not profits, to calculate AOV. In very simple cases (such as Koi-Planet), we can calculate costs and profits, but for mid-size companies with dozens of products and revenue lines in the tens or hundreds of millions of dollars, it can be a daunting task to determine profit and costs. Profit margins constantly shift as the company develops better processes, switches to other suppliers, launches new sales campaigns, and so on. Furthermore, accounting rules and regulatory issues can make it difficult to state profitability, so we use revenues, not profits.

Customer Lifetime Value

Customer lifetime value (CLV), which is also called *lifetime customer value (LCV)* or simply *lifetime value (LTV),* is the value of the revenue from the average customer over the lifetime of that customer. This means how much revenue you will earn from a customer over the years that the customer buys from you.

To find the CLV, multiply the AOV by the average number of orders by customers and the average lifetime of a customer.

$_____ Average Order Value × _____ Number of Orders by a Customer per Year × _____ Number of Years for Customer = $_____ Customer Lifetime Value (CLV)

CLV is a relatively new concept in marketing. Customer-centric marketing considers the customer as a person with needs and behaviors. The company can then provide ongoing products and services to the customer, which produces additional revenues. This leads the company into cross-selling (if the customer buys a digital camera, offer them a camera bag or a tripod), up-selling (offer advanced cameras), extended warranties, maintenance contracts, and so on. Software companies often use a lock-in strategy. They make it difficult for customers to switch to other tools. The company also plans for the product version to become obsolete, so the customer is forced to buy upgrades. This generates additional revenues from a customer.

Unica recommends its clients think of marketing as a service. Because the Web enables customers to shop anonymously and makes it easy for them to find another vendor, the buyer has more control over the transaction. However, you as the seller can differentiate yourself with better service, ensuring that the customer will stay with you. Consider the customer's point of view so you can offer additional appropriate products and services. With web analytics tools (such as Unica) and CRM tools (such as Salesforce and Sugar CRM), companies are able to manage customers on an ongoing basis.

Project Rate of Return

The next step is to apply the requirement for the project's rate of return. A marketing project can use a *project rate of return (PRR)* value, such as 25%. This is how much your company must earn on its marketing to be profitable. Your CFO may set a revenue threshold you have to meet in order to justify the investment.

We use PRR for our KPI calculations. Some companies may use internal rate of return (IRR), contribution margin (CM), or a combination of other metrics to determine profitability. In general, these numbers tell the marketing department how much they are expected to produce in revenues from their marketing investment.

The PRR is generally around 25%. This means the revenue will be four times the investment. In other words, if you invest $1 in marketing, you should expect $4 in revenues. The PRR can vary according to the type of company. If the company is 50 years old and established in their market, they can spend less and get more results. Their PRR can be 10%. If the company is new and wants to grow aggressively, they will spend more to acquire customers. The PRR can be 50%, 75% or higher.

We don't use ROI (return on investment). ROI is *profits divided by costs multiplied by 100*. To use ROI, you need to know the cost, but it is very difficult to determine costs in a mid-size or large business because it becomes a matter of definitions. Do you include fixed costs (such as the cost of the building, salaries, and interest)? Do you include variable costs (such as materials and outside services)? How do you allocate these costs across several hundred products, which may range in price from low to high? Costs may also vary according to the size of an order because of volume discounts. The company's accounting method (cash vs. accrual) also affects your calculations. To add more complexity, costs are constantly shifting. You find better materials, you find a cheaper supplier, your supplier runs out of a material and temporarily substitutes another, you upgrade the production machines, and so on. We have not even opened the discussion of corporate finance, merger and acquisitions, the effect of taxes and regulation, and so on. You can appreciate the difficulty of calculating costs in a global enterprise such as Toyota, SAP, or the Tata Group.

This is why we use revenues instead of profits or costs to calculate the CPL and cost-per-action. You only need to know the CLV and the PRR. You focus on getting leads and converting them into sales. These are the numbers that guide you to making profitable business decisions. We've found this works for our clients, even those with hundreds of millions of dollars in revenue.

Cost-per-Action

The next step is to calculate the cost-per-action (CPA). An *action* is the successful completion of a goal. You first define the goal (more leads, more sales, more registrations, views of a video, and so on) and then count the completions of that goal.

To find the CPA, multiply the CLV by the PRR.

$_____ CLV × 25% PRR = $_____ Cost-per-Action (CPA)

We assume the PRR is 25%. Your PRR may be different.

For many salespeople, CPA is cost-per-acquisition, which generally means they acquire a customer. If your goal is to get visitors to download a PDF document or watch a video, that isn't really an acquisition. That's a desired action (the visitor did what you wanted), so it's better to use the general term cost-per-action. It basically means the same thing.

Close Rate

The close rate (CR) is the ratio of how many leads turn into customers. If you get 40 conversions from 100 leads, that is a 40% CR.

To find the CR, divide the number of customers by the number of loads.

_____ Customers / Leads = _____ × 100 = _____ % Close Rate (CR)

Close rates can vary by industry and company. They can range from 2% to 50% or higher.

Cost-per-Lead

Finally, we calculate the cost-per-lead (CPL). This is how much a lead may cost. A *lead* is a prospect or a contact that you then convert into a customer. If a CPA costs $10 and you need ten leads to get one conversion, then those leads cost $1 each.

To find the CPL, multiply the CPA by the close rate (CR)

$\$\underline{\hspace{1cm}}$ CPA $\times$ $\underline{\hspace{1cm}}$% Close Rate = $\$\underline{\hspace{1cm}}$ CPL

Assumptions

Our KPI model has several assumptions and limitations. We assume a discount rate of zero, meaning that revenues earned in the future are worth the same as they are today. Most marketing projects have a short time horizon, so the discount rate generally doesn't matter.

You may need to adjust the KPIs several times over the course of a campaign. When you begin to optimize the campaign, the numbers will affect each other. You improve the CR, which increases the CPL, which produces more leads.

An advanced formula for CLV and AOV may distinguish between high-value and low-value customers and products. Work with your accounting team to develop appropriate models.

The KPIs will differ, depending on the type of site. There are several basic websites:

- **Lead generation websites** These sites get leads, registrations, or contact requests. Many of these sites produce leads that are closed by other teams, so the KPIs consider the CPL, not the cost-per-action.

- **Sales sites** These sites sell products or services. Our KPI model is best suited for sites that sell products, such as Koi-Planet.

- **Support sites** These sites offer support, FAQs, and information for products or services. Companies use them to reduce the cost of telephone support. If a support site does its job well, fewer visitors will contact the company (they got the solution at the website). For these sites, KPIs may consider the volume usage of the internal search tool, the reduction in support calls, and similar.

- **Informational websites** These sites offer content, such as information, videos, music, and so on. For example, there is Facebook, Education.com, and MySpace. These sites use advertising to generate revenue. They use other KPIs such as eRPM (revenue per million page views), eCPM (cost per million page views), time-on-site, and so on.

You can use our model to develop a KPI model that is suited to your industry, products, and website.

KPI Worksheet

Here is the KPI formula as a worksheet:

KPI	Explanation	Worksheet
Customer Lifetime Value (CLV)	The total revenue value of the customer.	\$_____ Avg. Order Value (AOV) × _____ Number of Orders by an Average Customer per Year × _____ Number of Years for an Average Customer = \$_____ CLV
Cost-per-Action (CPA)	How much are you willing pay to get a customer? Use the project rate of return (PRR) (let's assume PRR at 25%).	\$_____ CLV × 25% PRR = \$_____ CPA
Close Rate (CR)	How many leads turn into customers?	_____ Customers /Leads = _____ × 100 = _____ % Close Rate
Cost-per-Lead (CPL)	How many leads must you buy to get one customer?	\$_____ CPA × _____% Close Rate = \$_____ CPL

Work with your finance team to build a worksheet that matches your projects. You can download our worksheet from the book's website at Insider-SEM.com.

An Example: Selling Bags of Koi Food

Let's try out the KPI worksheet with an example. Let's assume Koi-Planet is selling bags of koi feed.

KPI Concept	Formula	Results
Average Order Value (AOV)	\$42,000 revenue per month / 420 sales = \$100 AOV	\$100 AOV
Avg. # of Orders per Year	4 orders per year per customer	4 orders
Avg. # of Years for a Customer	3 years	3 years
Customer Lifetime Value (CLV)	\$100 AOV × 4 orders × 3 years = \$1200 CLV	\$1200 CLV
25% PRR	\$1200 CLV × 25% PRR = \$300 CPA	\$300 CPA
Close Rate (CR)	20 sales / 100 leads = 20% Close Rate (CR)	20% CR
Cost-per-Lead (CPL)	\$300 CPA × .20 CR = \$60 CPL	\$60 CPL

In this example, Koi-Planet can spend up to \$60 for each lead and be profitable. The close rate (CR) is fairly low at 20%; if we improve that, the CPL will increase, which allows us to spend more on leads and be profitable.

Estimated KPIs or Actual KPIs?

The point of these calculations is to estimate the upper limits of your marketing expenditures that allow your project to remain profitable. If you know how much you can spend and stay profitable, then you can spend up to the limit. This sets a ceiling for your marketing spend.

Many books and articles about KPIs calculate these numbers the other way around: They start with how much you actually spent, look at how many leads you got, and then state that your leads had a cost of $10. That's a factual statement that doesn't give you any guidelines. What does it mean if you find that the CPL was $10? Was it profitable? Did you lose money? Could you spend $15 and still be profitable? Without including the PRR (or a similar number), the revenue value, and the CR, a factual CPL isn't useful.

Our KPI model combines several formulas into one larger formula to give you a way to calculate how much you can spend in marketing to produce the revenue you want. It also tells you how much you can spend per lead or action and remain profitable.

Why This Works

Books are available with hundreds of KPIs, but you only need a few to get control over your project:

- The CLV tells you how much a customer is worth in revenue. This is based on the AOV and the number of orders a customer makes during their life cycle.

- Multiply the CLV by the PRR to get the cost-per-action (CPA). The CLV is the value of the customer. The PRR tells you how much revenue you must produce to be profitable. By multiplying these, you'll know how much you can spend to get that revenue value. If you want $100,000 in revenues and the PRR is 25%, you can spend up to $25,000 for marketing. For every dollar you spend, you get four dollars back.

- Multiply the CPA by the CR to get the target CPL. The CR measures your ability to convert leads into sales. If you know half of your leads turn into sales, you need two leads to get a sale. If you can afford $10 for a CPA, you can spend up to $5 to get each lead. The CPL tells you how much you can spend to buy a lead.

All you have to find out is your CLV, your PRR, and your CR. With these, you can calculate the CPA and CPL, which tell you how to be profitable.

You have a great deal of control over the close rate. If your conversion is done on a web page, you can use multivariate tools to improve the close rate. If your conversions are done by a sales team on telephones or in person, use training and bonuses to motivate the sales team to improve the close rate.

The success of this formula depends on reliable data. Most companies have several years of sales data from the business intelligence (BI) tools and can quickly calculate these numbers. If you're starting a new project (or a new company), you can estimate/guess these numbers and then adjust them as you collect data. We will show you how to do this later in the chapter.

This formula works for both online projects (lead generation, e-commerce sales, registrations for social networking sites, and information distribution sites) and offline marketing projects.

Use CPLs to Manage Your Campaigns

The target CPL is the maximum amount you can spend for a lead. If you keep the actual CPL at or less than the target CPL, your campaign will be profitable.

In other words, the CPL is how much you can pay to buy a prospective customer. If you know your target CPL, you can buy the number of sales that you need for your business. This is why CPL is your most important KPI.

A high target CPL doesn't mean you must spend that much. It means you can spend up to that limit and still be profitable. It also doesn't mean you should spend as little as possible for a lead. Many marketers see advertising as a cost, not an investment, and they try to limit their costs. They generally underspend. If the KPI model shows they can spend $15 for a lead but they spend only $2 per lead, they will get few leads. If they are willing to pay up to $15 per lead, they will buy many more leads. As long as you are within your target CPL, you will be profitable. Spend up to the target CPL for the channel and buy as many leads as your sales team can handle.

If your competitors haven't calculated their CPLs, they will get nervous when CPLs go as high as $5. They refuse to pay $5, which means they lose the opportunity to buy customers. If your calculations are based on reliable data and you know $15 CPLs are profitable, you can spend $15 to buy more leads than your competitors.

Don't look at marketing as a cost. The goal of marketing isn't to reduce your costs. Your goal is to acquire customers to maximize your revenues.

CPL lets you manage your campaigns. You can use multiple channels such as Google, Yahoo!, and Microsoft PPC, along with Facebook, radio, TV, print, bulk e-mail, SEO, link building, direct mail, billboards, catalogs, coupons, and so on. The close rate will be different for each channel. This depends on many factors: the quality of your ads, the quality of your competitors, your unique selling point (USP), your sales team's close rate, and so on. Try the channels that are appropriate to your target audience. Measure the resulting KPIs and see where you can make profits. Track the KPIs in each campaign and compare the campaigns in terms of revenues against each other. If you keep the actual CPLs lower than your target CPL, the channel is profitable for you. This means you can increase the ad spend to get more leads and more sales. Turn up the volume!

You can assign the campaign to a staffer and give them the target CPL as their guideline. They can then manage the campaign, adjust bids and fees, and try out keywords and ads so long as they keep the average CPL at or under your target CPL. You can also give the target CPL to a marketing company or PPC agency and tell them to produce as many leads as possible within that CPL.

In some cases, CPL and CPA are the same. At an e-commerce website with a shopping cart, if the visitor buys, they become a customer. There isn't an intermediate stage of leads in the cycle.

In PPC (pay-per-click), you set bids by the keyword. But don't worry about the bids or costs for each keyword. Look at the average CPL for the entire ad group. As long as the ad group delivers leads within the target CPL, the ad group is profitable. This means it can be okay in an ad group if the CPL for some of the keywords is higher than the target CPL, as long as the average CPL for the ad group is within your target CPL. This allows you to use a kind of *portfolio management* for your pay-per-click campaigns. Some keywords may be high, but they are making conversions, and the more conversions you get, the sooner you reach the breakeven point.

We often meet people who say, "We've been doing great in SEO for the last three years, so we're not paying for PPC!" They think they're really clever. They are managing marketing as a cost, not an investment. When we sketch out this financial model and they realize how much they've lost in potential sales for the last three years, they move fast to set up campaigns in every channel.

Go After Your Competitors' Customers

You can also use these KPIs for competitive marketing. Once you've established your KPIs and you have a working model (optimized campaigns, actual KPIs, and so on), you can afford aggressive bidding campaigns to target your competitors' customers. You're helping their customers to get better products—namely, yours!

Set Your Baseline

When you start your project, set your baseline. Knowing your baseline, you'll be able to see if you are making progress. Use a time period for your project, such as sales the last month, the previous quarter, or the preceding year. The time period should be large enough that you have at least 1000 orders. If you have no data at all, start at zero.

How Much Data Do You Need?

You should use around 1000 data points as your basic set. Why 1000? Statisticians have shown that 1067 events are sufficient to draw conclusions with a 3% margin of error.

For example, if you have 1067 leads and you got 181 sales, that's a 17% conversion rate. You can expect the future conversion rate to be 17%, with a ±3% margin of error, which is 14% to 20% (3% below 17%, and 3% above 17%).

Of course, the more data you have, the better you can project the future. If you use fewer events, the margin of error will be greater. You can use more events to make predictions, but it improves the margin of error only slightly. With 2401 events, the margin of error is 2%. With 10,000 events, the margin of error drops to 1%.

We find that 1000 events with a 3% margin of error is sufficient to make decisions with a good level of confidence. For more, see "margin of error" in Wikipedia.

In Chapter 5, SEO, and Chapter 6, PPC, we state that you should have about 1000 impressions or clicks before you can decide whether to delete a keyword or ad. This is for the same reason. You need 1000 events to make reliable conclusions. Adjust the time span (yesterday, seven days, one month, and so on) until you get 1000 events so you can make decisions.

What about Impressions and Clicks?

As you can see, many of the numbers commonly used in PPC and analytics don't matter. Although it may be nice to know that traffic is up on your site, you should focus on conversions, sales, and profits. The following are not KPIs:

- Traffic increased by 24%.
- Clicks dropped by 10%.
- Page views are up by 7%.

Don't confuse KPIs with activity on your website. Those numbers come from the traditional IT's concern with data tracking. They have little to do with your business.

What about KPIs for Media Companies?

Up to now, we've looked at KPIs for companies that generate revenue through transactions, such as selling products or services. Let's briefly look at media companies. These generate revenue primarily through advertising. For media companies, the KPIs have different factors. The goal isn't an event or transaction. Instead, the media company generates revenue during the time the customer is on the website. For example, a media company may generate value through three primary methods: advertising impressions, clicks on advertisements, and actions taken by their customers for CPA advertisements. Using this as a baseline, we can calculate each of the KPIs as follows:

- **AOV**   If an average customer looks at ten ads per session, and one out of every ten customers clicks on a CPC advertisement, and one out of every 100 customers registers for a product demonstration offered by a CPA advertisement, the AOV is the sum of the value generated by each of those actions by an average customer. If we assume each ad impression is worth \$.01, a click on a CPC ad generates \$.30, and the registration for the product demonstration is worth \$5.00, then the AOV would equal $(\$.01 \times 10) + (\$.30 \times 1/10) + (\$5.00 \times 1/100)$, or \$.18.

- **CLV**   The CLV is the AOV multiplied by the number of times the average customer returns to a company's website without that customer having to be repurchased. If that customer returns four times without having to be prompted by another marketing campaign, then the CLV in our example is $4 \times \$.18$, or \$.72.

- **CPA**   In the same way that a transaction-based company uses PRR to calculate this metric, a media company must also calculate their target return to determine their target CPA. For media companies, the variable cost of delivering additional ad impressions tends to be very low. This allows the company greater flexibility to spend up to as much as the CLV to drive new visitors to the site and still generate incremental value for the business. This is because the contribution margin (CM) is positive up to the point where the cost of driving the last visitor equals the CLV. (See Wikipedia for more details on contribution margin.)

- **CR**   The conversion rate of a media company can be segmented based on the different advertising models or based on the channel the company is using to market to prospective customers. For example, a company may use a display advertising campaign as part of its portfolio approach to driving traffic, where the average impressions conversion from advertisement to visitors is 0.1%.

For those campaigns, the conversion rate would be equal to the click-through rate on the advertisements, which is 0.1%. In the case of PPC campaigns, the calculation is different. The action the company is looking for in calculating its CPA may be to drive more visitors to its site. For a PPC advertising model, every click becomes a visitor, so the conversion rate is 100%. These differences in channels are important for media companies.

- **CPL**   A media company may define a lead and a visit as the same, in which case the CPA and CPL are identical. If the company is using display advertising, its CR is the percentage of advertising impressions that converts to a visitor. In this case, the ad impression is the lead, so CPA and CPL are calculated with the CR.

How to Set a PPC Budget for a New Product

What if you're launching a new campaign and you don't have any data for your KPIs? How do you set your budget?

Google AdWords suggest the bids and a daily budget, but these are just their guesses. They have no idea of your average order value (AOV), close rate (CR), or your business model. Ignore their numbers.

To set the initial advertising budget for PPC, you'll need to calculate your CPL, as follows:

1. Estimate the number of sales you expect to make in one month. Use the minimum number of sales that you'll need to stay in business.

2. Guess at your close rate. For every 100 leads, how many will you convert into customers? Ten percent is fairly conservative. After a few months in business, you'll get better at selling.

3. Use your close rate to estimate how many leads you'll need to be able to make the minimum number of sales.

4. Calculate your target CPL. Talk with a few people with experience, make best guesses, and be conservative.

5. Multiply the number of leads by the target CPL. That's how much you'll have to spend per month to buy the leads you need.

6. Divide the monthly budget by 30 days to get the daily budget for Google AdWords.

For example, you want to sell 100 koi per month. You have a 50% close rate, so you'll need 200 leads to sell 100 koi. If the target CPL is $10 and you need 200 leads, you'll need to spend $2000 per month in marketing. Divide by 30 days to get the daily budget ($2000 / 30 days = $66 per day).

Watch your campaigns every workday. Yes, take weekends off. You need a break from all these numbers. Besides, you'll find from analytics that there are few buyers on weekends anyway. Try different ads and delete the ones that don't work. Keep your ad group's average CPL within your target CPL. It takes about four to six weeks to optimize a PPC campaign, so the numbers will fluctuate. The CPC will drop, so the number of clicks will increase. This means you'll get more leads. You'll get better at selling koi, so your close rate will improve. When your PPC account has reached optimal levels, you can recalculate your numbers. You'll know the actual CPC, conversion rates, and cost-per-conversion.

Work with your team to improve the close rate. Aim for a 30%–50% close rate. If you have a 50% close rate, see if you can get 75%. The more leads you close, the more results you get with the same advertising budget, so you can afford more for a CPL, which lets you buy yet more leads.

When you find it costs, for example, $12.53 to sell one koi, then in effect you know how much it costs "to buy a sale." You can then budget to buy the sales you want. If your sales team can only handle 20 leads per day, then budget what it takes to get 20 leads. There's no point in buying leads you can't handle.

How to Set a Budget for an Existing Product

If you have an existing product and you have data for the last six months (including number of monthly sales, AOV, CR, and PRR), you can calculate your CPL as follows:

1. Set the target for monthly sales.

2. Use the KPI worksheet to calculate your target CPL.

3. Multiply the number of target sales by the target CPL. That's how much you'll have to spend to buy the leads you need. This is your campaign's monthly budget.

4. Divide monthly budget by 30 days to get the daily budget for PPC.

Again, watch your results for the first few months. Because this is an existing product in an ongoing campaign, we're assuming you have optimized your campaign. Nevertheless, you can try to improve your close rate.

The Breakeven Point

Another important concept is the breakeven point (BEP). This is the number of sales you need to cover your costs. In some situations, it has additional benefits for your business.

Let's say we set up a small workshop to produce koi food. We hire four people to mix vegetables locally grown by organic farmers joyfully singing their traditional harvest songs. We add up the costs, which include monthly rent on the building, salaries, cost of vegetables, macrobiotic mango juice for the workers, and so on. Let's assume the total costs are $4000 per month. If a bag of koi food sells for $50, then we need to sell 80 bags to make $4000 to cover our costs.

This means we don't make any profit at all on the first 80 bags. We might think we have a 40% profit margin, but that's a mistake. The first 80 bags have zero profit. They merely cover the costs. So $4000 is our monthly breakeven point.

A very curious thing happens with the 81st bag. The cost for the 81st bag is only the cost of a bit of vegetables and the shipping bag. The 81st bag's profit margin may be 95%. All of your additional bags after the breakeven point are practically pure profit.

This means once you've covered your costs, you should use every possible channel to sell. The more you sell, the quicker you reach the breakeven point and the sooner you go into the high-profits zone. If Koi-Planet is shipping 1000 bags of koi food per month at $50 per bag, with a 95% profit margin on 920 bags, it's making good money (take out your calculator and calculate those numbers). With such high profits, Koi-Planet can aggressively target the market. It can bring in a Danish gourmet chef to make deluxe koi food, open up a production plant in China, and set up distribution in the European Union.

We've sketched out a simple model of the breakeven point. There are additional details, including the marketing costs, PRR, and so on. Again, talk with your finance team and develop a model that fits your company. This model works for companies with a high startup cost and a low cost-per-item. It also works for software companies, where the first few thousand sales cover the costs, and thereafter, it's basically free to create additional copies.

One of our clients sells a name-brand product that is used in Europe and the U.S. Many of you use it. It's great stuff. When we first met with their VP of Sales, we asked for the CPL. "Well, we haven't quite figured that out." We asked about their close rate. "We don't really know that either." So we paused for a moment and asked them about their sales strategy. "Oh, we just sell as much as we can!" Hey, that works. They had discovered the breakeven-point trick. By maximizing their sales, they reached the breakeven point, covered their costs, and had very high profit margins, which allowed them to grow explosively.

The Social Context of KPIs: Communicate Your Results

KPIs aren't just numbers. They help your career. At the director and C-officer level, KPIs are used to keep score. Your salary, bonus, and advancement will depend on KPIs. If you can define the KPIs, manage them successfully, and show that you reach your goals, you will do well.

You can consider several questions, such as how much improvement in the KPIs do I need to demonstrate success? How much revenue is produced by this KPI? What is the loss in potential revenue by not reaching a KPI? Can I get additional compensation based on my improvements in the KPIs?

A key question is to determine who controls a KPI. Who has the ability to make changes in strategies and tactics to improve the KPI? This can include the person who manages the channel, the webmaster, the graphics person, the sales team, and so on. By understanding and setting KPIs, you can give your team the direction they need to reach their goals, bonuses, and promotions.

When making presentations, keep your audience in mind. Are they owners, investors, directors, fellow managers, or your team? What do the KPIs mean to them? Which KPI matters?

These KPIs allow you to *measure marketing that makes money*. Marketing is no longer a mysterious hole in which we throw money and hope for the best. With AOV, CLV, PRR, CR, CPA, and CPL, the finance and marketing teams will be on the same page.

KPI and Analytics in Your Marketing Strategy

This combination of financial strategies and software tools is changing the way to do marketing:

- With KPIs, we can calculate the proper amount of marketing spend to produce maximum profitability.

- With analytics tools, tracking URLs, and unique domain names, we can track campaigns in multiple channels, such as PPC (Google, Yahoo!, and Microsoft), radio, TV, and print, plus other channels such as bulk e-mail, SEO, link building, direct mail, billboards, catalogs, coupons, and so on. With the automated rules in Omniture, Unica, and Offermatica, we can carry out thousands of campaigns in all of these channels.

- Through Google's global advertisement distribution platform, we can place advertising in multiple channels such as PPC, radio, TV, and print.

This lets us carry out multichannel marketing. We can use KPIs and analytics to compare the marketing channels against each other and find which ones produce the best results.

Conclusion

As you can see, analytics, SEO, and PPC aren't technical issues. They are at the heart of your business. By first establishing business goals and then defining the KPIs, you have the numbers that help you determine the limits for your campaigns and bids. You can set budgets and manage bids to get sales that produce the best profits. Just as you can optimize a website, you can optimize your sales. That's what this is all about: more leads and more sales.

Chapter 3
Analytics

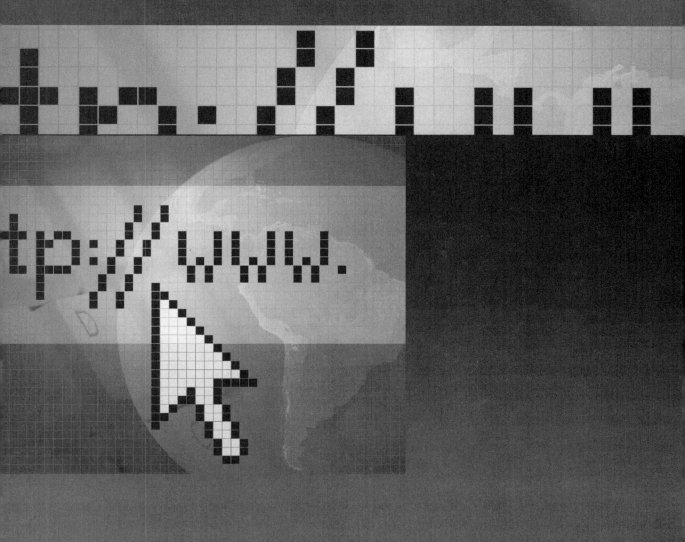

In this chapter, we show how businesses can use web analytics to manage their marketing. Although analytics comes from a type of software that has traditionally been managed by software engineers, it is not a technical issue. Web analytics is a business issue.

Analytics lets you take control of your marketing. You use it to manage your customer acquisition and marketing strategy. You see what works. Analytics shows you which half of your advertising works.

At the basic level, you place a few lines of code on web pages. When the visitor's browser opens the page, that code reports data about the visitor to the analytics software. It creates trends and charts to show the results. But it's more than that: Analytics uses data for actionable business decisions. You can set up campaigns to test, carry out those tests, and see the results. By knowing what visitors are doing on the website, you can manage their experience. By testing pages against each other, you can build better pages that produce more leads and conversions. By seeing which keywords produce revenue (and which ones don't), you can change the keywords to get more revenue. When you see that a part of the country sends lots of customers, you can refocus your advertising.

We also give you tips on vendor selection, discuss common issues with configuration, and provide a brief summary of several vendors. The chapter includes interviews with leading people at Omniture, Coremetrics, and Google Analytics. It follows up with a hands-on guide to Google Analytics.

Web Analytics as Your Business Tool

Peter Drucker, the leading management guru, writes in his key essay "The Purpose and Objectives of a Business" that the core purpose of a company is to create customers. The company does this by satisfying the customer's needs. This creates value for the customer, so they will select your products or services.

The question *What is the company's purpose?* opens a customer-centric discussion. What are the customer's expectations, behavior, and situation? Where is the customer located? This includes the customer's physical location (Berlin or Toronto); it also includes where the customer will be found on a marketing channel. The key question to ask is *What is the customer buying?* when they buy your product.

Many companies aren't very good at answering this question. They say they are in the business of selling products. People don't buy products; they buy solutions to their problems. By answering this question, you will begin to understand who your target audience is, where you can reach them, and how to develop your messaging.

Drucker writes that a company has only two essential functions: marketing and innovation. The function of marketing is to align the company with the customer's needs. By understanding the customer, the company can use marketing to offer what the customer wants. Marketing is essentially customer-centric. It focuses on the customer's point of view. If marketing is done well, the company doesn't have to worry about sales; the customers will want the product and the products will sell themselves.

The role of innovation is to keep the company in the market, which also means innovation should also be customer-centric. The company innovates by improving products, better marketing, and improving productivity (better quality, lower costs, and similar). Barry Jaruzelski and Kevin Dehoff's annual "Global Innovation 1000" report, published by Booz Allen Hamilton, points out the two major factors for successful innovations: Innovation is aligned to corporate strategy, and innovation happens when companies listen to their customers.

The task of management is to manage the company's performance and results to enhance innovation and marketing. This places analytics at the core of the company's management. You use analytics to manage marketing. Not only can analytics measure the performance of marketing (key performance indicators [KPIs], revenues, and so on), but it gives the company a view into their customers: where they are and what they are interested in. Analytics helps a company in both marketing and innovation.

Drucker, writing in 1974, added that the key measurements were haphazard and unclear. At the time, there weren't tools to define goals and measure progress. Analytics had not yet been invented. With analytics, you can now manage and measure your marketing performance. You can see how much revenue is produced by each channel, and you can compare the channels against each other. This is the foundation for the approach of evidence-based management (EBM).

Analytics tools are unlike most other software tools. For most companies, it doesn't really matter which word processor or browser the workers are using. Because analytics is software, many companies assume it's just another software tool and it's assigned to the workers. The company doesn't realize that analytics is involved with the management of the company. When analytics is successfully implemented in a company, the analytics team quickly becomes part of the core management.

To get the most advantage out of analytics, the company has to clearly define it's goals. By knowing the goals, the directors and managers can then determine the strategies and tactics. Let's look at these two:

- Strategy has to do with the company and its customers. Set the direction of the company, determine the company's strengths, or define the company's unique selling point (USP). This may also include a definition of the company's target audience or ideal customers. What type of customer do they want to attract? How does the company position themselves in the marketplace? How can the company increase brand loyalty?

● Tactics are the decisions that support and carry out the strategy. Tactical issues are day-to-day decisions in the channels. Tactics aim for growth and revenue goals, which are often defined by numbers such as KPIs. For example, the radio campaign's cost-per-lead is too high, so reduce the ads on radio stations that don't produce leads. The Google pay-per-click (PPC) campaign has good keywords and ads, so copy these into the Yahoo! and Microsoft PPC accounts. Give the list of the top PPC keywords to the search engine optimization (SEO) team so that they can improve the site's SEO.

If a company hasn't determined its goals, it will make poor choices in strategy and tactics. Everyone involved with analytics has to be clear about the company's goals and strategy because they are making the day-to-day decisions to optimize campaigns that create customers and produce revenues. When they know the company's direction, they can focus these optimization decisions.

This is why analytics should be done by people who have the company's interests at heart. In the beginning, you can use outside consultants to kick-start your analytics process. However, some companies leave the analytics entirely to consultants. That isn't a good idea, because the company is placing the ability to define their goals and tactics in the hands of outsiders. Consultants often look only at short-term tactics, such as optimizing for conversions or increasing leads. In general, you can work with outside consultants to train and support your team, but eventually, you should consider bringing analytics in-house or building a close partnership with the consultants.

Web Analytics, Quantitative Analytics, or Analytics?

The word *analytics* has several meanings:

● Web analytics is a tool that came out of engineering's web stats packages and was taken over by marketing departments. Web analytics collects website traffic data to learn how visitors behave in order to improve the marketing strategy. It uses key performance indicators (KPIs) to measure the results. Web analytics is done with software packages such as Omniture or Google Analytics.

● Quantitative analytics uses statistics and predictive modeling. PhDs in statistics and mathematics are trying to build models to manage companies according the mathematical rules, similar to how quantitative analysts (so-called *quants)* are trying to model stock market portfolios for Wall Street investment houses. This approach is not concerned with marketing or customers. Quantitative analytics is done with spreadsheets, mathematical software, and data warehouses. Thomas Davenport's *Competing on Analytics* (Harvard Business School Press, 2008) describes this quantitative approach to analytics.

When we use the word *analytics*, we mean the use of web analytics for marketing. Up to now, web analytics had to do with websites. As online and offline marketing are merging into one, it's better to just use the word *analytics*.

Five Steps Toward a Data-Driven Organization

Because analytics lets you measure your strategy and tactics, it gives you the ability to make decisions based on objective data. With analytics tools, you can carry out tests and see what actually works. You can compare campaigns and channels and then rank them by the generated revenues. Here are five steps for implementation of an analytics strategy:

1. *Identify your business goals.* These are the company's strategic goals, such as the company's unique value for customers.

2. *Identify business decisions or actions to be taken.* What campaigns and tactics can the company use to reach those goals?

3. *Establish benchmarking.* This includes the sales trends for the recent past. It also includes customer surveys, voice of customer (VOC), panel interviews, and competitive intelligence to determine the competition's market share and the company's position in relation to competitors.

4. *Set a timeframe for the goals.* This depends on how quickly your organization can move. Generally, you should expect four to six weeks to get campaigns underway. Don't try to launch too many initiatives at first. Start with one or two; let everyone learn how they work, and ramp up slowly.

5. *Measure the results.* Determine the KPIs, develop reasonable budgets, and collect the data. See how you can measure customer engagement, customer satisfaction, and so on.

This is not a one-time process. You won't do this once and expect the issue to be settled. This becomes an ongoing process that is reviewed again and again. You continually reevaluate your company's goals and strategy, look into new channels (which seem to pop up every 15 minutes), and use your tools to manage your campaigns.

Business Goals

Here are some ideas for your analytics projects:

- *Learn about your customers.* Use analytics to learn where your customers can be found. Find out what they prefer. Can you create a qualification process to identify the most promising customers? Set up marketing campaigns to place your marketing material where your customers are.

- *Increase customer retention and loyalty.* By helping your customers find what they are looking for, get what they need quickly, and feel good about the interaction with your company, you increase your customer loyalty. Use analytics to improve customer support and satisfaction. Create a customer satisfaction KPI that you benchmark your performance against.

- *Identify new market opportunities.* You can test new channels to see if there are additional customers. You can see which products get a strong response. This lets your business discover better audience segments as well as manage campaigns according to specific KPIs, such as managing a marketing site using the KPI of lead volume or managing customer support against your customer satisfaction KPI.

- *Automate your paid-search (PPC) campaigns.* The enterprise-level tools can be used to automate your PPC campaigns. These are based on rules that you create and manage. These rules are aligned with your business goals.

- *Reach your audience multiple times.* By being able to work in multiple channels simultaneously, you can reach your audience multiple times. This produces *campaign overlap,* where the campaign will be seen several times by the audience. It reinforces your campaign, similar to the use of repetition in TV advertising. Atlas Institute found that users who saw ads from multiple channels were twice as likely to convert. With analytics and marketing tools, you can manage your campaigns across multiple channels, including Web, radio, TV, and print.

- *Eliminate waste in campaigns.* Money can be saved by eliminating waste in campaigns. Use the remaining funds to expand the company's footprint in their current market or other new markets. If you find the market in one area performs well but another performs poorly, you can reduce or shut off the low-performing area and move the budget into the high-performing area. This also works for products: You can reduce your marketing spend on products that underperform. You can also reduce the marketing budget on channels that underperform.

The goal of analytics is to take better care of your customers. This is the same as a salesperson in a store who makes additional recommendations to a customer. This means helping them find what they are looking for, enabling them to pay for their purchases easily and seamlessly, or getting product information, as well as product comparisons, that allows your product to be compared against your competitors. Providing product or service comparisons wins you points in the online world. The search engines will drive more qualified traffic to your site, and that traffic will show up in your web analytics. Now, it is up to you to steer that traffic in the direction you want it to go. You can correlate sales with additional cross-sell and up-sell opportunities.

Very often, companies have difficulties in defining their business goals. This produces several problems.

Because they aren't clear about their goals, they don't have criteria for selecting the appropriate analytics tool. So they often buy the wrong tool and then they try to develop a strategy based on that tool. That bottom-up approach rarely becomes aligned with the company's core business strategy.

Or they just don't know what to measure. This often happens in startups, which sometimes are solutions in search of a problem. A group of engineers gets a great idea and builds a company without figuring out if there is a market for it. Many Web 2.0 startups have no business strategy. They assume they'll grow very fast, and when they have 20 million users, they'll then somehow figure out how to make money. Without a business strategy, they don't know what to measure.

This also happens in old, established companies where upper management has been in place for many years. They make good money, and that's good enough. If they grew the company, it'd just get in the way of playing golf in the afternoon. That's fine for their lifestyle, but it's difficult to implement an analytics solution because there isn't a clear business goal.

This isn't a problem only at poorly managed or casually managed companies. We've also seen this at large, successful companies that have great products and substantial revenues. Sometimes, too much success makes it difficult to develop a business strategy.

If you're having problems with analytics, it's often due to lack of clarity in the overall business strategy. Go to the CEO, the VPs, or the board of directors and ask a few simple questions: What's the goal? What value do we provide to our customers? What is our unique selling point (USP)? Whether it's a $20-billion dollar corporation or a mom-and-daughter shop, it comes down to the basics: They need to take care of their customers. Focus on your best customers and take care of them.

What You Can Do with Analytics

Analytics isn't a self-powered wonder tool. Like Luke Skywalker's lightsaber, it's all about how you wield it. Here are some points to keep in mind:

- You must clearly know what you want to accomplish. What are your business goals? By knowing your business goals, you develop your strategy. You can grow your customer base by using new channels.

- Next, you figure out how to measure those goals. What kind of data will let you measure that goal? You set the budgets and upper limits for ad spend. These are the KPIs that tell you how much you can spend to maximize your profits.

- Finally, you run campaigns, look at the results, and make decisions about what works and what doesn't work. Whatever doesn't work, you shut down. What works, you do more of.

Analytics will give you answers for business questions such as budget allocation, campaign effectiveness, content effectiveness, site engagement, traffic quality, pipeline, product affinity, cross-sell and up-sell opportunities, and so on.

You can use analytics to find new business opportunities, increase revenues, increase customer satisfaction, improve your market position, or find which products sell the best.

Analytics lets you unify the reporting for all forms of customer contacts, including web visits, web forms, store walk-ins, e-mails, click-to-chat and click-to-call, direct calls, and similar.

Analytics improves your website. By knowing your top keywords, you can make it easier for visitors to find your website when they search. By knowing which referring sites send customers to you, you can place ads or text with your link at those sites. You can use your site's internal search engine to improve the ability for visitors to find pages and products. You can improve pages so you get more leads and sales.

Analytics can also measure video. This includes videos watched on YouTube or downloaded to digital players. It can track which videos were opened and how much of each video (10%, 25%, 50%, and so on) was watched. By placing a unique URL in the video that viewers can visit on the Web, you can use analytics to track the leads and sales.

You can see what is going on via automated reports, interactive screens with drilldown, data combination and ad hoc queries, dashboards that present an overview of the KPIs, and alerts to let you know if the data for a KPI has dropped below an acceptable level. You can use this information to provide directions to your various partners, agencies, and consultants in marketing, web design, and so on. You can use all of this data to make decisions about your strategies and tactics.

Challenges in the Vendor Selection Process

There are several dozen analytics packages in the market. How do you select one? Here are several common problems in the tool-selection process:

- **Bells and whistles**   The advanced tools have hundreds of features. It's not a question of selecting the tool first and then adapting your business to it. You should first define your business goals and then select the tool that helps you to measure and manage those goals. It may well be that you only need a few features from one of the large tools. It's not the vendors' fault. Vendors are often faced with selection committees that demand a long comparison list, so vendors must show every feature.

- **Selection by committee**   You've seen those job descriptions that ask for someone with an engineering degree, an MBA, a PhD in statistics, plus project management, public speaking, and Photoshop experience. Are they looking for Superwoman? This is the result of a committee: Each member added items to the wish list. The committee should focus on the company's business goals. What is important? What do they want to measure? Make a list of questions the analytics tool should answer. You can also list future issues that your company can grow into, such as customer relationship management (CRM).

- **Generating reports**   People want analytics tools that can generate reports. Vendors don't want to lose the sale, so they give the customer what they want. Customers immediately set up dozens of automated reports that are sent out throughout the organization. People think they are doing their job because they are producing beautiful reports. Avinash Kaushik writes in his book *Web Analytics: An Hour a Day* that when he took over analytics at Intuit, he found the tool was sending out hundreds of reports. Out of curiosity, he turned it off. Nobody complained. Nobody actually read those reports. The focus on reports is the most common mistake. Analytics isn't about reports. It is for decision-making. The report is nice, but more useful is a short e-mail that explains what is going on and makes recommendations on what to do next.

- **Expensive is safe** If it's expensive, it must be better. Nobody ever got fired for buying IBM. Don't get side tailed by high prices. Focus on your business strategy: What information do you need to make strategic decisions? If you can get the same information with a free tool or a $49-per-month tool, that's your solution. Buy only what you need.

- **Technical issues** This one is complex. There are technical aspects to analytics, especially with the large packages, so the technical team will get involved. Let the IT team help you on the technical issues, but keep the project focused on the business goals. In many cases, the vendors have experience with installation, configuration, and customization, so they can help you here.

Select a vendor who has knowledge and experience with your industry. They can guide you with best practices. They can help you to select and define the goals and KPIs, as well as set up reports to collect the KPI data. They can also help you to set baselines so you know whether or not the process is working. This is one of the advantages of the paid tools. The free tools don't offer this.

Analytics is evolving fast. Whatever you select will be a temporary solution. In a year or two, the tools will change. The digital fusion of offline and online marketing has only started. Many new solutions and strategies will appear. What we can do today wasn't possible a few years ago. Nobody knows what these tools will be able to do several years from now.

A final note about data storage. It may seem that you would want to have access to the last five years of sales data, but things change so much that old data is not very useful. Your competitors are changing their strategies, new products and prices are available, and your customers are changing. So don't worry if a tool can't read old data or won't store data beyond a few years. Generally, the last year of data is sufficient.

How to Send Out Reports

Ideally, reports should be on one page. Simplify the dashboard or the report to just four or six KPIs. Use graphs, pie charts, and tables with only a few lines. On Google's search engine, nobody looks past the third screen of search results, and we suspect the same for your reports; nobody will read page 4.

The most important part of a report is your comments. It's your experience and judgment that are valuable. That's what tells others how to understand the reports. Here are some tips for creating your reports:

- *Add your comments.* Explain the report. What is going on? What are we looking at? Walk your readers through the reports. We launched a campaign on TV, and it produced this revenue at this cost-per-sale. Sales dropped last week because it was a national holiday. We lowered the cost-per-click by 50% and got rid of useless keywords, which caused the impressions to fall by 20%, but we improved the landing pages and focused on the top-performing keywords, so the number of conversions broke previous records.

- *Make recommendations.* Make suggestions on what to do. Here is where you really add value. No analytics tool can do this for you. Because you know the company's goals, the target customers, and what your company provides for them, you can make recommendations that result in effective change.

It often helps to follow up reports with in-person meetings to make sure the recipients understand the reports and can take action. Make sure they understand the goal and how it produces revenues. If they see the connection between the goal and the report and how it is measured by the KPI, they can make changes to improve the results.

Many analytics tools would be improved if the report required you to write a summary and recommendations before it went out. You could have the report sent only to you, where you add your comments and recommendations, and then send it out.

Here's an overview of titles, responsibilities, report frequency, and decisions:

Titles	Responsibility	Frequency of Reports	Actions Based on Reports
Executives and VPs	Define the company's strategy. Set overall business goals & directions of company.	Monthly and quarterly	Adjust strategy and goals based on results.
Directors	Select appropriate channels. Define KPIs. Set budget limits. Allocate budgets across channels.	Monthly and weekly	Modify or reallocate budgets.
Account managers	Make tactical decisions. Implement campaigns in the channels.	Daily and weekly	Optimize campaigns. Keep campaigns within KPIs.

Tips for Getting Started

The field of analytics is complex, and it may take too much time for your employees to learn this on their own. To avoid "expensive learning experiences," it's much better to bring in outside consultants at the various stages of selection, implementation, training, and ongoing support:

- **Selection**   The selection process can become complex because it often opens other issues. To select the appropriate tool, you need to know what you're going to measure, which means you'll need to know your company's goals. It might be best to hire consultants to guide you through this. If they are independent, they won't favor one particular solution.

- **Implementation and configuration**   There are a number of technical issues around installation and configuration. The quickest solution is to get help. In general, the vendor's technical installation team can help your team through this process.

- **Training**   You will need different types of training for the various levels in the company. Executives and directors will need to learn how to use analytics to manage the company. Account managers need to learn how to manage the channels, optimize accounts, understand the data, configure settings, and the like. Consultants can be brought in to train the team and support them afterward. These consultants may be independent or from the vendor.

- **Best practices and on-going support** The large vendors offer industry-specific playbooks that guide you in the best use of analytics for your industry. These include the essential KPIs, baselines, and so on.

Your vendor should always assign an account manager or a point of contact (POC). This is a person who works with you through the process: selection, implementation, training, support, and so on.

How to Handle Configuration and Setup

When setting up analytics, companies often run into several common issues. Half of the challenge is to get the analytics up and working correctly.

First, let's review what actually happens with analytics tools. You place three to five lines of JavaScript code on a web page. When the browser opens the page for the visitor, the JavaScript code is triggered. It contacts the analytics server and sends data to that server. The code includes your account ID, so the data is added to your account. When you open your analytics tool, the data is reported to you.

This means that to get good information, the tag has to be on the page. The tag has to be triggered, and it must be the correct tag. Sounds easy, no?

Let's take a look at the most common problems and what you can do to fix them:

- **Failure to tag all pages** To collect data, the tag must be on every page. Generally, sites have a template. If a change is made to a master page, it is carried out on all pages. In practice, some pages don't use the templates, so the analytics code will be missing. Work with the webmaster to make sure the code has been placed on all pages. For Google Analytics, EpikOne.com's SiteScan tool (free) checks to see if the tag is on every page at your site.

- **Broken tags** Sometimes, the analytics JavaScript code is saved in a word processor or sent by HTML e-mail. These may try to spell-check or format the code, which may change it. The easiest solution is to just replace the code with a fresh copy.

- **Multiple tags** Because it's easy (and free) to set up Google accounts, different people in a company may set up their own accounts. Some pages use account A, other pages use B, and yet others use C. If you're taking over the analytics at a company, review the tags (look at the account IDs in the tags) and make sure there aren't multiple accounts.

- **Tags and Web 2.0** JavaScript tags run only when the page has been opened. If the page contains Web 2.0 elements, the visitor will use those items and may spend hours on the page, but the page won't be reloaded, so the actions won't be tracked. PDF downloads, mouseovers, watching video, and so on can't be tracked by JavaScript tags. If you're using Web 2.0 items, check with your analytics documentation to see how to use event-tracking.

- **Technical issues** The technical team may be reluctant to add code that may cause problems. You can test a few pages to see if it works. If the technical team continues to delay your code, talk with their VPs or directors and show them how analytics will help the organization achieve its goals. If the site has a template, it's only a matter of pasting five lines of code into a single file. In general, it takes less than 15 minutes to add the tags for Google Analytics into a well-structured site.

- **Company politics** Another team may be campaigning for a different analytics tool. Or there are web stats tools or analytics tools in place and they don't see the need for yet another tool. There is no problem with multiple analytics tools on the same page. We've seen companies with three different analytics tools. Try several tools and see which one suit your needs.

The bottom line: work with your vendor and consultants. They have experience and can offer solutions.

Placing the Analytics Code on the Pages

To collect data, the code has to be triggered when the browser opens the page. If the page is long (perhaps the visitor has to scroll several screens) or the page isn't very interesting to the visitor, they may exit the page before the JavaScript has been triggered. In that case, there will be no data for the page. This means you won't know that your visitors are abandoning the page.

Analytics vendors generally recommend that the analytics code be placed at the bottom of the page. There is a reason for this: If the code conflicts with other code on the page, the other code should run first. It's more important that your company's code executes correctly.

If you find there is underreporting for pages (for example, long pages aren't showing the expected amount of traffic), move the analytics code to the top of the page or to the beginning of the body content. It can also be placed in the <HEAD> section of the page.

In general, place the analytics code at the bottom of the page unless there are good reasons for placing it elsewhere.

Why Don't My Numbers Match Up?

If analytics is all about data and reporting, it will surprise you that analytics doesn't deliver accurate data. The numbers are wrong.

This happens in all analytics packages, from Unica down to Google Analytics. In general, analytics reports for the same website may differ as much as 14%. You know the accounting department and the shipping department sold and sent out 100 koi this month, but your analytics tool tells you that you have only 86 sales. That's a significant difference. This also happens in PPC. Google AdWords, Yahoo! Search Marketing, and Microsoft adCenter all deliver slightly incorrect data for the number of clicks and the number of conversions.

If you are using both PPC and analytics, you'll find the numbers don't match across these two tools. The warehouse tells you they shipped 100 koi; the PPC tells you that you sold 95 koi, and the analytics tells you that you sold 90 koi.

There are several reasons for this. Analytics tools depend on cookies, but as many as 30% of users use anti-spyware tools to delete cookies daily. Computers and servers also sometimes lose some of the data traffic. Some vendors may give you cookie rejection reports, which can help you to estimate baselines. It also takes about 1.4 seconds for the page to open and the analytics JavaScript to be processed. If a visitor buys a product and the thank-you confirmation page starts to open but the visitor immediately goes to another site, the thank-you page's code isn't processed and the visitor won't be counted. You can improve this by getting them to stay a few seconds on the page. Add a few lines of text or a special offer to get their attention. You can also move the analytics code to the top of the page into the HEAD section.

This also means you shouldn't use analytics to track sales, revenues, or profits as the basis for reporting, compensation, commissions, or bonus because it may underreport up to 14%.

Don't worry about the specific values. If the tool is wrong by 4%, then assume it will be consistently wrong by 4% and look at the trend: Did sales go up or down? Does campaign A perform better than campaign B? If you want to know more about data quality, Stone Temple Consulting compared the data from seven analytics packages. Search for "Stone Temple 2007 Web Analytics Shootout Final Report" for more information.

Migration from One Analytics Package to Another

By now, many companies are using some form of analytics. So it's often a question of migrating from one package to another.

Don't turn one off and start the other. You should run both simultaneously for a few months and compare the results. As you've seen earlier, packages produce different results on the same website. If you switch from A to B, you may see a 9% drop. Or you may get a sudden 10% increase. This doesn't mean you should hand out dismissal notices or performance bonuses. The new tool will produce different numbers.

To smooth over the switch, collect data for both packages and develop formulas to convert the old numbers into the new numbers.

Vendors in Analytics

In 1995, IT teams needed to know when they had to add more servers to handle the visits to their websites. Thus, simple log stats packages were developed. These tools used log files to report website activity. Web servers produce log files, which keep track of requests made to the server, including which pages are clicked, which keywords bring visitors, which web browsers are used, when people come to the website, and so on. Log files also record the number of bytes downloaded along with each visitor's IP address. Engineering teams used these log stats tools to monitor performance, system requirements, and uptime. That's all they did: they did not track the cost-per-visit or any financial or marketing numbers. That wasn't an issue for the IT team.

In 1997, shopping cart software appeared, which quickly evolved into e-commerce applications during the web boom in 1998 and 1999. Sales and marketing departments began using web stats tools to monitor visitor trends, banner ad tracking, profits, and return on investment (ROI). These tools began to display data as graphs and pie charts.

After the dot-com crash in 2000, surviving companies and new companies had to concentrate on revenues and profits. Sales and marketing teams began to focus on lead generation and sales. They wanted to know the customer's activity and history: where they come from, how they got there, what they look at, how long they look, what they buy, and where they go. The web stats tools turned into web analytics tools.

The digitization of traditional media (radio, TV, print) and the use of unique URLs and tracking codes make it possible to use web analytics in offline channels. The last few years have seen a rapid evolution in analytics. The major companies change their strategy literally every year as they learn more about the market. Everyone agrees we will see more evolution in the next few years.

Previously, web analytics was reporting. Now, web analytics is used to drive the business. This moves web analytics to the top of the organization. CEOs, VPs, and CFOs are using web analytics to understand their business and make decisions.

Web analytics vendors include Omniture, Coremetrics, Webtrends, IndexTools, and ClickTracks. Unica is primarily an enterprise marketing management (EMM) vendor that also has an analytics tool. The large search engines have their own analytics tools: There is Google Analytics and Microsoft adCenter Analytics. Yahoo! bought IndexTools and may release it for free as Yahoo! Analytics.

The analytics industry is also undergoing consolidation. Google bought Urchin. JLHalsey bought ClickTracks. Omniture is apparently trying to buy the industry, so they bought Visual Sciences and Hitbox. And as previously mentioned, Yahoo! bought IndexTools.

Because of rapid evolution, we won't provide a detailed review of packages. They change too fast. To give you an idea of the differences, however, let's look at Omniture, Coremetrics, Unica, and Google Analytics:

- Omniture is an enterprise-level package for companies with extensive and complex marketing strategies. Omniture allows customized tagging. You can tag types or categories of content on different pages. This lets you track the visitor activity by category of content. Omniture also has event-triggered rules that can make changes to your campaigns. If you have 100 items in stock and the website sells the last one, it shuts off the PPC spending on those campaigns. It can increase or decrease ad spend based on rules you create. You can use automated optimization to monitor visitors on the website and modify the website according to their activity. Omniture starts at about $5000 for setup consulting services and costs $1000 per month, and it goes up from there based on the volume of traffic. You can purchase additional modules. You will have to invest in training and consulting services to get its full benefits. Omniture SiteCatalyst is an on-demand application service provider (ASP) solution.

- Coremetrics has developed in-house expertise across verticals such as retail, financial services, travel, and content. Coremetrics starts at about $750 per month, and goes up from there based on the volume of traffic. The data warehouse is included with the analytics platform. Besides providing a highly scalable and flexible reporting and ad hoc analytics solution, Coremetrics has invested heavily in a number of vertically-focused solution sets. They have developed in-house expertise and analytics across verticals such as retail, B2B, financial services, travel, content, and media. Coremetrics also provides an add-on suit of application aimed at optimizing online marketing functions. These include Coremetrics Search, which manages PPC in Google, Yahoo!, and Microsoft; Coremetrics Intelligent Offer, an automated recommendation engine; and Coremetric LiveMail, which enables integration of online customer behavior with 16 of the leading e-mail service providers.

- Unica is an enterprise marketing management (EMM) solution for companies to manage both online and offline campaigns. Unica offers a suite of products that manages the entire marketing department across the phases of analysis, planning, designing, producing, executing, and measuring. The web analytics solution is Affinium NetInsight, which can be licensed separately or together with other components of the Affinium suite. NetInsight On Demand starts at under $1000/month and goes up from there based on the volume of traffic. On Demand customers get an assigned Technical Account Manager. Unica also offers Best Practices services for data analysis, reporting, or strategic planning on an hourly basis or on a monthly retainer with a defined number of hours.

- Google Analytics was updated in spring 2007. Forrester Research ranks it as a solid candidate in the mid-level market. It is free and easy to install. With minor configuration, you can use it to track PPC campaigns in Yahoo! and Microsoft, along with campaigns in many other channels. It lacks advanced features of enterprise-level tools (such as EMM, bid automation, event-triggered rules, and so on), but that's also a good thing. Because the tool is simple, you can learn how to use analytics. Google doesn't offer consulting services or extensive support. If you need help, other companies offer consulting services.

We aren't recommending a tool. It's not "one size fits all." Find the tool that is appropriate for your business model and level of understanding. We recommend you start with one of the free tools, such as Google Analytics or Microsoft adCenter Analytics, so you can learn the basics of analytics. Whether analytics is hard or easy is a topic for debate, but in the beginning, the data tsunami is overwhelming. With a basic tool, you can learn how to use analytics for your business, and you'll be able to have a better conversation with Omniture, Coremetrics, and Unica.

Don't overbuy. Use tools that are appropriate for your goals. If Google Analytics is sufficient, go with it. We know a global oil company (annual revenues of over $250 billion) that uses Google Analytics. They only need to keep track of visitors and related activity, so Google Analytics is appropriate for them. Start with Google Analytics to learn about analytics and then consider one of the advanced packages such as Unica, Omniture, or Coremetrics.

Here are three interviews with key people at significant analytics companies. These interviews give you an idea of what their companies are currently doing and what they see coming.

Interview: Avinash Kaushik, Analytics Evangelist for Google

Avinash Kaushik is the analytics evangelist for Google and author of *Web Analytics: An Hour a Day*. He is also the cofounder of MarketMotive.com, a marketing consultancy. He is a frequent speaker at eMetrics Summit, Ad-Tech, Web 2.0 Expo, and SES. You can visit his blog on analytics, called Occam's Razor, at www.kaushik.net/avinash.

Q: Many companies ask about the high cost of investment in analytics. How do you address their concerns?

A: I think that people have become frustrated with ROI. These tools have been around for a while. People have found lots of data and lots of reports are generated. They also hired lots of people, but they haven't necessarily gotten much out of this. This is supposed to be such a data-rich process, but many companies haven't figured out what to do with it.

As a matter of fact, costs are going down every day. That's the most amazing thing. I think Google really lit a fire under the market by providing Google Analytics for free. So the cost of the tool isn't really an issue. If you want to start analyzing data, you can do it for free.

The amount of data isn't the point. The point is to get other people to use the tools. I talk about this in my book. I have this 10/90 rule. For every $100 you put in analytics, put $10 into the tool and $90 into people. At the end of the day, the tool won't produce the insights. It's the people who understand your business who will find the insights.

Start simple. Don't invest in the most expensive tool because it has tons of features. Start with something that matches your level of understanding and hire good people to help you gain insights from the tool.

Q: What are the most common mistakes you see in analytics implementations?

A: The biggest mistake companies make—regardless of free or paid tools—is that they don't invest enough in people. They can really help you make the most of your tools. Invest in consultants and train your team.

Second, make sure you have first-party cookies deployed. Check that you're capturing data correctly. Most of the tools are ASP, and they process the data for you. It's important to do periodic checks on how the data is being processed and make sure you have it set up correctly.

The third thing is a key failure by senior executives if they don't define the critical business metrics. You open an analytics tool, and it will spit out 200 different metrics, if not 20,000. I see a consistent failure in senior management. They don't sit down and define what is important for analytics. Put another way: You need to put forth the questions you want to get answered.

(continued)

Q: You talk about the Trinity Model in your book. But everyone is focused on conversions. A company's website is usually driven by sales or marketing, and they understand conversions because that's how they get evaluated and compensated. How do you convince them to move beyond conversions? Why should they care about outcomes and the customer experience? How do you sell this to a skeptical CEO?

A: Measuring conversions is a part of the puzzle and certainly a very important part, but it's not the complete picture. The average conversion rate in the United States for retailers is 1.8%. That means that 98% of people who come to your site don't convert. Now the interesting thing is a lot of people who come to your website never wanted to convert. For example, some people are just there to look at pictures or look for jobs. Others come to look for a store. Now how do you capture that conversion because you deserve the success?

For example, I was in a meeting with a CEO, and he said they were putting in a few million dollars in the site every six months. I said to him, "You are making $20 million dollars that's directly attributable online. And I'll bet you you're making another $50 million that you are driving to other channels." Then you have their ear. They listen because they want more credit. They're hungry. They want more bonuses. By speaking that language and showing them how to measure it, they usually can see why they need to pay attention to all of the potential outcomes.

The Trinity Model presents a three-part process to understanding and analyzing your data to get the fuller picture of website usage. Measure your data to know what's happening on your site. You should also measure outcomes, usually known as "use cases," to understand how people use your site. You should also measure experiences by using surveys and usability studies. Some of the questions I ask in surveys: Are you going to buy? Are you going to recommend us? Will you go to a store?

I tell people if you focus only on the conversion, you are solving for a minority of visitors. If you look at the 98% who do not convert, you will solve for a lot more people and understand the other reasons for why people come to your website. By providing a better level of customer service, you increase your website satisfaction and ultimately your revenues. The Trinity solves for this. It gives you a more holistic picture of what's happening on your website. Web analytics alone won't tell you that.

Q: When should a company look into benchmarking and competitive intelligence? When should it use services such as Hitwise, Nielson/NetRatings, and comScore?

A: I think it is very important to mention that each of these services uses a different method to collect data. Some data is accurate. Some data is not accurate. For example, comScore's panel consists of 120,000 people. If you're using comScore, you have to be aware of that. You can only use that data if you have a high-traffic website.

Alexa.com clearly tells you if a site has fewer than 100,000 unique visitors per month; Alexa will not be able to give you accurate trends about the site.

Services such as Compete.com and Hitwise use ISP-based methods to produce better results. They install software on ISP server to track all users anonymously. Compete has a lot of free tools. You should use this data to figure out what's going on.

For example, if you're spending a $100,000 on paid search, it's really a crime if you're not using competitive intelligence. Your competitors are using these services on you.

Competitive intelligence services tell you information such as the top keywords, market share, time-on-site, and behavioral, demographic, and psychographic information for both you and your competitors.

If you have a medium-sized business or higher, competitive intelligence can provide you tons of insights about what is working for your competitors. That's really the way to improve your campaigns by knowing which keywords to buy, which sites to target, and so on. Knowing your competitors' keywords and markets is a great way to make a ton of money.

Q: Can you use competitive intelligence to provide better customer service or address negative branding?

A: Yes, there are some things you can glean about what's going on in your market space. Here's an example: A major computer company had a buggy software package that produced error codes for users. The company realized a lot of people were writing bad reviews about their products, and those people were ranking high for those error codes. The computer company set up bidding on the error codes as keywords. This let them provide solutions on how to fix these problems instead of letting their customers go to complaint sites where they would just get more upset. The company solved the problems and turned these people into happy customers. There are definitely ways to counteract negative branding.

Q: John Marshall warns that we shouldn't pay too much attention to funnels. What do you think?

A: I think his point is true. When people create funnels, they think you come to the homepage, and then you go to the products page, and then you look at the product detail page, and then you call, and so on. This implies that a person's experience in a site is linear. It's not. With the Web, you cannot impose a path and expect your visitors to follow it. Because of search engines, there is no longer such thing as a homepage. When people search, they can jump directly into your site and bypass the homepage.

You can set up what are known as "content groups," which allow you to group pages by theme. That way, you can see the relationships between what people click on to arrive at certain areas in your website such as the product pages. This gives you a much better idea of what different visitor segments respond to. This lets you better measure your customer experience.

(continued)

If you have something that is linear, such as a shopping cart, and in order to purchase, the customer has to follow a series of steps, then you can set up a funnel. In this case, you are measuring the order's success/failure rate. This is one of the few situations where a funnel is appropriate.

Q: The current use of analytics is based on the classical model of the Web as a set of web pages where users move from page to page. Analytics tools measure those clicks. Web 2.0, blogs, RSS, and other new tools don't work this way. Is analytics appropriate here? Are there other tools?

A: Yes, the Web is becoming a very fluid medium. It is moving away from just page-to-page views and clicks to offering new forms of media consumption. Analytics tools can only tell you how many clicks you got for an RSS feed or how far people got in a video. This is known as event-driven tracking and analytics. But they can't tell you what your media consumption is or how many people subscribe to your RSS feeds on an ongoing basis. In this space, companies such as Feed Burner are creating innovative ways of capturing data and analyzing it. The analytics vendors are starting to wake up and will add real ways of tracking these media to show total content consumption. They will figure out better ways to add analytics and tracking codes that go beyond the limits of JavaScript and log files.

Q: Many of today's high school and college students don't use the traditional Web anymore. They don't even use e-mail. They use instant messaging, SMS on cell phones, messaging in Facebook and MySpace, Twitter, and other tools. What is the role of analytics here?

A: It's the same. The role of analytics at the end of the day is two-fold. First is to measure the impact you are having on your customer experience. Second is to understand if you're spending money wisely. Those are the two problems to solve.

Traditional analytics is going to die in a few years. We are starting to see the emergence of open platforms that will let you capture any type of data. It will be a flexible, open hierarchy in which a company can define the core things it wants to track. Some analytics developers have already developed apps to track activity in Facebook and the such. They are adding a lot more innovation to this field and will push the ability to customize our tracking features. Other analytics vendors will have to catch up with these new developments.

New metrics to quantify these new types of apps will need to be developed. I imagine they may be conversation metrics. This will change, but measuring and improving customer experience will remain.

Q: A company has a website. They want to add analytics. How do you advise them on selecting the right package?

A: Start simple. If you've never used an analytics tool, I recommend Google Analytics. Analytics is theoretical until you start using it. Once you start using it, you'll understand it very quickly. Use a free tool such as Google Analytics to explore the business questions you'd like to get insights and answers to. Write these questions down and then set up new analytics profiles to see if you can get useful data.

If your business needs more analysis, move up to a more sophisticated tool. Having experience with analytics tools makes the next vendor selection much easier.

Q: In your book *Web Analytics: An Hour a Day,* you recommend that a company should supplement their analytics with survey data. Why is this? How can companies use polling and surveys to supplement their web analytics?

A: There are two parts to a question: what and why. Analytics tells you the *what.* But it doesn't tell you *why* people do what they do on your site. Why do people bounce off a page? Why do they buy more of a certain product? Why does one campaign convert less than another? The *why* is missing from analytics. No analytics tool can tell you *why* a visitor came.

In conducting a survey, ask two questions. First, why did you come to our site? Second, were you able to complete your task at our site? This metric is your task completion rate. The third question: Were you able to complete your task, and why not? This is why surveys are important. Combining the numbers with the *why* is a powerful marriage that tells us specifically where we need to improve our site, what it is we need to improve, and why we need to improve it.

Q: What's the landscape for analytics? Where is analytics going in the next few years?

A: First will be the development of a more flexible architecture to capture data. The Web is moving away from page-driven sites.

Second, companies are now building tools to solve for the trinity. Analytics data can be combined and analyzed against other sources of data.

The third trend I see is automated decision making. This can lead to onsite targeting of video media, content, and products, and not merely be confined to targeted advertising, e-mail remarketing, or customer retention campaigns. This can be based on media consumption, application usage (RSS vs. IM), buying preferences, etc. We're heading in a direction where we will see more sophisticated forms of behavioral targeting.

Another shift I think will happen is web analytics will morph into a business analytics application. In larger companies, web analytics has been siloed and hasn't been

(continued)

a prevailing trend. Merging web analytics into other systems such as ERP, CRM, BI, etc., will become easier. Analytics will play a critical role in driving company decisions and outcomes.

Q: What are your top three tips for a small company?

A: As a small business, you are more agile than a large company. Don't overextend your analytics budget. Instead, try some free tools until you understand your business needs. Stretch these tools to their limit and use surveys and the Trinity Model to fill in your customer understanding. Focus on the analysis of data.

Make site optimization changes fast. Use multivariate testing tools, such as Google Site Optimizer, which is free.

You have the power now to go against your biggest competitors. You don't need to spend a half million dollars to get a rich understanding.

Q: What are your top three tips for a large company?

A: Simplify. You are too big and complex. Don't go out and buy the most expensive, biggest, meanest tool. The decision-makers in the large companies should sit down and define their key critical priorities. They must help their analysts focus on the key priorities. Focus their attention so they don't go on crazy rides in the wrong direction.

Second, connect your analysts with those who drive business initiatives. Don't let your analysts work in a silo. Promote open, flexible communication. This enables the data to drive change.

Third, don't focus only on conversions. At large sites, people come for many reasons. Offer your visitors surveys. Do both qualitative and quantitative analysis to understand the fuller picture around your website usage and customers.

Interview: Christopher Parkin, Senior Director of Product Marketing at Omniture

In this next interview, we'll look at the challenges companies face today in adopting analytics. Christopher Parkin, Senior Director of Product Marketing, will provide insights into how Omniture approaches this process and assists its customers in more fully adopting web analytics in their companies. As Senior Director of Product Marketing for Omniture, Christopher Parkin holds overall product marketing responsibility for

Omniture's SiteCatalyst suite of web analytics and online marketing solutions. Christopher is a graduate of the University of Utah with a bachelor of science degree in business communications.

Q: Chris, what do you find are the top challenges for organizations when they adopt analytics?

A: To get fully adopted in a company, web analytics needs more than just an executive sponsor. It requires executive adoption. The most successful companies using web analytics today have an executive point person who is channeling this information into other aspects of the organization and sharing with other executives exactly how the information is being used to make decisions for the business and soliciting their feedback, their interpretation of the analysis around business strategy, as well as informed decisions around specific tactics. In order to make that happen, we've crafted a *governance practice.*

This governance practice is in place with several large clients that have users of our technology distributed across multiple business units and multiple geographies. We put a governance plan in place so people know who the right contacts are in the executive and team strategy. Each individual who has a responsibility has the most appropriate view or lens into the data that fits their role and responsibility. This is one of the things we've truly learned along the way. It's about executive adoption, not just sponsorship. It's about democratization of the data; making sure that everyone from the executive level to the frontline worker has the appropriate lens on the information that they need to be most effective in their respective roles.

Q: What are the common analytics errors by beginners?

A: The potential for information overload can be detrimental. There is no lack of information whatsoever. It's like tossing your 16-year-old kid the keys to the Ferrari. You just don't do it! That's why we've taken actions to harness the information on the front end. The neat thing is, we can toss them the keys and give them the optimally configured vehicle from the word "go."

By adapting this practice, a company recognizes tremendous value gains relative to what they may have been using previously. Once we focus them on the key areas of their business, they have the foundation for developing a rich, robust analytics practice that is in tune with their business goals and strategy.

It is about what information you should be looking at, what is actionable, and knowing very specifically when you see the needle move in one direction or another, what are the actions that you should take to drive the success of the business. From there, a company can turn on more as they need. We don't want to overwhelm them at the start with the amount of available horsepower.

(continued)

Other areas include embracing a wide variety of business models with our out-of-the-box practices across our eight industry verticals. Each vertical has distinct reporting and data collection needs. We can get our customers set up with an appropriate and tailored configuration.

The data needs to be meaningful to that company. Many companies made a decision based on price three years ago. They learned price should not be the main decision factor and now they come to us.

Q: Who are the ideal users of Omniture?

A: Our customers have changed. We have been growing up rapidly. We have been moving beyond web analytics where our point of entry used to be more IT-oriented. It was the web analyst who was being asked by other business groups, "What's going on with the website?" Then over the last few years, we saw the more innovative top-tier brands moving more of their advertising spend into the online channel to chase the audience that had already moved there. Because their customers had moved there, they had to rush to fill the gap. They started to recognize that there wasn't a media channel as measurable as the Web.

This shifted our focus from the web analyst to seeing a lot more collaboration between the online marketing manager or interactive marketing manager and the web analyst. They needed to understand the behavioral nuances of visitors on the website and how to improve and plug the leaks in the conversion funnel. They also needed to look at the different areas they're investing in, in terms of the marketing mix, to make sure the right audience is driven to the website and that the number of those who convert is maximized.

The online marketing manager takes on a more strategic role within the company. They move from being the data jockey to having compelling information that enables them to make valuable business decisions. They are competing for marketing budgets against the other channels—whether it be tradeshows, direct marketing, etc. Analytics enables the marketing manager to illustrate a much better opportunity for optimizing their budget much more quickly than the other channels. The VPs of marketing and CMOs then drove us to start integrating a lot of information across many channels and marketing applications. That way, they could see everything in one central place to make informed decisions regarding their investment dollars. The online marketing manager has become a mini-CMO—without the title, of course.

Q: What is Omniture's approach with its customers?

A: We have been working for the last two years on packaging up our industry and domain expertise across a wide variety of industry verticals. Now when we sign up a customer—whether they are a mid-market customer or an enterprise-level customer—we apply what we refer to as the Fusion methodology to their business.

We get in and implement their solution, or we guide them through the implementation process to ensure the metrics we deliver are directly aligned with what we know to be best practices in their specific industry. In addition to that, we teach them about the specific reports we enable for them as part of the Fusion implementation and provide them with prescriptive guidance on the quick wins they can achieve by taking specific actions on the data they are looking at. We tailor the views into the information, help them achieve a stable set of information so they can drive greater democratization of the data, get people on board with the information they are looking at, understand how it applies to the business and why, and what they should do with respect to seeing variances in the business. Currently, we support eight different industry verticals using the Fusion methodology.

Q: How big should a company be to use Omniture? What is the threshold?

A: We've got some very small companies who recognize the value of competing on the Web. Many of our customers have identified smaller market niches where they can compete against larger traditional catalog and mail-order companies. They dedicate the time and resources to improve their customer's online experience and purchase volume. Because they do this, they often run up against the limits of less sophisticated analytics tools very quickly. They find the data analysis comes short of answering their key critical questions. This is often the point that they become aware that they need to switch. Our pricing starts at around $1000 per month for these smaller sites. That covers 500,000 unique visitors per month.

Q: Many people say "I have Google Analytics and it's free. Why should I pay for analytics?"

A: Google generates a large number of leads for our sales force! Google has been very good for the market in terms of driving awareness around the importance of using web analytics to understand where to invest, what works, and what doesn't.

As soon as people get in and look at it, the cylinders start firing. They start to recognize some success in their business by being able to measure what's happening, stop doing things that don't work, and do more of the things that do work. As the business grows, they see a need for better tools and they quickly see the limitations of Google Analytics. They also find they need customer service and a customized business strategy. Free isn't really free. You need to evaluate the quality of the software as well as the level of customer service and customization to your business model.

Q: How do I get started with Omniture?

A: It's easy. We have a lot of experience in helping customers migrate from one platform to ours. We can put a lens on the other system's data stream and start redirecting information onto our servers in a matter of hours. A lot of larger companies can't just turn off their analytics and start over with another vendor. For many of them, we take a phased approach that graduates them off the old system.

(continued)

Second, we look at the types of information they need to analyze. We can deploy a hybrid strategy, which can include page tags, direct data calls from servers, web logs, application logs, etc., that they can use to streamline data to our server for analysis. We can capture a lot of information directly from the servers. This is more in line with the newer technologies, including streaming media, Ajax, Flash Flex, and other Web 2.0 technologies.

Q: What is the future of web analytics? Upcoming trends you see?

A: Companies want to see multiple technologies that orchestrate together as well as understand the overall business impact of these various technologies. They want better ways of measuring the business impacts and outcomes of these technologies with regards to target audience. That is coming.

Q: What headway is Omniture making in predictive analytics and predictive modeling?

A: There are a variety of methods for doing that. One is having a dedicated engine that chews on the millions of transactions that a customer gets. It identifies needles in the haystack. One product we acquired was TouchClarity.

Whether you are a first-time visitor to a website or a loyal returning visitor, the system knows information about you through your web browser. Things like your screen resolutions, your IP address, time zone, keywords, and referring sites all get passed in. This is used to determine the content that is served up to an individual. We have a machine learning language that we use to serve content based on real-time user behavior. It relies on prior experience from a large user base to determine the outcome. The machine's brain and content-serving system work together based on previous content consumption patterns.

How would you like to walk into a store and see everything in that store set up exactly as you would like it? The customer sees this as a relevant, engaging experience. It doesn't rely on personally identifiable information (PII). It's simply to improve the website experience on a per-visitor level so companies can up-sell and cross-sell in a nonintrusive way.

Q: Are specific KPIs applied to this predictive modeling engine?

A: Yes, it depends on the industry. For example, a media customer of ours wants to know the repeat visitor frequency and the velocity of specific types of content when a visitor returns to the site. What content are they looking at and, second, how quickly is that content driving them deeper into the website. What are some natural pathing interpretations they might discern from that to go out and sell highly targeted advertising space to advertisers?

A media company has very different objectives from a financial institution, which is very interested in converting people to an online application for a product. Another application is the use of self-service online banking. A customer-satisfaction survey can show how well customers are able to complete their tasks online without a need to pick up the phone to call the customer service center. We want to avoid phone calls because they are expensive for the bank.

Q: Have you seen unexpected uses of analytics?

A: An interesting trend I am seeing is with our large automobile manufacturers and online clothiers recognizing the efforts they've put into their back office solutions such as ERP, supply chain management, etc., have reached their optimization peak.

We know that several large automobile manufacturers are using our technology as a leading indictor of demand. For example, people go to these sites and use the automobile configurator to select a make, model, color, different options, and enter in their ZIP codes. We are feeding that information back into the supply chain management systems to help manufacturers make much more informed decisions about the most popular cars and configurations they should be building and which markets to target. The purchase at a dealership is tied back into the system to understand the results of our sales modeling methods. This provides our customers with a new level of intelligence on how to better optimize their businesses.

For clothing retailers such as the Gap, they can do a preemptive launch to see what people are interacting with and understand what is most popular before launching an entire Spring line on what they think will be hot. They can use this information in two ways. First, they create in-store kiosks and displays that accurately represent how people will interact with the products. Second, they can tell their manufacturers what to make and how many items to make. This can prevent an after-season fire sale. The online channel gives you a much more reliable gauge of what your customers are looking for than many traditional testing methods such as focus groups.

Q: What are your top three tips for analytics?

A: First, go for executive adoption, not just executive sponsorship. Second, integrate your different marketing technologies with your web analytics to get a single version of the truth. Third, make incremental improvements on your business by focusing on what really matters vs. everything that you can focus on. Take a strategic approach to determine what your business should act on first. Once those things are performing well, add additional areas that can be optimized.

Interview: John Squire, Chief Strategy Officer at Coremetrics

John Squire is responsible for the development and management of Coremetrics Marketing Services and setting the company's vision of the market and technical strategy for Coremetrics Behavioral Analytics and Precision Marketing solutions. John holds an MBA with High Distinction from the University of Michigan and a B.S. with Highest Distinction in chemical engineering from the University of California, Davis.

Q: John, how would you describe Coremetrics' platform solution and what it offers businesses?

A: Coremetrics uses web analytics and digital marketing applications to build a complete set of customer behavior and marketing profiles. That comes from every single click that a person makes at a website. This is designed on top of a single data warehouse for a site. The business uses that information to help drive their digital marketing operations. Coremetrics creates this rich set of analytics to show how people perform at a website.

Q: What are the strong points of your analytics solution?

A: The base of Coremetrics has been building on top of LIVE profiles. LIVE stands for *lifetime individual visitor experience.* This builds on top of an eCRM system. We build a single customer profile that contains all of their activity. Coremetrics has been built natively on top of a massive data warehouse. This lets us look at these profiles to understand how people respond to marketing programs or how products or specific content affects visitor behavior.

As many businesses move from running a website to understanding the behavior of a customer both online and offline, we believe that this underlying infrastructure of a data warehouse build on top of customer profiles is going to be extremely valuable as we move into this melding together of offline and online programs.

The big differentiator between us and some of the other big analytics players is our solution comes with the data warehouse. It is included in our package. For instance, with Omniture, you're required to buy additional services and modules, including the data warehouse, in order to step up to the next level of service.

In doing research with Forrester, we found 45% of our clients have five people or more using web analytics in their companies on a daily basis. This tells us we're not building analytics for a single power user. Instead, we're building an analytics solution which lets everyone in the company access the data and do deep mining. There are no additional charges or package upgrades for segmentation, access to the data warehouse, correlating data, designing reports, etc.

We also have Intelligent Offer, our cross-sell/up-sell recommendation engine. Intelligent Offer allows you to automatically generate relevant offers for your visitors on the fly, purely based on their behavior.

Q: Who is your target market or ideal customer in terms of revenue and monthly traffic volume?

A: Our ideal customer is someone who is curious about using and analyzing their website data. Many of our customers have used Google Analytics and need to graduate up from merely site analytics to customer analytics.

Our ideal customer has some type of value event at their site, such as a conversion process, and they need to drive marketing, site optimization, or promotions. In retail, it's a sale. In travel, it's a booking. On a content site, it's page views per visit. For a B2B site, it's the number of leads and downloads. Our clients optimize their site to specific business goals.

Our smaller customers have about 50,000 unique visitors per month. Fees start around $750 per month, which includes the data warehouse. Our clients go up to multiple billions of visitors per month. Our clients are spread out across retail, financial services, travel, and content.

Q: Let me ask you the same question: Many people say, "I have Google Analytics and it's free. Why should I upgrade?"

A: There are a couple reasons. Many have to do with the depth of data they are trying to get to. Most of the time, they are trying to get to customer analytics to get a strong understanding of the business direction they need to go in. Google Analytics doesn't provide this depth of data analysis. This is why a lot of our customers upgrade.

Q: Coremetrics is well-known as a digital marketing solutions company. Can a customer get your analytics platform without employing your digital marketing services?

A: Absolutely. They can get on the analytics platform for their business intelligence needs. If they need our digital marketing services, this would be an additional option. Furthermore, they do not need to buy the analytics solution. We have other applications that manage e-mail campaigns, paid search, etc. These applications are modular and don't rely on our analytics platform.

Q: What is your "first-click" technology? You talk about this in your case studies.

A: *First-click* describes the ability to track through from the first marketing program to the last marketing program on a unique visitor basis. This enables marketing attribution. It provides visibility on all of the marketing programs that lead to a conversion. You can apply a time window, such as seven days, 14 days, 30 days, 60 days, or any other time frame you want. You can look at a specific program such as e-mail and then tie it back to any of those different click attributions.

This helps a company understand their most effective campaigns. As a result, companies can systematically reallocate their budgets.

(continued)

Q: I see Coremetrics has coined a term called *attribution management*. Furthermore, you have developed this capability in your software solution. Tell us, what is attribution management?

A: We're the only ones who do marketing attribution and deliver it as a standard solution. This is the ability to look at any single point in the sales process.

Marketing attribution focuses on three core questions. First, what is the reference scale you want to consider? Most people say, I want to start from a sale or another type of conversion. Second, do you want to look forward for attribution or backward for attribution? Third, what is the time window you want to look at? Is it over one session, three days, seven days, 40 days, and so on? This gives you a perspective on how much data to look at and how far in time, either forward or backward, you want to look at the influence. Coremetrics allows clients to compare many different time windows next to one another.

Clients want to see the value a campaign creates for them in a session when somebody clicks through. Then they ask, how much does this campaign lead to value in the next three days, seven days, 60 days, and so on? They can set thresholds to know how much value a campaign drives over the next 60 days. In doing this, they may see that 70% of the responses happen in one session, 10% more come in three days, the next 10% comes in over the next seven days, and then 3%, 2%, 2% over the rest of that 60-day time period. By seeing the response curve, they can see how much value a specific campaign brought in and how the responses correlate to conversion events.

If we flip that over to something like search, maybe this client gets only 20% of the value in the first session but between days 40 and 50, they see the last 30%. This means they should never count their search programs by what they just got in the first session. Instead, our marketing attribution management system lets them see that it took a lot longer for people who came from Google to respond to their products.

Forward means you have to look at the impact of a campaign on product demand going forward from a specific date. Backward looks at a specific event that happened. Look backward from 30 days and tell me which first and last programs drove a customer to our site. Let's say that the revenue value for a whitepaper download is $100. We allow our clients to assign partial credits across multiple campaigns and website visits. This is done over a specified time period.

Coremetrics calculates all of these values to show you that the first click got 40% of that $100 value, the second click got 30% of that $100 value, and then all the ones remaining get the remaining 30%. This lets a marketer accurately attribute this to their campaigns, rather than just the last click, which is the result of the hard work to build up momentum to sales. We have the ability to do total click and visit analysis. You'll need to have this understanding to show your boss the budget results. This is what we call "attribution management."

Q: What about privacy concerns with analytics?
A: Yes, data collection and web sensors are a debated topic. Data collection has worked up to now by using cookies. The vendors stored the visitor information in the cookie, including the referring URLs, all of the visitor's choices and actions, etc. This resided on

the user's computer. Omniture, WebTrends, and WebSiteStory did this. Over time, they realized they needed to do something about this because the cookie was sitting there with all of the things a visitor did across every single site they were collecting information on. This gave their systems access to all of your behavior across all the sites. This raised many questions around data collection, potential misuse of consumer data, and data privacy.

Coremetrics uses a unique ID with a permanent cookie. We get a session ID and a timestamp. This is the only information that is stored in the cookie.

With packet sniffing, user privacy has been a big concern. If someone opts out on the site, you do not have the right to go and get the data. This is the whole idea behind what the FTC put out as "notice and choice."

Whether the data is personally identifiable or not, there are privacy policies. This can put the larger companies in hot water if they don't adhere to this. They must also make sure their vendors and clients are adhering to these privacy policies.

There are a lot of privacy-sensitive people out there and they love to blog. As a large company, you need to be aware of these policies and challenge your vendors to make sure they keep you out of trouble.

Make sure you are doing server-side data collection and encrypting the personally identifiable information, and make sure this is not passed through in the web browser. This can be tricky because every application and company has a different way of constructing their calls, passing data, and encrypting data. Just make sure this is done on the back end and have good firewall technology deployed.

Q: What is Coremetrics' long-term vision?

A: The place where we see the market is headed is the connection of all these different networks, whether it's the large networks like Google, Yahoo!, MSN, or smaller networks like AOL or behavioral targeting networks like Revenue Science, Boomerang, and others. E-mail is one of the networks where you reach out and try to acquire new customers to come to your site and then convert those customers, whether it's through a transaction such as an online travel booking or opening a bank account online. There's a conversion process. The next stage is retention. How do I retain my customers through all of the marketing mediums? When you spend time acquiring customers, you need to spend the time to retain them.

Our vision is there's a large set of networks where your customers or prospective customers will learn about your brand or service offerings. A business needs a way to connect these to advertise more effectively. This is driven by a set of databases or applications that sit on top of your website visitor data. Advertising is transitioning from an art to a science in which various optimization rules and algorithms are applied to present the best offer or information to a specific person at the right time.

Resources

A number of resources for analytics are available, including blogs, books, training, consultants, and so on. Several are listed here. We have an up-to-date list at our book's website at Insider-SEM.com.

Blogs about Analytics

Analytics is evolving rapidly. The best resource is blogs, where news, ideas, and tips are distributed and discussed. Use an RSS reader and subscribe to the following blogs:

- Google Analytics Blog at http://analytics.blogspot.com/.

- Avinash Kaushik at www.kaushik.net/avinash.

- Eric Peterson has a blog at www.WebAnalyticsDemystified.com/ weblog. He also hosts the Analytics Forum on Yahoo! at http://tech.groups.yahoo.com/group/webanalytics/.

- Justin Cutroni at www.epikone.com/blog.

- John Marshall at www.marketmotive.com/marshall/.

- Matt Belkin of Omniture at www.omniture.com/blog.

- The Web Analytics Association blog at http://waablog.webanalyticsassociation.org/.

- Our blog at www.Insider-SEM.com/blog.

There are additional blogs on analytics. You can add all of these to your RSS reader by fetching our OPML file for your RSS reader at our book's website.

Books on Analytics

The following books are recommended:

- *Advanced Web Metrics with Google Analytics* (Sybex, 2008), by Brian Clifton. Technical documentation of Google Analytics with details on filters and configuration. A must-have book for Google Analytics.

- *Web Analytics: An Hour a Day* (Wiley Publishing, 2007), by Avinash Kaushik. The author is the Analytics Evangelist for Google. Avinash focuses on analytics as part of business. This is the best general book on analytics.

- *Google Analytics Short Cut* (O'Reilly, 2007), by Jason Cutroni. For advanced users, this e-book has lots of details about filters, regex (regular expressions), e-commerce configuration, and so on.

- *Actionable Web Analytics* (Wiley, 2007), by Jason Burby and Shane Atchison. A useful hands-on guide to analytics in e-commerce.

- *Multichannel Marketing* (Sybex, 2007), by Akin Arikan. An overview of methods in multichannel marketing. The author is a senior manager at Unica.

- Forrester Research is writing a series of well-researched articles. Titles include "The Business Case for Web Analytics" (August 2006), "Where to Get Help with Web Analytics" (December 2007), "Google Analytics Brings Basic Web Analytics to the Masses" (September 2007), "Omniture Delivers Powerful Web Analytics for Large Enterprises" (September 2007), "ClickTracks Offers Data Visualization and Basic Analysis" (September 2007), "HBX Analytics Offers an Easy-to-Use Tool for Business Users" (September 2007), "The Web Measurement Planner's Checklist" (April 2007), and "Five Tips for Web Analytics Success" (June 2006).

- *Web Analytics for Dummies* (Wiley, 2007), by Pedro Sostre and Jennifer LeClaire. A basic guide to analytics.

- *Web Analytics Demystified* (Celilo Press, 2004), by Eric Peterson. The author has worked at top analytics companies and uses all of the major tools. (See WebAnalyticsDemystified.com.)

As more books appear, we will review them at our website.

Organizations and Trade Shows

The analytics industry is fortunate to have a professional association. You should consider membership.

- **Web Analytics Association**   The central resource for the analytics industry. You can find information, events, conferences, and job postings. Certification is also available (Stephanie Cota, coauthor of this book, is on the analytics certifications committee). See WebAnalyticsAssociation.org for more information.

- **Emetrics Summit**   Trade show for the analytics industry. See Emetrics.org for more information.

Courses and Training

There are several opportunities for training in analytics:

- Online courses at the University of British Columbia, offered in partnership with Web Analytics Association (http://www.tech.ubc.ca/webanalytics).

- Omniture offers certification (http://www.omniture.com/en/education).

- Training in analytics, KPIs, online business strategy, and multichannel marketing (http://www.Insider-SEM.com).

Conclusion

The analytics industry is headed toward consolidation and standardization. Just as Salesforce is the tool for CRM and Microsoft Excel is the standard spreadsheet for accounting, a few large companies will offer full suites of analytics tools along with integration to subvendors and services. This will allow partners, suppliers, agencies, contractors, and so on to collaborate on marketing projects and share data and results.

Analytics tools are becoming proactive. They include automated decision-making capabilities. PPC campaign management tools allow you to design rules to manage keywords based on performance. If a keyword is producing sales, it will adjust the bid to the optimal position. If keywords and ads are performing above-average in Yahoo!, the tools could also automatically copy those into Google and Microsoft PPC and test them as well.

Bid automation will be added to other channels. Through Google, you can place bids on ads in radio, TV, and newspapers, so why not automate the bid management for those channels? As the bidding model spreads throughout the advertising industry, the analytics tools will add the ability to manage those bids according to business goals and revenue data.

That opens the ability for automated marketing management across multiple channels. Ad placement could be automatically managed across thousands of newspapers, radio stations, and TV stations around the world, in dozens of languages, wherever the audience responds favorably.

Automation is extending into webpage optimization. Multivariate tools and A/B split testing tools can quickly find a combination that works better, but those tools require that you select the winning combination. By adding automated decision-making, the tool can select the best combination. But it's clear that one combination doesn't fit all customers, so an automated page optimization tool will generate pages for different types of visitors, using their demographics, interests, location, and similar profiles. By drawing from the data warehouse, these tools can use a customer's past shopping history, credit rating, and so on to offer versions of products, tailored to the visitor's needs. Based on your business goals and the activity of visitors, these tools can build on-the-fly versions of pages that are adjusted for an optimal experience to each visitor cluster. This doesn't adjust only the landing page; it can create and adjust all pages on the website so the entire website appears as an optimized presentation.

This process is only beginning. There is lots of room for innovation in analytics-driven marketing.

Chapter 4
Google Analytics

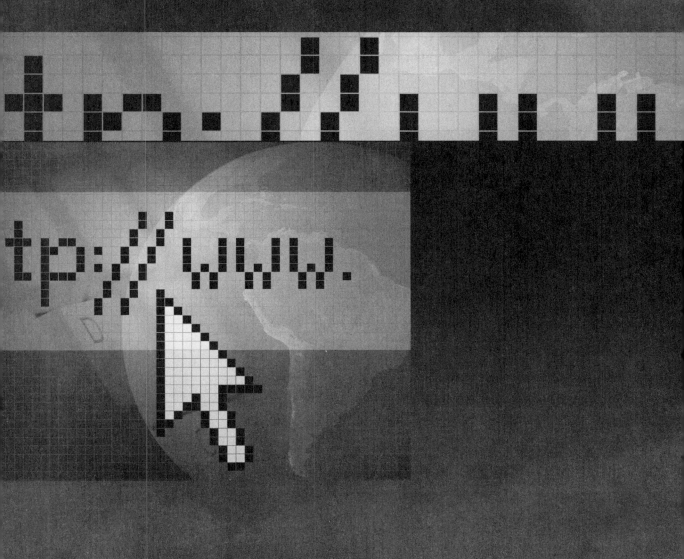

Before you try to select a large analytics package, you should become familiar with analytics. You do this by using one of the free tools. By understanding a free analytics tool, you will be able to have meaningful conversations with the sales people, ignore the bling-bling, and make the appropriate choices.

The only way to understand analytics is to actually use it. We'll use Google Analytics for this because it's widely used, free, and easy to install. You can do the same with Yahoo! Analytics and Microsoft Analytics. We will first show you how to install and configure it, then we'll show you how to use it by looking at the most useful reports.

Here are several good reasons for you to use Google Analytics:

- It's free.

- It's a good mid-level package.

- It's linked with Google AdWords.

- You can use it to learn analytics and see if you need a larger package.

You can use Google Analytics to manage pay-per-click (PPC) paid search accounts in Google AdWords, Yahoo! Search Marketing, Microsoft adCenter, and Facebook, plus other services. You can also use it to track search engine optimization (SEO) campaigns. You can use Google Analytics to track other campaigns such as bulk e-mail, radio ads, TV ads, ads in newspapers, postcards, and so on.

Can a free tool be any good? You'd be surprised to know how many Fortune 1000 companies use Google Analytics.

Install and Configure Google Analytics

Let's start with the installation and configuration of Google Analytics. After that, we'll show you how to use it.

Define Your Goals

Before you start, you need to set a clear goal for your analytics project. What is the purpose of your website? It usually comes down to a simple statement: "I want more _____." You want more conversions, sales, leads, registrations, downloads, uses of the FAQs, and so on.

You need to have a clear goal in mind. Analytics without a goal is a mere collection of data, and these tools can churn out a tsunami of numbers. A goal allows you to focus on the numbers you need. With a clear goal, you can use analytics to figure out which visitors produce the highest conversions and returns. You can target your marketing to find more of them.

Sign Up for Google Analytics

If you already have an AdWords account, click the Analytics tab and sign up. If you don't need an AdWords account, go to www.google.com/analytics and sign up.

Install the Tracking Code

Google Analytics gives you a few lines of JavaScript code for you to place on your website. This tracking code lets analytics capture activity at your pages. There are two versions of the tracking code: the legacy code and the new tracking code.

The legacy code is the old tracking code. Google will support this until the end of 2008. If you have this code on your site, switch to the new tracking code. Here's an example of the legacy code:

```
<script src="http://www.google-analytics.com/urchin.js"
type="text/javascript">
</script>
<script type="text/javascript">
_uacct = "UA-1234567890";
urchinTracker();
</script>
```

Here is an example of the new tracking code:

```
<script type="text/javascript">
var gaJsHost = (("https:" == document.location.protocol)
? "https://ssl." : "http://www.");
document.write(unescape("%3Cscript src='" +
gaJsHost + "google-analytics.com/ga.js' type='text/
javascript'%3E%3C/script%3E"));
</script>
<script type="text/javascript">
var pageTracker = _gat._getTracker("UA-1234567890");
pageTracker._initData();
pageTracker._trackPageview();
</script>
```

Why switch? The old tracking code had a problem with HTTP and HTTPS. If you had HTTPS pages on your server and you used the HTTP code, the code would send a warning to the visitor that unsecured elements appear on the page. A hack was required to get around this. The new tracking code handles both HTTP and HTTPS pages, which resolves this issue.

The new tracking code can also track Flash events, JavaScript events, PDF downloads, views of videos, outbound links, and clicks. You can also change the session timeout and the time limit for a conversion from six months to whatever you want. It also processes faster. To learn more, go to Google Analytics Help and search for "55597."

Place the tracking code on the pages you want to track. Place the code at the bottom of the HTML, just before the </BODY> tag, but not inside a table. If the tracking code is not on a page, the page won't be tracked. Although you don't need to have it on every page, we generally put the code on all pages in a website.

Within minutes, Google Analytics will detect the tracking code. Data will show up in your reports within three hours. The data is updated every three hours.

If you are using frames or Ajax, place the tracking code in the <HEAD> section. If the code is in the body of an Ajax or frames site, Google Analytics can't detect it.

tip

Use an include to place the tracking code throughout the site. This places the code in an external file, which is then automatically inserted into every page. This lets you update and modify it across all pages. This also ensures that there aren't unintended multiple versions of the Google Analytics tracking code on your site.

The Problems with Installing Analytics

Easily 50% of the trouble with analytics is in the installation. These problems include the following:

- **Incorrect installation of tracking code**   For analytics to work, the tracking code must be on the page. If the code is missing, placed incorrectly, or was changed incorrectly, the analytics won't get data. There's a free tool by EpikOne that scans your site for the Google Analytics code and finds mistakes. Visit SiteScanGA.com.

- **Company politics**   In some companies, bureaucratic inertia and internal politics can make it difficult to get the tracking code installed. The IT team may refuse to install the code for weeks (or months), usually because they don't see it as a priority. Another team may be campaigning for a different analytics package. Or perhaps another team already has an analytics package and doesn't want another. Also, sales teams earn their commissions on sales, and they don't want to share their commissions with other groups. A good solution is to use a small team to manage the analytics.

- **Multiple Google Analytics accounts** It's too easy to create accounts in Google Analytics. We've seen companies that set up as many as five accounts for the same site, but they don't realize there are different accounts, so they switch randomly from one to the other. Check the account number in the tracking code. Decide which account is the official account and delete the extra ones.

To resolve these problems, meet with the head of IT. Explain how analytics will be used to manage the marketing, which will reduce costs and increase revenues. When they understand what you want, they'll work with you to implement this.

After you've installed analytics, the next problem is using it. It's very easy to generate pretty charts with lots of numbers. But people quickly learn to ignore those. You'll need substantial dedication to get others to use the information to make decisions and changes.

Create Profiles

The next step is to create profiles in your analytics account. Think of a profile as a project in Google Analytics. You can set up different projects. A project contains the reports and data for a website. For example, you can set up three profiles for three different websites. You can also use projects to manage a directory within a website.

You can also set up several profiles for the same site. Each profile can be for a different type of user, such as the CEO, the webmaster, and the PPC manager. Each profile will have different types of reports. The CEO gets high-level reports on traffic, goals, and so on. The PPC manager gets reports on top keywords, ad placement, and so on.

If you don't understand this right away, don't worry. Profiles are a bit unclear to explain. Go ahead and follow the instructions and set up a profile. You can easily change it later. You won't break anything. One of the great things about Google Analytics is that you get lots of do-overs.

You can have up to 50 profiles in an account. This lets you track up to 50 websites and up to five million page views per month. If you sign up for an AdWords account, you get another ten million page views.

To create profiles, click Add Website Profile and enter the URL, as shown next.

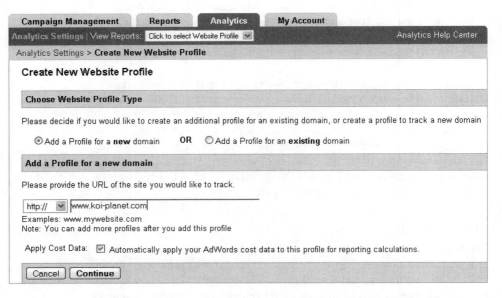

To add another profile for the same website, select Add a Profile for an existing domain, as shown next. Give the profile a name, such as Webmaster (you can edit these names later).

For now, create profiles named Executive, Marketing, SEO, PPC, Webmaster, Link Building, and Test Profile, as shown here.

Website Profiles					
« Prev 1 - 10 / 10 Next »		Show 10 ▼ Search		⊕ ⊖	
Name	**Reports**	**Settings**	**Delete**	**Status**	
1. Test Profile	View Reports	Edit	Delete	✓ Receiving Data Conversion Goals (2)	
2. PPC	View Reports	Edit	Delete	✓ Receiving Data Conversion Goals (1)	
3. SEO	View Reports	Edit	Delete	✓ Receiving Data Conversion Goals (1)	
4. Webmaster	View Reports	Edit	Delete	✓ Receiving Data Conversion Goals (1)	
5. Executive	View Reports	Edit	Delete	✓ Receiving Data Conversion Goals (1)	
6. Link Building	View Reports	Edit	Delete	✓ Receiving Data Conversion Goals (1)	
7. Marketing	View Reports	Edit	Delete	✓ Receiving Data Conversion Goals (1)	

If you later find that you don't need some of these, delete them. It's better to create them early so they can start collecting data.

Configure the Profile

The next step is to configure the profile. You'll follow these steps for each profile.

In the Settings page, click Edit. This has four sections: Main Website Profile, Conversion Goals, Filters, and Users. Let's go through each one.

Main Website Profile

You can change the profile name and the default page. You can also turn on Site Search. To do this, click Edit (upper-right corner of the box) in the Main Website Profile, as shown next.

Profile Settings: Koi-Planet.com

✓ Receiving Data (Check Status)

Main Website Profile Information	Edit
Website URL:	http://www.koi-planet.com
Default page:	index.html
Time zone country or territory:	United States
Time zone:	(GMT-08:00) Pacific Time
Exclude URL Query Parameters:	
Apply Cost Data:	Yes
E-Commerce Website:	No
Site Search:	Don't Track Site Search

This opens a window with several settings to edit. Let's go through these.

- **Set Default Index Page**   You should set the default index page. Enter the name of your main page, such as index.html or index. asp. There's a reason for doing this. When someone comes to a website, they can type either the domain name (such as site.com) or the domain name plus the home page (for example, site.com/index. html). To visitors, these are the same. But for analytics, these are different. If you don't set the default index page, Google Analytics will treat these as if they are separate pages (for example, site.com/ and site.com/index.html). This splits your data across two pages. By adding the default index page, you combine data for both into one page.

- **Apply Cost Data**   If you are using Google AdWords, turn on Apply Cost Data. It collects the data (cost per click and so on) from the AdWords account. Be careful, though. If you have campaigns for multiple websites in your AdWords account, this will use the total ad spend of the account. For example, suppose you have three websites and each one has a $1000 ad budget. If you use analytics to track only one of the sites, it will use the total ($3000) from your AdWords account (you can fix this with filters).

- **Exclude URL Query Parameters**   If your site uses session IDs, you can enter these here so the analytics will ignore them. Otherwise, each user session will appear as a different page and you'll have thousands of lines about the same page. Ask your webmaster if your site is using session IDs and add those.

- **E-commerce Site**   If your site uses e-commerce transactions, turn this setting on. You'll also need to add tracking code in the e-commerce shopping cart. How this is done will depend on your shopping cart's technology. See your shopping cart's documentation for details. For details on modifying the tracking code, search for "e-commerce" in Google Analytics Help.

- **Site Search**   If your website has an internal search box, turn this setting on. Later, we'll show you how to use this.

If you are using Google AdWords, you need to check that the tracking URLs are turned on in Google AdWords. These are normally on by default, but someone may have turned them off. To check this, go to Google AdWords and select My Account | Account Preferences | Tracking and turn this setting on.

 tip *If your site uses variables, analytics may ignore them, so all pages will appear to be the same page. Use mod_rewrite to convert dynamic URLs into static URLs. This has an additional benefit: Google can index those pages as unique pages. See http://httpd.apache.org/docs/1.3/mod/mod_rewrite.html for more info.*

Conversion Goals

In the Conversion Goals panel, shown next, you assign goal pages so you know when a conversion happens.

Conversion Goals and Funnel [?]				
Select up to 4 conversion goals for this profile, and define the funnel pages leading up to each goal.				
	Goal Name	**URL**	**Active Goal**	**Settings**
G1	Koi-Thank-You	http://www.koi-planet.com/thank-you.html	On	Edit
G2	(Goal not configured)		Off	Edit
G3	(Goal not configured)		Off	Edit
G4	(Goal not configured)		Off	Edit

Let's first review conversions. When someone buys a product at your website, they are converted from a visitor into a buyer. *Conversions* is the sales term for a successful completion of an action that you wanted the visitor to take, such as signing up in a form, buying a product, downloading a product specs PDF, watching a sales video, and so on.

When someone comes to the koi website, they look around and read about our koi. When they've decided on the breed of koi, they fill out the order form and click Submit. This brings them to the thank-you page. The only way they can reach the thank-you page is by placing an order, so whenever the thank-you page is viewed, we know a conversion took place.

We place the code on the thank-you page, as shown next, so we can track the number of conversions.

Goal Settings: G1

Enter Goal Information

Active Goal:	⦿ On ○ Off
Match Type [?]:	[Head Match ▾]
Goal URL:	http://www.koi-planet.com/thank-you.html
	(e.g. For the goal page "http://www.mysite.com/thankyou.html" enter **"/thankyou.html"**)
	When the user navigates to this page, they have reached the conversion goal (Checkout Complete, Registration Confirmation, etc.).
Goal name:	Koi-Thank-You
	Goal name will appear in Conversion reports.
Case sensitive ☐	Goal value (optional): 1

Define Funnel (optional)

A funnel is a series of pages leading up to the Goal URL. For example, you might define the checkout steps that lead up to a completed purchase as a funnel. In this example, the funnel generally would not include individual product pages -- rather, it would consist only of those final pages that are common to all transactions.

The Defined Funnel Navigation report will show you how effectively you retain visitors throughout the conversion process.

Note: URL should not contain the domain (e.g. For a step page "http://www.mysite.com/step1.html" enter **"/step1.html"**).

	URL (e.g. "/step1.html")	Name	
Step 1			☐ Required step [?]
Step 2			

Google Analytics allows up to four goals per profile. If you need to track more goals, set up additional profiles. To add a goal, click on Edit (under Settings). To set up the goal, fill out the following items:

- **Goal URL**   Enter the thank-you page's URL.

- **Goal Name**   Give the goal a name, such as Sale, Lead, or similar.

- **Goal Value**   When you've calculated your conversion's value (see Chapter 2, KPIs), enter this here. Don't skip this. You need to calculate the value for each goal.

- **Define Funnel**   We recommend that you skip this for now. It will be covered in the section *Funnels* later in this chapter.

In some situations, you may not have a thank-you page. It may be sufficient if a visitor comes to a target page, such as your contact page or your services page. You can add the target page as a goal. You can also set a folder as a goal. A visit to any of the pages within the folder will count as a conversion. These are called *microconversions*.

You can repurpose a goal for a new project. If you use the same thank-you page URL, the old data will continue to be displayed. You can change the thank-you page's URL slightly (from thankyou-001.html to thankyou-002.html, for example) to purge the old data.

> **tip** *Even if you don't have e-commerce, you can still use goals. If you are advertising on your site, divide the ad revenues by the number of visitors to find out how much each visitor is worth (for example, $10,000 in ad revenue per month divided by 50,000 visitors is 20¢ per visitor). If you increase the number of visitors, you increase your ad revenues. Or if you have a consulting business, divide the number of submitted forms it takes to get a consulting project by the value of that project (for example, $50,000 divided by five forms to get $10,000 per form). By knowing these values, you can set your promotion budgets accordingly.*

Filters

By blocking irrelevant data, you can improve the quality of the reports. For example, your own employees may be looking at your website, so you want to exclude that internal traffic from your analytics. In the next few sections, we'll show you how to set up several basic filters.

Filter to Use Lowercase   When visitors use search engines, they type keywords in various capitalizations. They use lowercase, uppercase, and a mix of both. For example, they search for koi food, Koi Food, Koi food, and koi Food. This example will be reported as four different keywords, although they are actually the same keyword.

By using a filter that converts all keywords into lowercase, the analytics combines the data for those keywords. Here is how to create a lowercase filter:

1. At Filter Type, select Custom filter.

2. Name the filter (for example, "Convert to lowercase").

3. Select Lower Case.

4. In Filter field, select Campaign Term.

Filter to Exclude IP Addresses   The analytic tool tracks all the visitors to the website, including your own visits. If your company's employees are visiting the website, that can create false traffic. If your company uses their website as the home page on company computers, you'll get inflated traffic numbers. This filter blocks out your internal traffic. Here is how to exclude IP addresses:

- First, you need to find your IP address. This is easy to do. At your computer at your office, visit WhatIsMyIPAddress.com. It shows your computer's IP address, as you can see here. Copy your IP address. If you use your computer at home to look at your work, use the website to find your home IP address. If you have employees who work offsite, ask them to send you their IP address.

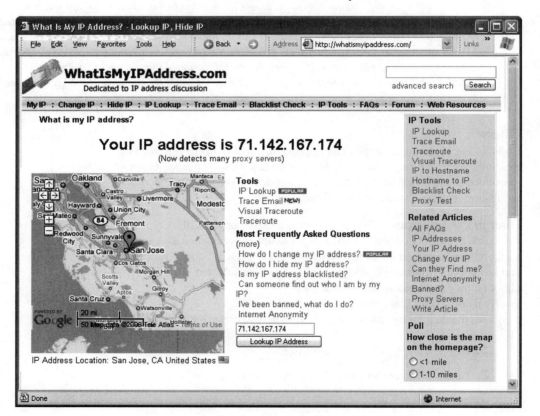

- The IP address has to be edited for Google. Change the IP address by adding a slash before each period (for example, change 123.456.789.012 to 123\.456\.789\.012).

- If your company has a range of IP addresses (such as 123.456.789.010, 123.456.789.011, 123.456.789.012, and so on), you can filter out the entire range. Search the Help for "range of IP address" for a list of options on how to do this.

- If your company has multiple offices (Palo Alto, New York, Beijing), you will have several IP addresses. Add as many IP addresses to your list as necessary.

- Look at Traffic Sources and see if there are sites with significant traffic that should not be tracked. If you see a URL that generates lots of traffic but zero conversions, you can filter it out.

- Be careful: Google has an error in some of their pages. They add a closing slash and a closing dot to the IP address, such as 71\.142\.167\.174\. (note the final slash and dot). This is not valid. It should be 71\.142\.167\.174 (no final slash or dot).

Don't forget that you have these filters. If you've excluded your company's traffic and you're now testing a form, you'll wonder why conversions don't appear. It's because you excluded your own traffic. Remember the Test profile? Don't add any filters to that profile. Use it as a test box where you can see everything that is going on.

Filter to Exclude a Domain Name   You can also filter out a domain name. This ignores all the traffic from the employees at that URL. However, this may not be a good idea. Often, the website is hosted at a large ISP that hosts many companies. If you block the domain, you may also filter out data from all other domains that are hosted by that ISP. In general, you should filter the IP address, not the domain name.

Search and Replace Filters   Search and replace filters can replace a term with another one. For example, you can replace product ID numbers with descriptive words. Suppose the file IDs look like this:

```
/docs/document.cgi?id=1000
/docs/document.cgi?id=2000
```

Using the search and replace filter, you can convert "1000" to "books" and "2000" to "magazines." This makes your reports more useful for people who are not familiar with the ID codes. For more about this, search for "Advanced Filters" in Google Analytics Help.

Filter to Select Only One Folder   You can also create a filter that reports on only one folder. To do this, set Filter Type to "Include only traffic to a subdirectory." Then enter the name for the subdirectory, as shown next.

Note that you need to use a special format: If the folder is named /koi-food, enter it as **^/koi-food/** and save the changes.

Enter Filter Information

Filter Name: `Koi Food`

Filter Type: `Include only traffic to a subdirectory`

Subdirectory `^/koi-food/`   What do the special characters mean?

Apply Filter to Website Profiles

Available Website Profiles

```
PPC
SEO
Webmaster
Executive
Link Building
Marketing
Test Profile
```

`Add »`

`« Remove`

Selected Website Profiles

`Koi Food`

`Save Changes` `Cancel`

Custom Filters   You can create many kinds of filters. Custom Filters offers many options:

- **Regular expressions**   Filters can use regular expressions (regex), a database method for processing search patterns. You can find many regex tutorials and FAQs on the Web (for example, www.Regular-Expressions.info).

- **Lookup tables (LUT)**   These allow you to use a list of X and Y values. Although this feature is listed, it is apparently turned off for most users.

- **Advanced filters**   This feature allows you to use regex to create customized filters for e-commerce, ad campaigns, and so on.

For more details, use Help and search for "custom filters."

Manage Filters   Once you've created a filter, you can apply it to the other profiles. Here are the steps to follow:

1. Click on Filter Manager.

2. Click Edit to open a filter, as shown next.

3. The lower pane shows the profiles that don't use the filter (Available Profiles) and the profiles that do use the filter (Selected Profiles). Select one or more profiles and add them.

Filter Manager

Existing Filters			+ Add Filter
« Prev 1 - 3 / 3 Next » Show 10 ▾ Search			⊕ ⊖

	Filter Name	Filter Type	Settings	Delete
1.	My IP Address	Exclude	Edit	Delete
2.	Koi Food	Include	Edit	Delete
3.	Use Lowercase	Lowercase	Edit	Delete

 note   *Filters are applied in the order they are listed. The results of a filter are used for the next filter.*

Users

You can grant others access to your analytics account. Before you do this, they must have a Google Gmail account. Here are the steps involved:

1. Click on Access Manager.

2. Click Add User.

3. Enter the Google Gmail address and name.

4. Select the type of access: View Only or Administrator. If the user has Administrator status, they can see all profiles and reports in your account.

5. For users to access the analytics account, they go to www.google.com/analytics and log in with their Google Gmail and password.

How to Create Tracking URLs

One of the best features of Google Analytics is the link with Google AdWords. AdWords feeds information to Google Analytics about the cost-per-click, the budgets, the keywords, and so on.

If you are only using Google AdWords, you can skip the rest of this section. Just remember you can use Google's URL Builder to track online campaigns, such as PPC in Yahoo! or Microsoft, e-mail newsletters, banner ads, link building, and so on. You can also track offline campaigns, such as radio ads, TV ads, newspaper ads, postcards, and the Goodyear blimp. This lets you track visits, conversions, and revenues.

Google AdWords and Google Analytics are linked by default. If you are using Yahoo! and Microsoft PPC, you need to track those. If you don't tag that data, Google Analytics will treat it as organic data. In other words, a visit from Yahoo!'s PPC appears to Google Analytics as organic (nonpaid) traffic from Yahoo! If you tag the data, Google can tell whether it is paid or nonpaid traffic and apply the cost data. This applies to any PPC service you may use.

To use the tool, go to Google Analytics Help and search for "URL Builder." Select the first link in the results and then follow these steps:

1. Fill out the boxes.

2. Click Generate URL.

3. The tracking URL appears in the bottom field, as shown next. Copy and paste it into Notepad.

Google Analytics URL Builder

Step 1: Enter the URL of your website.
Website URL: * `http://www.koi-planet.com/koromo-koi.html`
(e.g. *http://www.urchin.com/download.html*)

Step 2: Fill in the fields below. **Campaign Source**, **Campaign Medium** and **Campaign Name** are required values.

Campaign Source: *	Google	(referrer: google, citysearch, newsletter4)
Campaign Medium: *	PPC	(marketing medium: cpc, banner, email)
Campaign Term:		(identify the paid keywords)
Campaign Content:		(use to differentiate ads)
Campaign Name*:	Summer	(product, promo code, or slogan)

Step 3
[Generate URL] [Clear]

`http://www.koi-planet.com/koromo-koi.html?utm_source=Google&utm_med`

The following is an example of a tracking URL:

http://www.koi-planet.com/?utm_source=google&utm_
medium=ppc&utm_campaign=summer

The tracking URL is made up of several attributes, such as source or campaign. These allow you to pass information to the analytics tool. In the example, you can see that the source is Google, the medium is PPC,

Name	Required?	Description	Example
Campaign Source	Yes	The source, such as Google, Yahoo!, Los Angeles Times	utm_source=google
Campaign Medium	Yes	How the campaign will be delivered—PPC, e-mail newsletter, postcard, and so on.	utm_medium=ppc
Campaign Term	No	If you are using PPC, add the keyword.	utm_term=koromo
Campaign Content	No	Differentiate links to the same page. A page may also have three links to the same offer. You can test which works better.	utm_content=photo utm_content=text utm_content=buybutton
Campaign Name	Yes	Differentiate campaigns, such as name of products, spring, promotion codes, and so on.	utm_name=summer

TABLE 4-1   Explanation of the items in a tracking URL, along with examples.

and the campaign is our Summer campaign. Table 4-1 lists the attributes, along with an explanation and examples.

You can use the tool to generate a tracking URL and then edit it to create more URLs. You can use these as links in your Microsoft PPC, your e-mail newsletters, and so on.

The URL Builder documentation uses a plus sign to combine two words (for example, utm_term=koromo+koi), but URL Builder's result uses %2B to combine two words (for example, utm_term=koromo%2Bkoi). The second version is correct. Google may fix this at some point.

tip *If you plan to use a URL in postcards or on the radio, it must be short and easy to remember, such as Koi-Planet.com/Summer, because people will have to type these. But tracking URLs are often very long and ugly. Nobody will want to type those. Thankfully, several solutions are available. A 301-redirect lets you point the short URL to the long URL. Visitors type Koi-Planet.com/Summer, which is converted into a longer tracking URL. (For more about 301-redirects, see the 301-redirect FAQ at Insider-SEM.com.) Another way is to buy a URL for your campaign, such as SummerKoi.com, JulyKoi.com, and so on. URLs are only $7 at low-cost services such as GoDaddy.com.*

Use Event Tracking with Flash, Ajax, and Web 2.0

With event tracking, you can track user actions instead of pageviews. This lets you track Flash, including Flash movies, embedded AJAX page elements, page gadgets, and file downloads. This lets you track your visitor's activity on Web 2.0 sites.

The reports appear in Content | Event Tracking. This can be valuable information. For example, Honda created a page that lets visitors select the options for their car: colors, interior, features, and so on. All of this was created in Flash. By tracking the visitors' options, Honda was able to learn what the market really wanted. They could do inexpensive market research. In another example, a Hollywood studio used event tracking to test trailers for a new movie. By watching at what point people abandoned the trailers, they improved the final version.

For details, visit http://code.google.com/apis/analytics/docs/.

Schedule Reports

The next step is to set up automated recurring reports. On the first of every month or every quarter, Google Analytics will send you a report by e-mail. You can add multiple e-mail addresses so others get the reports. Here are the steps to follow to set up this feature:

1. Click the Email icon.

2. Click the Schedule tab.

3. Add the e-mail addresses. Separate the e-mails with commas.

4. Under Subject, you only need to add "Monthly" or "Quarterly." Google will add a longer subject header. Look at the far right of the window to see the subject header, as shown next.

5. Select the format. You can get reports in PDF, XML, CSV (spreadsheet), or TSV (text file) format.

6. Select the schedule: weekly, monthly, or quarterly.

7. Check the Include Date Comparison box. The report will include a this-week-vs.-last-week, this-month-vs.-last-month, or this-quarter-vs.-last-quarter comparison so you can see if the trend is up or down.

☑ Send Now	⊙ Schedule

Send to others: (Separate multiple addresses with a comma)

    maggie@koi-planet.com,
    eurydice@koi-planet.com,

☑ Send to me

Subject: Quarterly

Description:

    Quarterly analytics report for
    Koi-Planet.com.

Format:
- ⊙ 📄 PDF   ○ 📊 CSV
- ○ 📄 XML   ○ 📄 TSV

Date Range/Schedule: Quarterly (sent first day of each quarter) ▼

Include date comparison: ☑

Schedule

Preview

To: maggie@koi-planet.com, eurydice@koi-planet.com,

From: eurydice@gmail.com

Subject: Analytics koi-planet.com 20071217-20080317 (Quarterly)

Attachment: 📄 PDF

Quarterly analytics report for Koi-Planet.com.

To manage your reports (add or delete recipients, and so on), click Settings Email. Select the report and make your changes. You can also delete a report.

We suggest you set up a team strategy session to review the reports at the beginning of each quarter. By discussing the items in the reports, plus taking requests for missing items, you'll quickly develop useful dashboard reports.

Weekly reporting sounds tempting, but don't use it. Most people look at weekly reports for a few weeks and then ignore them. Weekly reports generally don't have enough data to show trends. We recommend quarterly reports.

Tailor the Reports for Each Profile

You can create automated reports for the various job titles and functions in your company. Create a profile for each job function and then create automated reports for that profile.

Each profile should get only the reports relevant to their job title. There's no use in sending information to people who can't act on it.

Table 4-2 provides some suggestions for profiles, dashboards, and reports.

You'll notice that we put goals at the beginning of most of these. Work with your teams to get them to focus on the company's goals.

Too Much Data?

If you are getting 500,000 visits or more per month, your reporting may slow down. When this happens, you can reduce the amount of data sampling. Instead of collecting 100% of the data, you can collect a smaller percentage. Because you have a very large sample, the margin of error

Profile Name	Audience	Dashboard Reports
Sales & Marketing	VPs, directors, and managers in sales and marketing	Goals, SEO, PPC, keywords, revenues, funnel, traffic sources, referrers, campaigns comparison, bounce rates, internal search, map, and site overlay.
Executive	CEO and top staff	Goals, overview of site activity, campaigns comparison, plus a map of a country or state.
SEO	The SEO team	Goals, paid and nonpaid keywords by conversion, entrance pages, internal search, referrers.
PPC	The PPC team	Goals, paid and nonpaid keywords by conversion, ads by conversion, ad positions, internal search, entrance pages, campaigns comparison, and a map.
Webmaster	The webmaster, web graphics, and IT support	Reports to improve the web pages or highlight technical issues at the website. This includes bounce rates for entrance pages, traffic trends, site overlay, funnel, internal search, browsers, resolution, languages, JavaScript, and Flash.
Link Building	The link building team	List of referrers, ranked by conversion.

TABLE 4-2   Some suggestions for profiles, dashboards, and reports.

will be insignificant. To collect, for example, 50% of your data, add the following line to your analytics tracking code:

```
pageTracker._setSampleRate(50)
```

If you're working with very large data sets, consider an enterprise analytics package such as Omniture or CoreMetrics.

How Long Does It Take for Data to Appear?

After you've added the tracking code to your website, data will begin to show up within three hours. Let it run for a few days and then look at the data and ask yourself the following questions:

- Do the traffic volumes make sense? Is your reported traffic in relation to your sales? If the reported traffic is too low, perhaps the tracking code is missing on key pages.

- Look at the list of content pages. Are any significant pages missing in that list? If a page is missing, check the page's source code to see if the tracking code is present.

- Is there data in the goals? Does it match your data from CRM or other tools?

Using Google Analytics

If the goal data is missing or too low, check the pages and settings to see what is wrong.

Google Analytics has over 50 reports. Most of us call these *views, screens, pages,* or *panels.* However, Google Analytics calls them *reports,* so we'll use that name in this book. As shown next, a Google Analytics report may show you a graph for a time span, a pie chart, and a numeric breakdown of the data.

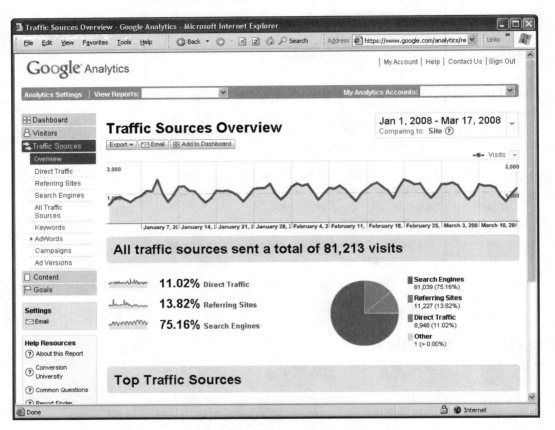

Using the Dashboard

The Dashboard is your collection of favorite reports. You can add and remove reports in the Dashboard. After a few weeks, you'll find the reports that you like and you'll add those to the Dashboard.

You can configure the Dashboard as you like. To see how to do this, let's add a report and then remove it:

> **1.** At the far left, click Visitors and then click Languages. This shows a list of visitors' languages (English, French, and so on). Click Add to Dashboard to add this report to your dashboard, as shown next.

Traffic Sources Overview

2. Click Dashboard to return to the dashboard. Your new report appears at the bottom of the page.

3. To move the report, grab the gray bar and drag it to a new location.

4. To remove a report from the dashboard, click the close button at the far right in the gray bar.

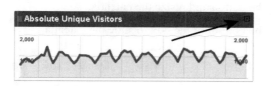

Setting the Date Range

In the calendar box, shown next, click the down arrow to open the calendar.

Feb 1, 2008 - Feb 29, 2008
Comparing to: Site (?)

You have three ways to change the calendar span: click on dates in the calendar, use a timeline, or edit the dates.

Here are some points about clicking on the dates in a calendar:

● To select a week, click the side tab.

● To select a month, click the month heading.

- To select a range, as shown next, click the first date and then the second date.

- To scroll to another month, click the scroll arrows.

The timeline, shown next, lets you pick dates from a horizontal timeline. Here are some points to keep in mind:

- Click inside the calendar to activate the grab buttons.

- Grab the button and resize the calendar.

- Grab the bottom of the box to slide the calendar.

Finally, you can also edit the dates in the text box. Click and change the dates, as shown next.

You can also compare one time span against another: this week vs. last week, this month vs. last month, this quarter vs. last quarter. To do this, click the arrows next to Site and select Date Range. In Timeline, a green box appears next to the blue box, as shown next. The green box has the same number of days as the blue box. You can click in the box and resize each box independently. You can also slide them so you can compare June and October, for example. Click Apply, and a new graph shows both date ranges. The thick blue line shows the current (or recent) time span; the thin green line shows the previous time span. This lets you quickly compare two trends.

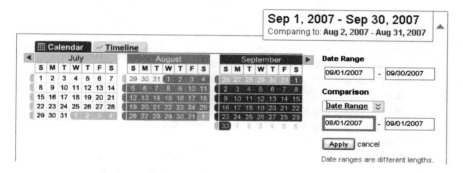

If you don't do a comparison, you get the following chart:

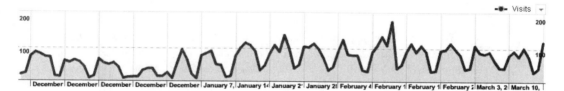

If you compare the period with the previous period, you can see the improvement. The thick line is the current period; the thin line is the previous period:

Dec 1, 2007 - Mar 17, 2008
Comparing to: **Aug 15, 2007 - Nov 30, 2007**

Let's look at the trends. You can see the weekly traffic cycle. Traffic starts to grow on Tuesdays; it peaks on Wednesdays and ends by Thursday. Weekends are quiet. If your site's traffic has a weekly cycle, this lets you know when to send out announcements and new releases. When you launch campaigns, do so on a Tuesday at 9 A.M. for New York City. This places your ads in front of people when they'll likely see it. The worst time to launch a campaign is Friday afternoon because traffic drops on the weekends.

Some industries have seasonal trends. As data streams in over the year, ski resorts see a drop in summer and a spike in late fall and winter. Garden supply vendors see a spike in early spring. Some industries aren't affected by seasonality and have a steady flow of traffic throughout the year.

There are also holidays. You'll see significant traffic drops in the U.S. for Easter, 4th of July, Thanksgiving, Christmas, and New Years. These are often four-day holidays and people are away from their computers. If you're managing campaigns in China or Europe, look for traffic drops on the major holidays there as well.

Watch your visitor trends for the year and use that to plan campaign releases. You can see when traffic starts to climb. Be ready with campaigns for those early buyers.

In general, look at traffic for the last 60–90 days. It sounds good to be able to see a year or more of data, but with so many changes on the site and in the marketplace, most data from a year ago isn't very useful.

tip   To see data for only one day, click twice on that day in the calendar. The first click selects the start day and the second click sets the end day, which in this case is the same day. This lets you isolate a single day and look at its numbers in the various reports. For example, if you sent out an e-mail to 10,000 customers, this lets you review the results, day by day.

Comparing Metrics

You can also compare two metrics to see if there are trends that affect each other. Click the arrow and then click Compare Two Metrics. Use this in the Visitor or Traffic Sources section, where you can compare traffic vs. goals. For example, in Traffic Sources | Search Engines, click on a search engine and then open the tool. Click on Compare Two Metrics and leave the first metric (blue) on Visits, as shown next. Set the second metric (orange) to one of your goals. The graph shows both trends, so you can see if they move up together or whether one goes up and the other goes down.

The number of conversions follows the number of visits, which is expected. On February 9th and March 9th, bulk e-mails were sent out to

customers, which produced two spikes that were independent of the general
website traffic.

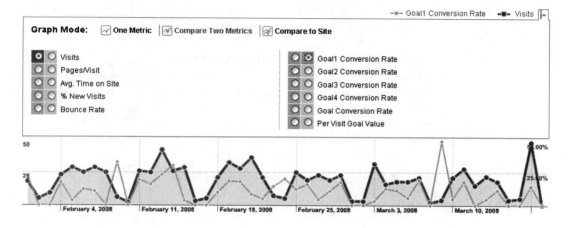

Navigating in Google Analytics

At the left side is a vertical navigation bar that contains general topics
(Visitors, Traffic Sources, and so on). When you click one of those, a
submenu appears. The reports appear in four categories:

- **Visitors** These reports show you information about your visitors
  (city, language, and so on) and their computers (version of Java,
  browser, OS, and so on). By knowing this, you can make changes to
  your website.

- **Traffic Sources** These reports show you which search engines or
  websites your visitors come from. You can also see which keywords
  and ads produced results. By knowing this, you can advertise
  effectively and cut waste.

- **Content** These reports provide information about your web
  pages, the top pages, and the links on your pages. With this
  information, you can improve your pages.

- **Goals** These reports help you study your conversions. Where did
  those conversions come from? How much did you earn? Which
  campaigns produce more?

For example, if you want to go to the site overlay item in the Content
section, select Content | Site Overlay.

We will go through each of these menus later in this chapter.

Best Practices in Analytics: Using the Top Reports

Let's go through the top analytics reports and how to use them to improve your conversions. You should try these so you're familiar with them and can choose the ones that are appropriate for your project.

Find the Keywords That Bring Conversions

Let's find the keywords that visitors type into search engines to come to your site. By knowing what they search for, you can target those keywords in the research or purchase phase of the buying cycle. You can use these in your SEO or PPC paid search projects. Here are the steps to follow:

1. Go to Traffic Sources | Keywords.

2. Increase the time span to three or six months to get a large list of keywords.

3. The default report opens with ten keywords, as shown next. To see a longer list, go to the lower right of the report and increase Show Rows to 50 or 100.

4. You can sort the columns by clicking the column headings.

Search sent 654 total visits via 178 keywords

Show: total | paid | non-paid   Segment: Keyword ▾

	Site Usage	Goal Conversion			Views: ▦ ● ≣ ≛	∿
Visits ⑦ **654** % of Site Total: **84.06%**	**Pages/Visit** ⑦ **2.88** Site Avg: 2.77 (4.01%)	**Avg. Time on Site** ⑦ **00:01:08** Site Avg: 00:01:05 (4.44%)	**% New Visits** ⑦ **93.27%** Site Avg: 93.83% (-0.59%)	**Bounce Rate** ⑦ **39.45%** Site Avg: 43.19% (-8.66%)

Keyword	Visits ↓	Pages/Visit	Avg. Time on Site	% New Visits	Bounce Rate
1. koi	139	3.12	00:01:21	91.37%	25.90%
2. (content targeting)	70	3.86	00:01:43	94.29%	27.14%
3. koi fish	59	3.29	00:01:13	100.00%	33.90%
4. ornamental goldfish	54	1.50	00:00:30	100.00%	74.07%
5. koi for sale	38	3.16	00:00:53	76.32%	13.16%
6. koi farm	21	3.43	00:00:58	95.24%	33.33%
7. koromo koi	15	1.93	00:00:16	93.33%	53.33%
8. koi planet	14	3.14	00:00:44	85.71%	50.00%
9. asagi koi	11	2.27	00:02:24	90.91%	36.36%
10. planet koi	11	4.18	00:01:01	100.00%	18.18%

Find Keyword: containing ▾ [   ] Go   Go to: 1   Show rows: 10 ▾   1 - 10 of 178 ◄ ►

The report opens at the default Site Usage tab. However, conversions are what counts, so click on the Goal Conversion tab, as shown next. (This assumes you've set up conversion goals.) Now you can see the keywords that actually produce conversions.

Search sent 1,423 total visits via 210 keywords

Show: total | paid | non-paid   Segment: **Keyword** ⌄

Site Usage	**Goal Conversion**							Views: ▦ ● ☰ ± ～

Visits ⑦ **1,423** % of Site Total: 60.81%	Goal1: ⑦ **16.58%** Site Avg: 15.04% (10.25%)	Goal2: ⑦ **0.35%** Site Avg: 0.56% (-36.75%)	Goal3: ⑦ **0.00%** Site Avg: 0.73% (-100.00%)	Goal4: ⑦ **9.28%** Site Avg: 8.76% (5.88%)	Goal Conversion Rate ⑦ **26.21%** Site Avg: 25.09% (4.49%)	Per Visit Goal Value ⑦ **$22.00** Site Avg: $0.00 (0.00%)

	Keyword	Visits ↓	Goal 1 Info	Goal 2 Buy Koi	Goal 3 Food	Goal 4 Pumps	Goal Conversion Rate	Per Visit Goal Value
1.	koi	514	2.53%	0.19%	0.00%	1.75%	4.47%	$0.00
2.	(content targeting)	198	27.27%	1.52%	0.00%	15.15%	43.94%	$0.00
3.	koi fish	136	13.24%	0.00%	0.00%	11.03%	24.26%	$0.00
4.	ornamental goldfish	74	37.84%	0.00%	0.00%	25.68%	63.51%	$0.00
5.	koi for sale	43	79.07%	0.00%	0.00%	4.65%	83.72%	$0.00
6.	koi farm	38	0.00%	0.00%	0.00%	0.00%	0.00%	$0.00
7.	koromo koi	30	30.00%	0.00%	0.00%	13.33%	43.33%	$0.00
8.	koi planet	19	10.53%	0.00%	0.00%	10.53%	21.05%	$0.00
9.	asagi koi	16	12.50%	0.00%	0.00%	6.25%	18.75%	$0.00
10.	planet koi	15	13.33%	0.00%	0.00%	0.00%	13.33%	$0.00

Find Keyword: containing ⌄ [   ] Go   Go to: 1   Show rows: 10 ⌄   1 - 10 of 210 ◀ ▶

To see the keywords that came from PPC, click Paid, as shown next. This shows your successful PPC keywords. You can increase bids on those; you can create ad groups around those keywords, and you can search for additional similar keywords. You can also see which keywords have low conversions, and you can delete those keywords. You can also add the top keywords to your SEO.

Search sent 869 paid visits via 46 keywords

Show: total | paid | non-paid   Segment: Keyword ⌄

Site Usage	Goal Conversion						Views:

Visits (?) 1,423 % of Site Total: 60.81%	Goal1: (?) 16.58% Site Avg: 15.04% (10.25%)	Goal2: (?) 0.35% Site Avg: 0.56% (-36.75%)	Goal3: (?) 0.00% Site Avg: 0.73% (-100.00%)	Goal4: (?) 9.28% Site Avg: 8.76% (5.88%)	Goal Conversion Rate (?) 26.21% Site Avg: 25.09% (4.49%)	Per Visit Goal Value (?) $22.00 Site Avg: $0.00 (0.00%)

	Keyword	Visits ↓	Goal 1 Info	Goal 2 Buy Koi	Goal 3 Food	Goal 4 Pumps	Goal Conversion Rate	Per Visit Goal Value
1.	koi	514	2.53%	0.19%	0.00%	1.75%	4.47%	$0.00
2.	koromo koi	135	13.33%	0.00%	0.00%	11.11%	24.44%	$0.00
3.	(content targeting)	38	0.00%	0.00%	0.00%	0.00%	0.00%	$0.00
4.	koi fish	32	15.62%	3.12%	0.00%	6.25%	25.00%	$0.00
5.	koi for sale	19	10.53%	0.00%	0.00%	10.53%	21.05%	$0.00
6.	koi farm	14	7.14%	0.00%	0.00%	0.00%	7.14%	$0.00
7.	buy koi fish	11	0.00%	0.00%	0.00%	0.00%	0.00%	$0.00
8.	koi fish for sale	9	11.11%	0.00%	0.00%	0.00%	11.11%	$0.00
9.	koi ponds	9	0.00%	0.00%	0.00%	0.00%	0.00%	$0.00
10.	pond koi	7	0.00%	0.00%	0.00%	0.00%	0.00%	$0.00

Find Keyword: containing ⌄ [   ] Go   Go to: 1   Show rows: 10 ⌄   1 - 10 of 210 ◄ ►

To see the keywords that came from non-PPC (that is, organic or natural search), click Non-Paid, as shown next. This shows the keywords that people typed into search engines. Your site showed up in the results and they came to your site. By clicking the Conversion tab, you can see which keywords brought conversions. Use this list of keywords to improve your SEO. You can also add those keywords to your PPC.

Search sent 554 non-paid visits via 172 keywords

Show: total | paid | non-paid   Segment: **Keyword** ⌄

Site Usage	Goal Conversion					Views:

| Visits (?) 1,423 % of Site Total: 60.81% | Goal1: (?) 16.58% Site Avg: 15.04% (10.25%) | Goal2: (?) 0.35% Site Avg: 0.56% (-36.75%) | Goal3: (?) 0.00% Site Avg: 0.73% (-100.00%) | Goal4: (?) 9.28% Site Avg: 8.76% (5.88%) | Goal Conversion Rate (?) 26.21% Site Avg: 25.09% (4.49%) | Per Visit Goal Value (?) $22.00 Site Avg: $0.00 (0.00%) |

	Keyword	Visits ↓	Goal 1 Info	Goal 2 Buy Koi	Goal 3 Food	Goal 4 Pumps	Goal Conversion Rate	Per Visit Goal Value
1.	"asagi koi"	166	29.52%	1.20%	0.00%	16.87%	47.59%	$0.00
2.	"ornamental goldfish"	72	38.89%	0.00%	0.00%	26.39%	65.28%	$0.00
3.	12 types koi	40	80.00%	0.00%	0.00%	2.50%	82.50%	$0.00
4.	koromo koi	29	31.03%	0.00%	0.00%	13.79%	44.83%	$0.00
5.	asagi blue	16	12.50%	0.00%	0.00%	6.25%	18.75%	$0.00
6.	asagi for sale	13	15.38%	0.00%	0.00%	7.69%	23.08%	$0.00
7.	asagi koi	12	8.33%	0.00%	0.00%	0.00%	8.33%	$0.00
8.	asagi koi colors	6	0.00%	0.00%	0.00%	0.00%	0.00%	$0.00
9.	asagi koi for sale	6	16.67%	0.00%	0.00%	0.00%	16.67%	$0.00
10.	asagi koi for sale.	6	66.67%	0.00%	0.00%	50.00%	116.67%	$0.00

Find Keyword: containing ⌄ [   ] Go   Go to: 1   Show rows: 10 ⌄   1 - 10 of 210 ◄ ►

You'll notice that we talk quite a bit about koromo koi, but our visitors are actually interested in asagi koi. Hmm… maybe it's time for a board meeting and a change of direction.

If you set a value in the goal configuration, this report shows the value of conversions. Go through your key performance indicator (KPI) calculation (see Chapter 2, KPIs) to determine these values.

You can save this report to the Dashboard. However, you can only save either the paid or the nonpaid report, not both at once. Select one and then click Add to Dashboard. Go back, select the other, and add it to the dashboard as well.

You can export the list of keywords. At the upper left of the report, click Export and select CSV (for spreadsheets) or TSV (for text editors), as shown next.

Keywords

Export ▲ | ✉ Email | ⊞ Add to Dashboard
🔳 PDF | 🔳 XML | 🔳 CSV | 🔳 TSV

Be sure you look for misspellings as well. Very often, misspelled words have high traffic. Add these misspellings to your website. At the bottom of the web page, add a sentence that includes the misspelled word. For example, *fish* is often misspelled as *fsih,* so at the bottom of the page, add a sentence such as "Were you looking for koi fsih?" The search engines will find this misspelling and add it to their index.

You can also track PPC from Yahoo!, Microsoft, and Facebook. Google AdWords already tags the clicks, so Google Analytics knows that traffic from Google is either paid or nonpaid. Use the URL tagging tool to create tags for your PPC campaigns in Yahoo! and Microsoft. This allows Google Analytics to distinguish between paid and nonpaid traffic from them (without URL tagging, the PPC keywords appear to be nonpaid). To do this, see the section How to Create Tracking URLs earlier in this chapter.

Find the Keyword Positions That Bring Conversions

Wouldn't you like to know whether your ad works better in position 2 or position 7 in Google? With the Keyword Positions report, you can see the number of clicks (and conversions!) for every position in Google. Here are the steps to follow to set up this report:

1. Go to Traffic Sources | AdWords | Keyword Positions and set the time span. When you open this report, you don't see very much. At the left is a list of keywords from AdWords; at the right is blank screen, as shown next.

Keyword	Visits ⌄ ↓	Position breakdown:	Visits ⌄
koi	137 ▶		
(content targeting)	70 ▶		
koi fish	58 ▶		
koi for sale	33 ▶	**Choose a keyword to see its performance across ad positions.**	
koi farm	21 ▶		
koi fish for sale	5 ▶		
buy koi fish	5 ▶		
pond koi	4 ▶		
koi ponds	4 ▶		
Find keywords containing ⌄ [ ] Go		Show rows 10 ⌄ 1 - 9 of 9 ◀ ▶	

2. Click a keyword on the left side. The right side now shows you a Google search page. Your keyword showed up in Google in those positions. It shows you the number of visits (clicks).

The top keyword (koi) was clicked only twice when it was in the blue box at the top of the page, but it got the most clicks in position 8 (33 clicks), as shown next. That's unexpected.

Keyword	Visits	Position breakdown:	Visits
koi	137		
(content targeting)	70	Top 1: **2**	Side 1: **12**
koi fish	58		Side 2: **14**
koi for sale	33		Side 3: **15**
koi farm	21		Side 4: **14**
koi fish for sale	5		Side 5: **17**
buy koi fish	5		Side 6: **15**
pond koi	4		Side 7: **15**
koi ponds	4		Side 8: **33**

Find keywords containing [ ] Go   Show rows 10   1 - 9 of 9

3. Now click on the dropdown menus to see conversions. This shows you which positions brought conversions. It may well be for your campaign that position 4 works better than position 1. For Koi-Planet, positions 3, 4, and 5 produced the most conversions. Write down these optimal positions and then lower or raise your bids to get your ads in these positions.

Keyword	Visits	Position breakdown:	% New Visits
koi	137		Visits
			Pages/Visit
(content targeting)	70		Avg. Time on Site
		Top 1: **3.00%**	% New Visits
koi fish	58		Bounce Rate
			Goal1 Conversion Rate
koi for sale	33		Goal Conversion Rate
			Per Visit Goal Value
koi farm	21		Side 3: **13.33%**
koi fish for sale	5		Side 4: **11.00%**
buy koi fish	5		Side 5: **13.06%**
pond koi	4		Side 6: **8.00%**
			Side 7: **9.00%**
koi ponds	4		Side 8: **6.97%**

Find keywords containing [ ] Go   Show rows 10   1 - 9 of 9

Find the Ads That Bring Conversions

Just as with keywords, we can see which ads produce conversions. Here are the steps involved:

1. Go to Traffic Sources | Ad Versions, set the time span, and then click the Goal Conversion tab. Your ads are listed by their headings, along with their conversions.

2. For this to work, your ads should use unique headings. If several ads have the same heading, their results will be combined.

3. Look at these three reports (keywords, keyword position, and ad versions). Use your top keywords to write better ads. Look at the positions of the converting ads and adjust the bids.

> **note** *If you are managing your bids by hand, this is a great tool to help you determine your bids. If you're using automated bid management (ABM), you don't need this feature.*

Find the Referring Sites That Bring Conversions

The Referring Sites report shows you the list of websites that sent traffic to your site. Those sites have links to your site, and people clicked on those links to come to your site. You can also see which links brought you conversions. Here are the steps to follow to set up this report:

1. Go to Traffic Sources | Referring Sites and increase the time span to six months.

2. Look at the top entries, as shown next. Are there sites that should not be on there, such as your own company, your ad agency, or similar? If you don't filter these out, their traffic and activity will be tracked along with visitors, which may inflate your data. Export the list of sites and create filters to exclude the sites that shouldn't be in the report.

		Views:
Site Usage	**Goal Conversion**	

Visits ⑦	Pages/Visit ⑦	Avg. Time on Site ⑦	% New Visits ⑦	Bounce Rate ⑦
83	**2.25**	**00:00:40**	**98.80%**	**60.24%**
% of Site Total: 10.57%	Site Avg: 2.78 (-18.87%)	Site Avg: 00:01:05 (-37.90%)	Site Avg: 93.89% (5.23%)	Site Avg: 43.31% (39.09%)

Source	Visits ↓	Pages/Visit	Avg. Time on Site	% New Visits	Bounce Rate
1. 🔲 insider-seo.com	57	2.26	00:00:37	100.00%	63.16%
2. 🔲 images.google.com	7	1.86	00:00:46	100.00%	71.43%
3. 🔲 att.net	2	1.50	00:01:01	100.00%	50.00%
4. 🔲 dogpile.com	2	3.00	00:00:20	100.00%	0.00%
5. 🔲 goodsearch.com	2	1.50	00:02:16	50.00%	50.00%
6. 🔲 images.google.nl	2	1.50	00:00:02	100.00%	50.00%
7. 🔲 my.att.net	2	2.00	00:00:24	100.00%	50.00%
8. 🔲 andreas.com	1	5.00	00:03:04	100.00%	0.00%
9. 🔲 ariadna.elmundo.es	1	1.00	00:00:00	100.00%	100.00%
10. 🔲 charter.net	1	4.00	00:00:49	100.00%	0.00%

Find Source: containing ▾ [   ] [Go]   Go to: 1   Show rows: 10 ▾   1 - 10 of 16 ◄ ►

3. Now click on Goal Conversion. This shows the referrers that bring converting traffic.

4. Look at the first 10–20 referrers. Next to the name is a tiny double-box icon, as shown next. Click it to open the referrer's website. What kind of website is sending traffic to you? Is this a magazine or a blog? A company website?

4.	🔲 dogpile.com	2
5.	🔲 goodsearch.com	2
6.	🔲 images.google.nl	2
7.	🔲 my.att.net	2

This allows you to manage the link building. With Yahoo! Site Explorer, you can see the complete list of sites that link to you. With Google Analytics, you find that only a fraction of those links actually results in traffic to your site. By looking at conversions, you'll see that only a few of those actually produce conversions.

For example, one of our clients has 18,836 inbound links. That sounds good, until you find that only 3,249 sites (17% of the 18,836 links) actually produced visitors in the last three months. Of that, only 54 sites produced conversions (and the bulk of conversions came from only a few of these sites).

Use the Referring Sites report to find the sites that produce conversions. Contact those sites and place pages or links at those sites. Look for similar sites. Use Placement Targeting and the Content Network in Google AdWords to place ads (both text and images) on those sites and related sites.

Find the Cities and Countries That Bring Conversions

Using the Map Overlay report, you can see where your visitors are on a map of the world. You can zoom in from continent to country to state to city. Which state or city sends you lots of traffic?

You can also view this information by conversion. See if California converts better than New York. You can even see this by city. You can find your key customer base and target ads to them. You can also use this report to select cities and regions for your ad campaigns in radio, TV, and newspaper. Here are the steps to follow:

- Go to Visitors | Map Overlay.

- At the upper right, click the dropdown menu to select Conversions.

- Select a conversion, and you will see which countries, states, or cities produced the highest conversion rates. If you assigned a conversion value, you'll see which states or cities produce the most revenues, as shown next.

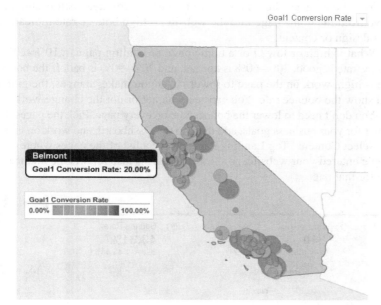

Lower the Bounce Rate

Avinash Kaushik, the Analytics Evangelist for Google, says the bounce rate is "a very lovely number." And he's right. The bounce rate is easy to understand, it's very powerful, and when you make a change, it clearly shows you if your change was good or bad. The bounce rate is the measure of your page's relevancy to your visitor's search. How well does your page resonate with your visitors? You get all that in one simple number.

First, what is bounce rate? If someone comes to your web page and leaves from the same page, they didn't go further into your website. They looked and exited. That means they "bounced" in and out of your site.

Is this always bad? It depends. On a blog, it's normal that someone comes, reads the blog, and exits. Your blog will have a high bounce rate (80% or more) and that's okay. Web 2.0 sites will also have a high bounce rate because there are often no further page visits within the site. If you go to Google Maps, there really isn't another page to visit from there.

If you have a landing page for a product, you expect visitors will click on information pages or open the shopping cart. A landing page should have a low bounce rate. A high bounce rate is a bad sign; your visitors aren't interested. You aren't offering a reason to learn more or buy.

Your home page should also have a low bounce rate. Visitors should move from the home page into the website. A high bounce rate indicates poor design or content.

What is high or low? For a home page or landing page, a 10%–20% bounce rate is good, 30%–60% is normal, and 70%–90% is bad. If the bounce rate is high, work on the page to lower it. As you make changes, the graph will show the bounce rate. You can see whether or not the change works.

You don't need to lower the bounce rate on every page. Pick the pages that matter for your business goals, add them to the Dashboard, and work on those.

Select Content | Top Landing Pages to see a list of the pages where people entered your website, as shown next. This also reports the bounce rate for that page.

Landing Pages   Views: ▦ ● ☰ ±

Entrances ⑦	Bounces ⑦	Bounce Rate ⑦
785	**340**	**43.31%**
% of Site Total: **100.00%**	% of Site Total: **100.00%**	Site Avg: **43.31% (0.00%)**

URL	Entrances ↓	Bounces	Bounce Rate
1. /index.html	602	236	23.20%
2. /koromo-koi.html	81	36	24.44%
3. /koi-fungus.html	52	42	40.77%
4. /	41	19	46.34%
5. /site-map.html	4	3	75.00%
6. /about.html	2	2	100.00%
7. /thank-you.html	1	1	100.00%

Find URL: containing ▾ [   ] Go   Go to: 1   Show rows: 10 ▾   1 - 9 of 9 ◄ ►

To improve the bounce rate, first try new headings and opening text. Put your top keywords in the heading and the opening paragraph.

Add product shots. Add links to pages that offer additional information, comparisons, FAQs, and similar. Use prominent buttons and place them above the fold.

The best way to test changes is with Google Website Optimizer. This multivariate testing tool lets you create dozens of permutations of a page, each slightly different, and it tests all of them to find the best combination. You can quickly lower the bounce rate and get higher conversions. Google Website Optimizer is inside Google AdWords, and it's free to use. When you make changes, you'll be able to see changes in the trend.

The Dashboard also shows a bounce rate, but that's the average of all pages at your website. An overall average is misleading because many pages have a naturally high bounce rate. Don't pay attention to the average bounce rate.

 tip   *Improve the bounce rate before you launch your campaigns. If you have a 70% bounce rate and you start a campaign that brings 100,000 people to your landing page, 70,000 will leave. If you lower the bounce rate to 30% (which is quite feasible; we've lowered bounce rates to 21%), you'll get 40,000 more visitors with the same budget.*

Go to a Wider Web Page

If your website's width was designed for small monitors and most of your visitors now have large monitors, you're leaving empty space at the right and left sides of your screen. You could fill that space with your products. A narrow page design pushes the end of your page "below the fold" (below the bottom of the screen) where visitors won't see it. By using the full width of a screen and presenting your products and services above the fold, you increase the opportunity for conversions.

Go to Visitors | Browser Capabilities | Screen Resolutions and look at the list, as shown next. Note that 800×600 is the smallest monitor setting, but 1024×768 is the usual size for today's monitors. Click on Goal Conversions and see if there is a relation of conversions with monitor width.

If there are only a few conversions from visitors who use 800-pixel width, switch your website design to 1024 pixels. Discuss this report with your web designer and redesign the site.

Site Usage	Goal Conversion				Views:
Visits **18,751** % of Site Total: 100.00%	Pages/Visit **4.32** Site Avg: 4.32 (0.00%)	Avg. Time on Site **00:03:07** Site Avg: 00:03:07 (0.00%)	% New Visits **57.48%** Site Avg: 57.47% (0.02%)	Bounce Rate **36.54%** Site Avg: 36.54% (0.00%)	

Screen Resolution	Visits		Visits	Screen Resolution contribution to total: Visits
1. 1024x768		**7,063**	37.67%	
2. 1280x1024		**3,291**	17.55%	
3. 1280x800		**2,892**	15.42%	
4. 800x600		**922**	4.92%	
5. 1440x900		**831**	4.43%	
6. 1152x864		**725**	3.87%	
7. 1680x1050		**651**	3.47%	
8. 1400x1050		**618**	3.30%	
9. 1280x768		**349**	1.86%	
10. 1920x1200		**282**	1.50%	

Find Screen Resolution: containing [ ] Go

Go to: 1   Show rows: 10   1 - 10 of 86

Where Do Visitors Click on Your Website?

Site Overlay is another very popular report. First, set the time span in the calendar to the last 90 days and then go to Content | Site Overlay. A new window opens up. At first you see your website, and then little rectangles are added next to the links at your website. The rectangles show you the number of clicks. Better yet, the bar shows which links got the most clicks, as you can see next.

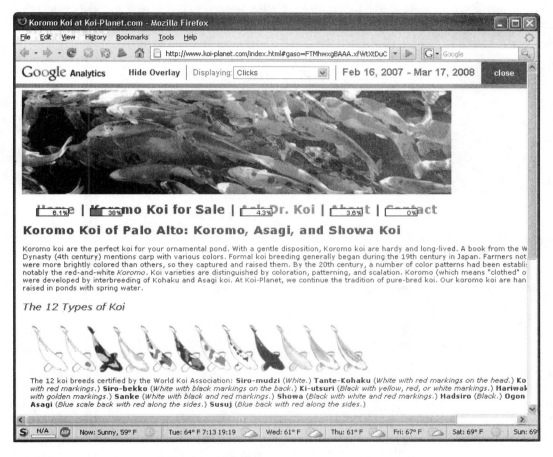

This means you can quickly see which links on your page get the most traffic. At the top of the window, you can select clicks, goals, or values. The color bars change to show which links produce conversions or revenue. Move the most productive links to the top left of the page. You'll get more sales just by doing this.

Site Overlay gets lots of attention in meetings because it's easy to understand and gives you very clear information that lets you make decisions.

Just like maps, this report shows very complex information in an intuitive and visual way. If only more reports could be shown this way! Regrettably, this tool doesn't work on some sites with Flash, frames, and so on. You'll have to try it on your website and find out.

Funnels

A funnel is the click path of visitors through a website. You set up a series of pages that make up a path-to-conversion, such as a landing page, a product details page, an order page, and a thank-you page. The funnel then shows you how many people move from one page to the next. It also shows you how many people exit a page.

To use funnels, go first to Settings and add the series of pages in the funnel. Then go to Goals | Funnel Visualization to see the funnel, as shown next.

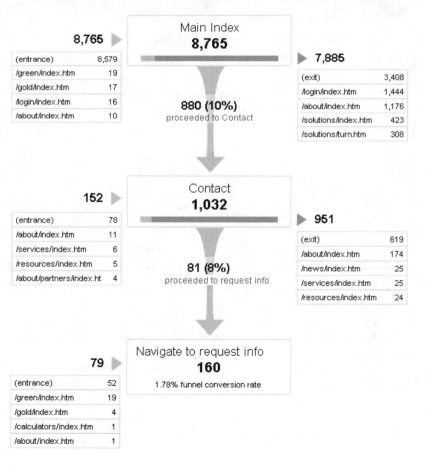

Funnels work best for improving the pages in a clearly defined conversion path. You can set up funnels, see how many people entered each page, how many went to the next page, and how many exited the page. You can use multivariate testing to improve these pages.

But at a large site, there can be thousands of possible paths. Visitors appear to click around almost randomly. They may leave the website, which is reported as an exit (an abandonment) in the funnel, but they come back. You may find that the most common path is only a fraction of all conversion paths.

In this case, it's better to use funnels where a stage can be a collection of pages. Let's say you've created a silo for a product, so there is a landing page and ten subpages for the options, comparisons, features, reviews, and so on. Finally, there is a purchase page and a thank-you page.

There are two ways to add the subpages (the ten pages) to the funnel. You can place the ten pages in a folder and use the folder name as the path. However, sites generally don't place products in folders. All files are on the same level, so you use the product name in the file names for the subpages (for example, koifood-reviews.html, koifood-compare.html, koifood-contents.html). You set up the funnel and set the Match Type option to Regular Expressions Match. Add the word that is common to all subpages (in our example, koifood) and use a regex statement to mark it—for example, koifood(.*)\.html. This adds any page that contains the word to the funnel. (This feature works for a small site, but don't use it for a large site. In general, don't use asterisks in regex statements because this matches everything, which slows down the processing.)

> **tip** *Meet with your webmaster and discuss the Site Overlay, Monitor Width, and the Funnels reports. Widen your website's design and move links around to make it easier for customers to get what they want. Improve the pages in the funnel. These changes will increase conversions at the site.*

What Do Visitors Search for at Your Website?

If you have a search box (properly called *internal site search*) in your website, the Site Search report shows you what people search for in your site's internal site search.

To use this, you first need to have a search box at your website that lets visitors search your site. You also need to turn this feature on in Google Analytics. Go to your profile's settings and in Main Website Profile Information, click Edit. The last item is Site Search. Turn this on. You are then asked for your query parameters. Go to your website and search for "koi." When the results page shows up, copy the URL and paste it into a text editor. Look at the URL and find the search term. It may be very long, but it will include a section such as &q=koi, which means "the query is koi." Q is the query parameter, so type **q** into the analytics site search setup.

Go to Content | Site Search. The Search Terms report shows the keywords your visitors used in your site's search box. See if there are topics that your visitors can't find in your navigation or on your pages. You can also see the pages where people begin and end their searches. You can either improve the page, improve the navigation, or add new pages. The Content | Site Search | Destination Pages report shows you the pages they selected, which also means the pages they found useful. You can also add your visitors' search terms to your SEO and PPC project. This can give you ideas for new products or features for your company because it shows what your visitors want to buy from you.

If you don't have a search box at your website, consider adding one. This lets you learn more about your visitors. You can see what they are seeking at your website, you can discover new ideas for products, and so on. Visitors who use a search box are highly motivated and generally convert better.

When you're looking for a search box tool, you have several issues to consider. First, it should be scalable to your growth. If you're building a social network site, you could end up with 50 million users. The search tool should be able to handle that. In any case, it should allow you to use your website's look. It should automatically index your site to refresh its index. You may also want to be able to add results or use additional results from a lookup table so you can suggest links. This allows you to cross-sell and up-sell.

For small and medium sites, you can use Google's search box. A $100-per-year version is available that removes the Google logo and lets you customize the search box. Large sites such as Home Depot and Gap use Endeca's enterprise-level search technology.

Microsoft's Search Server 2008 allows companies to search files and documents inside their corporate network. The tool includes online administration, reporting, and provisioning. It is free (see www.microsoft .com/enterprisesearch).

tip *Over the years, Google has released various search boxes for webmasters. Some of these don't work with Site Search. If you don't get results in Google Analytics, upgrade your search box to the latest version (see www.google.com/coop/).*

Compare Everything

The final best-practices report is the Total Campaign Comparison, which lets you compare goals and revenues for all of your campaigns, including direct traffic, referring traffic, PPC paid search (Google AdWords, Yahoo!, Microsoft adCenter), nonpaid search engine traffic (SEO), e-mail campaigns, radio, TV, and so on.

To use this, you first set up URL tagging for your various campaigns. When this is done, you can use Traffic Sources | All Traffic Sources. Use the dropdown menu to select Medium and then select the Goal tab. All of your campaigns are displayed in a comparison table.

As Google releases new reports and tools, we will review them and add to this list. See Insider-SEM.com for more.

Summary of Best Practices

Here's a summary of the best reports and how to use them:

- To find the keywords that bring conversions, look at the paid and nonpaid lists, displayed by conversions. For successful PPC keywords, increase bids, create new ad groups, find similar keywords, and add them to the SEO. Look at the list of successful nonpaid keywords. Use these to improve your SEO. Look for search terms that you don't carry. Add new pages or products. Add misspellings to your website as well as to your PPC.

- To adjust your bids, find the keyword positions that bring conversions. You may find that position 4 produces the most conversions, so there's no point in placing high bids to be in the top position.

- To improve ads for better conversions, look at the conversion rates for ads. Delete weak ads and write new versions of strong ads.

- To find referring sites that bring more conversions, visit the top referrers' websites. What types of website are they? Are they blogs, social networking sites, sites for students or moms? Contact those sites and place pages or links at those sites. Look for sites that are similar to the ones that send customers. Use placement targeting in Google AdWords to place ads on those sites and related sites.

- Find the cities and countries that brought conversions. Use the Map Overlay to find which state or city sends you traffic that converts. Create PPC campaigns with geographical targeting to target those cities. Add pages to your website for visitors from those cities.

- To lower your bounce rate, select Content | Top Landing Pages and look at the bounce rate for your top entrance pages. You can lower the bounce rate by putting top keywords in the heading and the opening paragraph. Add product shots. Add links to pages that offer additional information, comparisons, FAQs, and similar. Add a prominent Buy Now button and place it above the fold. Use a multivariate tool, such as Google Website Optimizer. Aim for 20%–30% bounce rate.

- Review your website design. If you get few conversions from 800-pixel-width visitors, increase your website design to 1024 pixels wide. By using the full size of the screen and presenting your products and services above the fold, you increase your opportunity to get conversions. Look at the Site Overlay to see which links get the most traffic. Put these links at the top.

- Look at your funnels to see where people abandon your conversion path and use multivariate testing tools to lower the abandonment rate.

- Add internal site search to your website and use Site Search to track the terms. This shows you what your visitors want to find at your site. Improve the navigation. Add new pages, new products, or features. Add these terms you find here to your SEO and PPC.

- Compare all campaigns against each other. Look at goals and revenues for your multichannel campaigns. If a campaign doesn't produce conversions within your target cost-per-action (CPA), delete it. Focus on the campaigns that are profitable.

Reports That Don't Matter

Many of the remaining analytics reports either provide useless numbers (they don't support decision-making) or can be misleading. Numbers look important, but Avinash Kaushik asks, "So what?" And you should, too. Here's a list of some of these reports and why they don't matter:

- **Page Views**   This report tells you the number of pages visitors have viewed. You may notice it doesn't include conversions. That's because the number of page views has little to do with conversions. You can increase page views by putting pictures of kittens on your website, but this won't increase sales. Don't pay attention to page views.

- **Visits**   If 200 visitors each visit your site twice, that's 400 visits. But if you have zero sales, so what?

- **Unique Visitors**   You may have 200 visits, but it turns out there are only 50 unique visitors. They visited your site four times each. So what? It doesn't matter if there are 50 or 5000 if they don't buy.

- **Average Number of Page Views**   This report tells you that the average visitor saw 4.5 pages per visit, for example. This report also doesn't include conversions because there's no relation between page views and buying. It's also easy to manipulate this number. If you want more page views, you can break up your pages into smaller ones, which forces your visitors to visit lots of pages.

- **Time on Site**   This report tells you how long people are spending on your site. It sounds good that people are spending 20 minutes on your site and that this number has increased every month for the last year. There's a reason for this, though. New browsers such as Firefox and IE 7 allow tab browsing, which means you can open multiple web pages in various tabs simultaneously. While you're looking at the first tab, the other tabs are open in the background and the clock is ticking for all of them. Time-on-site is increasing, but nobody is looking. This also happens when a visitor gets a phone call or goes to lunch and doesn't exit your site. Ignore this report.

- **Bounce Rate**   This report provides the average bounce rate for all pages. However, the average for all pages is meaningless. Some pages, such as blogs, have naturally high bounce rates. Instead, look at the bounce rate for your top entrance pages, such as landing pages and the home page. Ignore the average bounce rate.

Other Reports

There are yet more reports in Google Analytics, several of which are interesting. Let's cover those so you'll know what is available.

Also note that in the course of writing this book, we saw draft versions of reports that Google Analytics may add in the future. When these appear, we'll discuss them in the updates at this book's website, Insider-SEM.com.

Visitors

The Visitors section tells you about your visitors and their computers. Here's a list of the reports you'll find in this section:

- **Visitors | Benchmarking**   This report compares your site with similar sites. You can also compare your site against other industries. Don't pay much attention to the general numbers. Look at the Top Landing Pages comparison to see how your landing pages compare against your industry. To use this, you give permission to Google to share your data anonymously. You can try this report, and if you don't need it, just turn it off.

- **Visitors | Languages**   This reports shows which languages your visitors speak. Should you translate your pages? For example, if sufficient conversions are coming from South America, you can consider translations *para nuestros amigos*. You can also translate keywords and try PPC paid search campaigns in those languages.

- **Visitors | Browser Capabilities | Browsers**   See which browsers your audience is using. For example, if many visitors use Firefox, you should test your website for compatibility with Firefox.

- **Visitors | Browser Capabilities | Screen Resolutions**   If you're thinking about redesigning your website, you can see what monitor size your audience uses. If the visitors with 800×600 monitors produce few conversions, you can use a wider layout.

- **Visitors | Browser Capabilities | Flash**   If your Web 2.0 site uses Flash, see what version of Flash your visitors are using. Don't force them to upgrade.

- **Visitors | Browser Capabilities | Java Support**   This shows you how many of your visitors use Java.

- **Visitors | Network Properties | Network Locations**   This shows the visitor's ISP. (Don't worry about this. It's not very useful.)

- **Visitors | Network Properties | Hostnames**   This shows the URL that users are visiting at your site. If your site is koi-planet.com, this report will show koi-planet.com as the hostname. If other URLs are listed, they could have copies of your content and your analytics tracking code. Don't worry about this report either because it is very unlikely anyone would do this.

- **Visitors | User Defined**   This allows you to collect additional information from forms at your website. When you first open this report, it shows "not set." For example, you can use a form that asks visitors for their job title or age group. This lets you segment visitors by title, demographic, and so on. You can then study the segments along with their bounce rates and conversions. Be careful with this: The more you ask in a form, the fewer responses you'll get.

Traffic Sources

The Traffic Sources section tells you about your traffic stream. Which search engines or websites sent traffic to you? Which keywords and ads produced results? This lets you focus your advertising on the sites that produce conversions. Here's a list of reports available in this section:

- **Traffic Sources | Direct Traffic**   This shows the visitors who type your URL (or use a bookmark) to get to your site.

- **Traffic Sources | Referring Sites**   This shows the sites that sent traffic to your website.

- **Traffic Sources | Search Engines**   You can see which search engines send traffic to you. This report also shows the general market share for the search engines. You can distinguish this by paid or unpaid. If we add up all of our clients, Google has 90%; Yahoo! has 6%, and Microsoft has 3%. This is somewhat interesting, but not useful. When you make your SEO changes, the big three will pick up your website anyway. For PPC paid search, go ahead and set up campaigns on all three and compare the results.

- **Traffic Sources | All Traffic Sources**   This combines the previous reports: direct, referring, and search engines. First, set up URL tagging for your various campaigns. Next, use Traffic Sources | All Traffic Sources. Use the dropdown menu to select Medium and then select the Goal tab. This lets you compare goals and revenues for all of your campaigns, including AdWords, Yahoo!, Microsoft adCenter, Facebook, direct mail, e-mail campaigns, radio, TV, and so on.

- **Traffic Sources | Audio Campaigns**   You can track the traffic for your radio campaigns. This shows the number of impressions (potential listening audience), the number of ad plays, the cost, and the cost-per-thousand (CPM). You can compare the audio impressions with your traffic to see if there is any correlation between radio ads and traffic spikes. If you use unique URLs and tracking URLs, you can track the conversions and compare radio campaigns against campaigns in other media.

- **Traffic Sources | TV Campaigns**   Similar to radio reporting, you can track TV campaign in Google Analytics. It shows the number of impressions, ad plays, costs, and CPM.

To track newspaper ads (print campaign), use unique URLs and tracking URLs. The data shows up in Traffic Sources.

Content

This section shows information about pages at your website. You can select a page and then learn all about it: what page the visitor came from and which page the visitor went to, along with which keywords brought visitors to the page. You can also see which pages produced conversions. Here's a list of the reports available in this section:

- **Content | Overview**   You can look at a page and see where people come from and where they went after they left the page. However, this report shows only the traffic among pages within your site.

To see the list of websites that sent traffic to your site, use the referrer report. (To see where your visitors go, use Content | Outbound Links report.) Along the right side, click Navigation Summary. Click the Content dropdown menu and select a page.

- **Content | Top Content**   Shows a list of pages by file name.

- **Content | Content by Title**   Shows a list of pages by title. This report uses the TITLE tag in the HEAD section, and it requires that you use a unique TITLE tag on every page. If multiple pages have the same title, they will be reported as one page, which causes misreporting. This report is useful for small sites, but sites with tens of thousands (or millions) of pages won't have meaningful unique TITLE tags. If you have a small site (under a few hundred pages), this report may be more useful than the Top Content report, because the titles will make sense. You can use Google Webmaster Tools to find which pages have duplicate titles and fix that. Because this report shows the page's traffic, you can use this to improve your page's TITLE tag. Try different TITLE tags, based on top keywords from analytics and PPC, and see if the traffic improves.

- **Content | Content Drilldown**   This report lets you view your folders. If you have pages within folders, this report lets you select a folder and then view the pages within the folder as a group.

- **Content | Top Landing Pages**   This report shows the pages at which visitors enter your website. For example, your home page may show 100,000 views in the Top Content report, but 80,000 visits in the Top Landing Page report. This means 80,000 people started at your home page, and another 20,000 came to the home page from other pages within your site. This report is useful for improving the bounce rate because these pages are the first thing your visitors see. If you have 10,000 pages at your site, use this report to see which pages bring you the majority of the traffic. You'll find that you'll need to do SEO work on only a few pages.

- **Content | Top Exit Pages**   This shows where people left your site. Be careful with this report. People have to leave a site from somewhere. An exit page doesn't mean it is a bad page.

- **Content | Outbound Links**   This shows the sites where people go after they left your site.

- **Content | Navigation Summary**   At Content | Overview, select a page. Along the right side, click Navigation Summary. This shows what page the visitor came from and which page the visitor went to.

Goals

The Goals section covers your conversions. What can you learn about your conversions? If you can get an idea of which visitors are converting, you can create campaigns to target those groups and get more conversions.

To use this section, you need to set up goals, which also means you've calculated your KPIs.

As stated in the last chapter, you shouldn't use analytics to track revenues, profits, commissions, and your bonus because it will underreport by 10%–20%. Instead, use analytics to track relative amounts of trends, referrers, and keywords.

Here is an summary of the reports in this section:

- **Goals | Overview**   Click your goals (Goal-1, Goal-2, Goal-3, Goal-4) to look at each of them.

- **Goals | Conversion Rate**   If everything stays the same, use this report to see if your conversion rate is trending up or down. But nothing ever really stays the same, does it? There are always new products, new competitors, and new campaigns.

- **Goals | Goal Verification**   This shows the pages that people visited before they converted. You can also set a directory as the goal. This lets you know how the pages within the directory (the silo) are performing.

- **Goals | Reverse Goal Path**   Use this report to see the different combinations of pages that were viewed in a conversion path. Study the most common paths and improve them.

- **Goals | Value**   This shows the trend in goal values for the various goals.

- **Goals | Abandoned Funnels**   Shows the funnel abandonment rate. This report isn't very useful, though. Visitors often leave to check something and then come back, but that still counts as an abandonment.

- **Goals | Funnel Visualization**   Use this report to see the funnel as an image. You can see where visitors entered the funnel. You can also see where they went when they abandoned the funnel.

Export and Send Reports

Analytics allows you to share reports with your team. You can make one-time reports or you can set up automated reports that go out to a distribution list on a set schedule.

Export the Reports

Export allows you to export the report you're viewing. Click Export, select the format (PDF, XML, CSV, TSV), and then either open the report or save it to disk.

Email Reports

The Email button lets you send a report or set up a scheduled report by selecting the Send Now or Schedule tab. Here are details about both tabs:

- The Send Now tab allows you to send a report immediately via e-mail. Navigate to the report you want, or go to the Dashboard, and click Email | Send Now. Add the recipients and separate them with commas (for example, jing@koi-planet.com, sales@koi-planet.com). Select a format (PDF, XML, CSV, TSV) and type the word of the day.

- The Schedule tab lets you send reports on a schedule. You can set up weekly, monthly, or quarterly reports. These appear on Mondays, the first day of the month, or the first day of the quarter. Add the recipient list and select the format. In the Subject field, we add "Monthly" or "Quarterly" so we can distinguish the reports. Be sure to turn on Include Date Comparison. This lets you compare trends by looking at this month vs. last month or this quarter vs. last quarter.

It's usually better to have the report sent only to you. When you get the report, write a short e-mail that explains the trends (what is going on), make suggestions and recommendations (what the company can do about it), and attach the report. This written summary is more useful to your team than the report by itself.

Modify or Delete Reports

To modify a report, click the Settings Email button. Then select a report by clicking its heading. You can add/remove recipients, change the format, and so on. You can also delete reports. Click the tiny garbage can icon to delete the report.

Weekly (sent weekly)
Reports: Dashboard
Recipients: jing@koi-planet.com,sales@koi-planet.com , eurydice@gmail.com
Attachment: pdf

Monthly (sent monthly)
Reports: Dashboard
Recipients: jing@koi-planet.com,sales@koi-planet.com , eurydice@gmail.com
Attachment: pdf

Quarterly (sent quarterly)
Reports: Dashboard
Recipients: jing@koi-planet.com,sales@koi-planet.com , eurydice@gmail.com
Attachment: pdf

Limitations of Google Analytics

So you can fully understand Google Analytics, let's look at its limitations. The main issues are the lack of training and lack of advanced support. The tool is free, but you'll have to pay elsewhere for training and support. Here are some points to keep in mind:

- *Google Analytics doesn't control the PPC.* It reports on the trends in PPC, but you have to go back to AdWords to make the changes. In contrast, Omniture allows you to modify bids or delete PPC keywords within their tool. Omniture also manages the PPC toward business goals.

- *Google Analytics hasn't released an API.* An API would allow other companies to develop better interfaces, data visualization, and reporting tools. It would also allow you to export the analytics database to a business intelligence (BI) data warehouse, so you can correlate the website data with the company's business data.

- *Google Analytics doesn't offer much support.* There are some FAQs, a bit of online documentation, and a user group. In contrast, Omniture offers over 1500 FAQs and several dozen implementation handbooks, each tailored to specific markets, extensive training both online and in person, and expert consultants to solve technical issues.

Google Analytics is free, but free isn't cheap. As you can see, analytics can substantially increase your sales. You will also cut waste in marketing and sales. To get these results, you need to invest in people to develop their skills. You'll need to find experts who can help your team to take advantage of analytics. You'll also have to pay to send your team to advanced training. All of these "non-tool expenses" will be greater than the cost of any analytics tool.

When you're finally comfortable with Google Analytics, you can look at larger packages, such as those from Omniture, CoreMetrics, and Unica, and see if there are any features you need.

Google Analytics' FAQs and Support

Here is a short list of resources for Google Analytics. We have an up-to-date list at Insider-SEM.com

- Basic e-mail support is available at Google Analytics. You can contact support at Analytics-Support@Google.com.

- For FAQs and documentation, see the Google Conversion University (click the link at the top of Google Analytics).

- You can find case studies at www.google.com/analytics/case_studies.html.

- Be sure to read the Google Analytics blog at http://www.analytics.blogspot.com.

Conclusion

You should use Google Analytics for at least three months before you begin to look at larger packages. It takes time to set up KPIs, goals, and goal values. You'll set up a dashboard with your favorite reports and several months later, you'll realize some of these reports don't really matter. Ask your coworkers for feedback and you may find other reports are useful. You can then begin to look for missing features in the larger packages.

Chapter 5
SEO

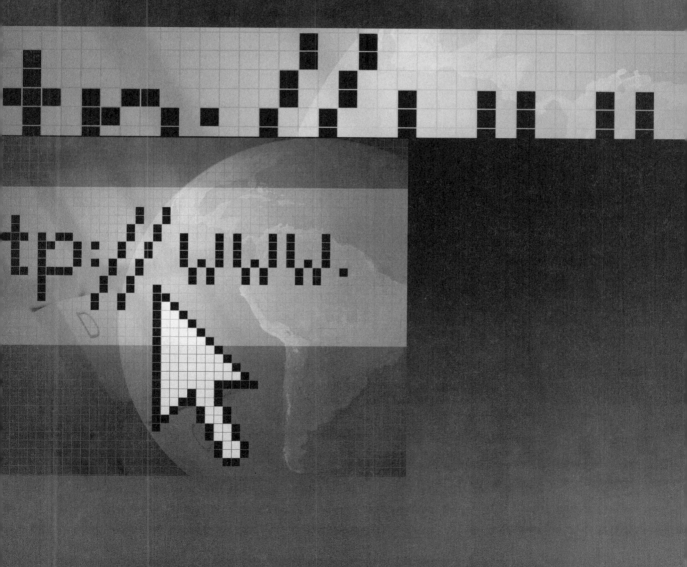

This chapter shows you how to use analytics to manage your search engine optimization (SEO). You use SEO as part of your marketing strategy to increase leads and sales. We show you what search engines are looking for and how they rank pages. We also show you how to optimize your website's HTML code to make your pages indexable by the search engines, along with tips to get people to select your page from the search results. The chapter also covers ways to improve your website's content. This chapter also includes an interview with the Shari Thurow, a leading expert in the SEO industry.

What Is SEO?

SEO stands for *search engine optimization.* In short, this involves making changes to a web page so your visitors can find it in a search engine. But there's more to it than that.

The Traditional Approach: Faith-based SEO

For many years, SEO was about getting to the top of the search engines. Why was number one important in traditional SEO? Quite simply, it was the easiest way to measure success in traditional SEO. Everyone could type their favorite keyword, look in a search engine, and see their ranking.

Unfortunately, companies often chose the keywords that they wanted to rank on, not the keywords that customers actually used. Koi-Planet .com will show up number one on a search for "koi planet" simply because that's the company's name. But it's unlikely that someone who wants to buy a koi will use a company name. They are looking for koromo koi. Without analytics, there wasn't a way to match searches with conversions. But the webmasters could see their ranking, so they used that.

Another problem has been the lack of direction from Google. Aside from a cryptic directive to "build better pages," Google hasn't helped much, which has led to lots of confusion and misinformation. The SEO forums are filled with bad advice. Scammers take advantage of Google's silence to offer dubious services.

A deeper problem with classical SEO was the focus on a technical fix. Webmasters used various technical strategies to produce more traffic or higher ranking. But they didn't have a business strategy or work toward business goals because they couldn't measure cost-per-lead or cost-per-acquisition. There wasn't a business basis to SEO.

New SEO: Analytics Changes the Game

The introduction of analytics has changed SEO. Analytics lets you manage the SEO according to your business goals. Analytics shows you which keywords bring visitors to your site. You see how much each keyword produces in conversions, leads, and sales. You know which sites sent traffic that converted. By knowing bounce rates for your top entrance pages and using multivariate tools, you can measurably improve your pages and show the increase in profits. You can also compare the cost-per-lead and cost-per-acquisition against pay-per-click (PPC), radio, TV, newspapers, and other campaigns. With analytics, SEO can be managed just as you manage PPC and your other sales and marketing campaigns.

The goal of SEO is not to be number one in the search engines. SEO is part of your business strategy, which means the goal of SEO is to increase your conversions and sales. You measure success by showing an increase in leads, conversions, or sales. You measure this with analytics.

The Main Search Engines

There are hundreds of search engines, but only a few are important. Look in your analytics software and see which search engines send traffic to your site. For most of our clients, the search traffic comes from the Big Three: Google (90%), Yahoo! (6%), and Microsoft (3%). Make sure your site is in these.

Google's rules are stricter than those of Yahoo! or Microsoft. If you do well with Google, you'll be fine with the other two. Therefore, concentrate on building pages for Google.

Specialty Search Engines

There are also specialty search engines (also called *vertical search engines* or *portals*). Nearly every market has its own portals and search engines. For example, LuxuryLifeStyle.com caters to wealthy consumers. By being listed in portals, you get traffic that doesn't depend on Google. Get a list of over 600 specialty search engines and portals at http://info.vilesilencer.com.

When you buy links in those sites, use URL tagging so you can track the results in analytics. If a portal has a fee, you can see if the site sends you enough traffic and conversions to justify the fee. When you talk with the portal, ask for a free month so you can see if they produce profitable traffic.

Don't depend on Google for all of your traffic. Google constantly changes their search engine, and many websites that had been at the top for years suddenly drop down. If your pages aren't findable, your sales will collapse. Try to diversify as much as possible.

The Links in the Search Engines

When a user employs a search engine, they see two types of links: unpaid links and paid links, as shown next. The unpaid links are the result of the search engine's technology. They scan the Web, find the websites, and rank the results. (The paid links, which are paid advertising, appear on the right side of the page. Sometimes, paid links are also placed at the top of the page. This is covered in Chapter 6.)

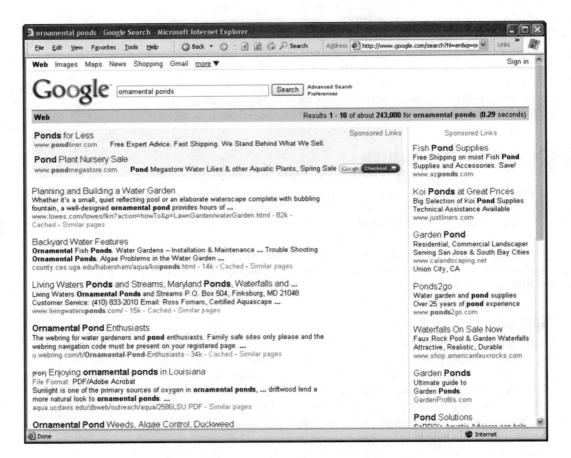

Unpaid links are also called *natural* or *organic results*. This term is misleading because there's nothing natural about it. Search engines use complex rules to produce these results, and people use SEO to improve the ranking.

This chapter covers the unpaid listings. You'll learn how to make your page findable by your target audience.

The Three Types of Searches

To understand how to get your pages to rank well, you should understand what search engines want. If you can build pages the way search engines want them, your pages will show up at the top.

For search engines, there are three types of searches:

- **Navigational**   You are searching for the official website for an organization, a company, an office, or a person.

- **Informational**   You are searching for information. You want to learn about a subject or how to perform a task. This can be text information at a web page, a how-to video, and so on.

- **Transactional**   You are searching to get something. You want to buy a product or service; you want to hear a song, watch a video, or download a PDF; you want to use a tool or service at a website.

Keep in mind that your website may show up in different ways for each of these searches. Here are some examples:

- If someone is looking for your company, that's a navigational search. If they use your company name, most likely you'll be at the top. Google will show your main website to people who are searching for your site.

- If someone is trying to learn about a product or service, Google will show the pages with the best information about that topic. For your site to show up in that search, you need to have authoritative information on your site. On the flip side, this means that pages with not-very-useful information will not show up for these searches.

- If someone wants to buy a product or get a service, Google shows the most credible vendors or suppliers for that item. To rank high, your site should be a reliable merchant. This also means pages that are only affiliates won't be in the results.

If your website offers information—such as U.S. Department of Agriculture information on farming, a hospital's guide on preventing diabetes, an adoption agency's information for hopeful parents, or a company's manuals for digital cameras—you should offer authoritative and complete information. Search engines will therefore give your site preference.

For merchants, this means the original manufacturer has an advantage. If you are the manufacturer of a product, create landing pages that clearly show you produce the product. You will rank higher. If you are a reseller, write informative pages so you can rank higher than your competitors.

How Does Google Rank the Results for Searches?

How does Google decide which pages will rank for the three types of searches? Google uses software (the algorithm) to evaluate pages. Google also has people who work as Quality Raters. Google collects the millions of daily searches, sorts these by frequency, and sends them to people who evaluate the search results by authority, usefulness, and relevance.

The first ranking is for official sites. These are the official pages for a country, a government office, an organization, a company, a city, or a person. Examples include the Bundestag.de (the parliament of Germany), RedCross.org, Guinness.com, BCN.es (the city of Barcelona), and the page for Muhammad Yunus. If yours is the authoritative site, it will generally be the number-one result for a navigational search.

The second ranking goes to pages with information. This means the page should be comprehensive, high quality, and authoritative. Ideally, this is a page by a college professor or graduate student with an overview of a topic. It should be neutral and factual. It should not be too broad or too detailed. Wikipedia and other encyclopedia articles tend to rank highly.

The third ranking is for pages that are relevant. For Google, this means the page matches the user's search. If the page answers an aspect of the search, it has some useful details, or it has partial information, then it appears in the search results.

Below these are pages that are either not useful or spam. If Google doesn't think a page is appropriate for the search, they may lower its ranking.

Google also gives preference to things that have names, such as countries, organizations, institutes, cities, companies, products, brand names, people, and the titles of books, films, and music.

Often, a page may rank high but doesn't fulfill these criteria. This only means the page is at the top for now until someone writes a better page. Just because your page has been at the top for the last five years doesn't mean it will stay there. If Google's reviewers find better pages (official, informational, or relevant), those pages will move up.

What Lowers Your Ranking

Your page's rank may be lowered for several reasons:

- If you're offering information (free PDF, free download, free book, and so on) but the visitor must first register, your page will be rated as unavailable.

- If there is any erotica on the page, the page is rated as porn. If you have a page with 49 photos of the University of Florida women's swim team in swimsuits and one photo is provocative, the entire page is rated as porn. You should put that one image on another page.

- If you use any methods to mislead the search engines, your page is marked as webspam. Webspam includes pages with redirects to other sites, keyword stuffing (too many keywords or inappropriate use of keywords), content text from Wikipedia or other sites, or a parked domain. Parked domains are old domains that have traffic from other sites but have been taken over and now have different inappropriate content.

Which Language Do You Use?

Results are also sorted by language. Search engines classify a page as German, Chinese, Arabic, Hebrew, and so on. Google works in 43 languages, and they sort pages into those languages.

Google shows search results in the language used to perform the search. Therefore, someone searching in China will see results in Chinese, not Japanese, Italian, and so on. The search engine knows this because the user is in Jilin, China (location), has their browser set to Chinese (browser settings), is using Google China (Google.cn), and is using Chinese search terms (language).

The exception is English. The European Union uses English as the common language. Nearly all colleges and universities in Asia and the Arabic world use English to teach courses in technical and scientific subjects as well as economics and business. Therefore, Google always shows pages in English for the results of a search in another language. Someone in Holland or Vietnam will see results in English, along with their results in Dutch or Vietnamese.

Wherever you are, write a page in your language and a copy of the page in English for the rest of the world. If you are in Denmark, write your pages in both Danish and English. If you are in Australia and you want to sell your products and services to Japan, write in both English and Japanese.

Here's a list of the languages Google currently supports: Arabic, Armenian, Belarusian, Bulgarian, Catalan, Chinese (Simplified and Traditional), Croatian, Czech, Danish, Dutch, English, Esperanto, Estonian, Filipino, Finnish, French, German, Greek, Hebrew, Hungarian, Icelandic, Indonesian, Italian, Japanese, Korean, Latvian, Lithuanian, Norwegian, Persian, Polish, Portuguese, Romanian, Russian, Serbian, Slovak, Slovenian, Spanish, Swedish, Thai, Turkish, Ukrainian, and Vietnamese.

Google's Quality Raters

Google isn't just an algorithm. Google also hires thousands of college students to evaluate and rank websites. These Quality Raters work from home, all over the world, in the 43 languages. They are given lists of terms to search and websites to visit. They check the links that show up in search results. Are these official, informational, or transactional (shopping) sites? Is the page authoritative, useful, relevant, not relevant, spam, or porn?

They also judge whether a shopping site is a real merchant or not. The more complete a merchant site is, the higher it will be ranked. They lower the ranking for sites that are merely affiliates. They look for whether a site lets visitors view their shopping cart contents, has a return policy, and provides full contact information (including a physical address), a shipping charge calculator, a "wish list," the ability to track FedEx orders, a gift registry, user feedback via forums, a privacy policy, and so on.

If your website is honest, this is a good thing. Google gets rid of scam competitors.

Want to be a Quality Rater? Earn $15 per hour and work from home on your own schedule, in your pajamas, pretty much anywhere in the world. Search for "google quality rater" and send in your resume.

Write Good Content

So what's the secret to ranking in the search engines? The short answer is, Write good content. But what does that mean? Here are some points to keep in mind:

- *Be authoritative.* If your site is the official page for your town, your hospital, or your company, make it clear that it is the official page. If your page is about a person (such as the home page for Tom Hanks or Ang Lee), make it obvious to Google's team that this is the official page. Google gives preference to the official site if people are looking for a city, organization, company, or person.

- *Offer expert information.* Write a page that fully answers what someone wants to know. It should be as good (or better!) than an encyclopedia article. It should be good enough to be published in a major magazine. If you're writing about Venice, write like a *Lonely Planet* guide. If you're writing about Chinese food in New York City, describe the regional styles, include recipes, add maps, and rate the restaurants. If you're writing about Bangalore, India, add your photos. When you add a list of recommended sites or products, go ahead and place yourself at the top of the list.

All this work is not easy, but that's the point. People search for information and they want the best results. The search engines want to provide those results. The best pages will be at the top.

We know, however, that many sites won't be able to do this. If you're selling handmade jewelry in Bombay or you're the webmaster for a small clinic in San Francisco, it's not feasible to write such articles. Many companies and organizations don't have the resources to write encyclopedia-quality articles.

In that case, you can use PPC to place ads for your organization, products, or services in the search engines. By knowing your profits and costs, you can manage the PPC so it will be profitable.

An Overview of SEO Methods

Before we delve further into this chapter, here is an overview of methods in SEO:

- **Internal architecture** How the structure of the website affects the search engine's ability to index your site, and how you can modify the link structure to improve this. You do this by turning the site into a collection of themed sections.

- **Keyword research** How to use analytics to find the keywords that produce conversions at your site. You use the keywords in the selling proposition (USP).

- **USP** By knowing your website's business goal, you create a unique USP statement that lets you focus your efforts and lets your customers know why they should select you as the vendor. With a USP, you can write the various tags, headings, and body text.

- **Meta tags** The HEAD section of a web page contains three tags: the TITLE, DESCRIPTION, and KEYWORD tags. Use the keyword research and USP to write these tags.

- **BODY tags** The BODY section has the text that visitors see on their screen. You'll use the keywords and USP for the page heading and the introductory sentence.

- **Sitemaps** The two types of sitemaps are HTML and XML. We cover both of these and how they work.

- **Issues in SEO (Ajax, Flash, spam, and so on)** We provide a few notes about technical issues that can cause problems in SEO, along with some tips.

The point of these methods is to make your site indexable. However, that doesn't mean your site will rank well; it only means your site can be indexed and found by the search engines.

Google doesn't care about the technical quality of your page. They care about the content. It's possible for your page to rank very high even if you don't do any SEO work. If your page is significant, it will rank higher than a page that is technically perfect but not significant.

A page isn't ranked by keywords. You can have the main keyword twice or a hundred times on the page; that doesn't matter. Google looks at the concept of the page. Does the page answer the user's search? If the user searches for "flocks of Antarctic penguins" and the page shows a collection of photos of penguins but the keywords aren't in the page, it will rank high anyway.

Keyword density tools, repetition of keywords at the bottom of the page, and so on will not help, and in fact may hurt. If Google thinks you're trying to influence the search engine, they may lower your page's ranking.

Old-fashion SEO was the use of technical methods to influence Google. The early search engines used algorithms to index keywords, and by knowing what they indexed you could influence the results.

But those easy days are over. Google has learned how to evaluate and rank pages. With a combination of software and people, they provide the best results for your searches, whether you're looking for companies (navigational), recipes for falafel (informational), or to buy a koromo koi (transactional).

In this chapter, we show you how to create pages that are easy to index, are easy for searchers to select in the results, and serve your business goals.

Enough theory. Let's get started.

Internal Architecture

In the traditional method of building websites, a home page leads to all pages in the website. This works because people can easily figure out context from visual cues. If links are big and at the top, they're important. Links with images of credit cards and shopping carts lead to the payment page. People know which sections to visit (and which to ignore), just by looking at a web page.

Set a Clear Business Goal for Your Website

The purpose of your website is to make conversions in leads, sales, and so on. With a clearly defined business goal, you can build the website toward that goal. This gives direction to your web developers, graphics designers, copy writers, and so on.

Search engines, however, are literal. They can't use visual cues to figure out the context. All they see is plain text. If the page doesn't explicitly state the topic, the search engine won't be able to index it correctly. If the Google spider comes to a website where all pages are linked to each other, the spider won't know what the site is about, as illustrated next.

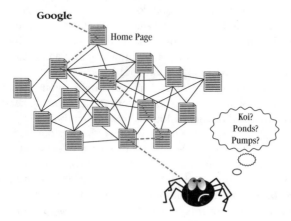

There is a way to improve the indexing of this site. This process has several names: internal architecture, silos, and themes. The website's linking structure is modified to turn the website into several sets of pages, as shown next. With these changes to the website's link structure, it becomes possible for people to browse the website and for search engines to index the site. It provides a better result for the visitors; they see everything about their search in a set of pages.

To convert the website into sections, you change the way the links work. Instead of links that allow the search engine spider to hop from a section into another, you mask the links to the other sections. The spider sees only the pages in the section and nothing else. This is done by adding a NoFollow attribute to the link, which tells the spider to ignore the link. Here is an example: Visit my <a href="http://www.koi-planet.com/" rel="nofollow">koi website</a>.

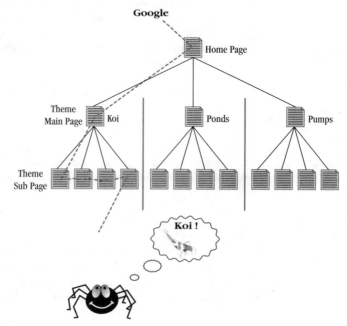

For people, the link is clickable, and they can click the link and go to the next topic. But the nofollow code tells the search spider to ignore the link.

Start by creating a list of your major products or services. Each product has a collection of pages that belong to that product. The silo has a main page and several subpages. The collection of pages should fit into a theme about that product. If the silo is about koi food, then all the pages in the koi food silo are about koi food. The main page states the product's USP, such as organic koi food. The subpages add details about koi food: food for fingerling koi, active koi, senior koi, and nursing koi; a comparison of koi food; how to make your own koi food; and so on.

The subpages should offer useful information for your visitors. Here are ideas for additional pages: FAQs; history of the product, service, or industry; how to make repairs; solutions to common problems; additional help, tips, and ideas; ideas of additional uses of your products and services; extra information; how to extend the life of your products; reviews of your products and services; reviews of competitors' products and services; reviews of books and magazines for your products and services; comparisons of your products and services against competitors; research material; and so forth. For more ideas, look at your competitors' websites. You can also look at e-mails from your customers. Ask your top customers for tips and ideas about your products. Add comment boxes to your web pages and ask your visitors to write suggestions.

You should also create an additional silo for your company. The theme of this silo is your company itself (not the products or services). It's an "about us" silo. This silo can include pages about your company, such as contact information, maps to the office, the key team, history of the company, information for investors, press releases, and so on.

By making these changes, your pages will be easier to find in the search engines—and conversions, leads, and sales will increase.

 tip *You can use Microsoft Visio to create a view of your website's file tree. However, this only works if your site has a few hundred pages. For sites with tens of thousands of pages, there isn't a feasible way to view the file tree.*

You only need to do SEO work on the pages where the majority of your visitors arrive.

Use your analytics to make a list of your entrance pages, sorted by incoming traffic. These pages are called *entrance pages*. Other pages may have more traffic because people are moving around within your site, but the entrance pages are where people enter your site. These pages attract visitors.

Focus your SEO efforts on these entrance pages, which are usually the website's home page, the product pages, services pages, FAQs, the support page, and the "contact us" page.

Find Keywords That Produce Conversions

The next step is to identify the keywords for each page. The keywords are the search terms that users will type into a search engine to find your page.

The best keywords aren't the ones you think should be in the site. The best keywords also aren't the ones that produce the most traffic. Your best keywords are the ones that produce conversions.

A number of tools and resources are available to help you to find keywords. Your goal should be about two or three keyword phrases per target page.

> **note**   *As people use search engines, they have learned how to get better results. They find the more keywords they use in a query, the better the results. People now generally use three words in a search. We say "keywords," but we mean keyword phrases with three or four words, such as organic koi food.*

- **Analytics**   The best keywords will be in your analytical report. The keyword reports in analytics will show you the keywords that visitors used to find your site. Better yet, it will show you the keywords that customers used. These are the keywords that produce conversions.

- **Google's Keyword Tool**   You can enter a few keywords, and Google's Keyword Tool shows you additional keywords. In addition, it looks at a web page and recommends keywords for that page. If you have a well-written, focused page, Google will give you lots of good keywords. This also means you can enter your competitors' websites and get keywords for those pages. You can enter competitor pages, Wikipedia pages, industry sites, and so on. This tool is in your AdWords account. You can also use it without AdWords by going to https://adwords.google.com/select/keywordsandbox.

- You can find additional keyword research tools at Wordtracker.com and KeywordDiscovery.com. Many people like these tools, and you should try them out.

- **Competitors' meta-keyword tag**   Visit your top five competitors' websites, select View | Source, and look at the tags in the <HEAD> section. Print out their product pages and look for keywords.

- **Brand names** Add your product names to the list. If you sell Hiromi Koi pellets, add the product name (Hiromi Koi Pellets) to your keyword list.

- **Company names** Add your vendors to the list. If you sell Koi pellets by Hiromi Corp., add the company name (Hiromi Corporation) to your keyword list.

- **Misspellings** Add misspellings to your keyword list. For example, add *goldfsih*. Search for *goldfsih* and see how many have misspelled it. Add these misspellings at the bottom of your page by writing "Were you looking for *goldfsih?* We have goldfish." That lets the search engines index the misspelling on your page.

In your research, you may find several thousand keywords. But which ones get the most traffic? Set up an AdWords account, add the keywords, and let it run for several weeks. AdWords will show you which keywords actually get clicks. If you want to test keywords and you don't yet have the website or the product pages ready, point the ads to a related company.

The next step is to turn your keywords into a sales message that resonates with your customers. This is called the *unique selling proposition (USP)*.

Writing Your Unique Selling Proposition

A unique selling proposition (USP) is a short statement that explains why a customer should buy from you instead of your competitors. What is the unique value that a customer gets from you?

The USP isn't merely what's unique about you. Perhaps your salesmen are dressed in gorilla suits. That's unique, yes, but not a reason to buy from you.

The USP is something customers get from you that they can't get from your competitors. Customers always thinks of themselves as special, and faced with a sea of identical suppliers, they select a company that appeals to their needs. For example, you offer onsite installation and configuration for a certain product. You have a patent. You wrote the book. You are the exclusive distributor in your region. You're licensed or certified by the manufacturer. You offer a 90-day warranty. These are all reasons for your customers to buy from you and not elsewhere.

Few of your competitors have probably thought about their USP. To customers, your competitors are identical and there's no particular reason to buy from any one of them. By stating your USP, you help your customers see why they should buy from you.

The USP is also called the *unique selling point, unique value proposition* (UVP), or *point of difference* (POD). These are all ways of differentiating your product from your competitors' products.

If your company or product is new, you shouldn't compete against an established competitor on the same USP. Because they are established, you are affirming their USP (and their products!). Instead, offer a feature that other companies don't have.

In many cases, there isn't a difference between you and your competitors, especially if all of you are resellers of the same product or you offer a generic service. For example, offshore companies are alike. Some use offshore teams in India; others are in China, Russia, or Mexico. But that doesn't matter to the customer, so it's not a benefit. If you're in a situation where there is no difference between you and your competitors, add a benefit that makes you unique. For instance, the offshore company could offer an onsite account manager. As an example, there are many koi farms in the U.S., but let's say our site is the only koi ranch that raises koromo koi, which are a certain breed of koi. So we use that in the USP for Koi-Planet: "The Only Supplier of Koromo Koi."

Add Your Keywords to Your USP

Now combine your keywords and USP. The goal is a short sentence that uses the top two or three keywords and describes your USP, your page's purpose, and your product or service. Here are some guidelines:

- Use a short sentence that your grandmother will understand. "Empowering agents to dynamically leverage verticals" doesn't say anything to most people. Say it in plain English that your grandmother will understand.

- The best USP is a spoken phrase, not a written sentence. Ask friends and coworkers to say your USP. It's good when it doesn't sound awkward.

- Write a USP for each of your products. If you have three products, write three USPs.

 tip   *Test your USP with PPC. Put your USP in a series of ads. You'll quickly see which USP works best.*

Okay, now you have your list of keywords and your USP. The next few pages will use both.

The Website's URL

If you don't yet have a URL for your website, put your main keyword in the website's URL. If people are searching for koi, they will more likely click on Koi-Planet.com than BillAndDeborah.com. The point isn't to feed the keyword to the search engines. The point is to let searchers know that you have what they are seeking. Keep the following points in mind:

- Put your main keyword at the beginning of the URL. Koi-Planet.com is better than Planet-for-Koi.com.

- If you already have a URL such as BillAndDeborah.com that doesn't match your keyword, consider changing your URL. You can set up a redirect on the old site to point to the new site. Another solution is to buy URLs for each product, such as Koromo-Koi-Planet.com, Asagi-Koi-Planet.com, and so on.

- If you don't yet have a URL, use AdWords (see Chapter 6) to help you to find a good URL. Run an AdWords campaign with several thousand keywords for ten business days. You'll see which words get the most traffic and clicks.

The URL doesn't matter too much. If you already have a URL, work with that. If it's BillAndDeborah.com, then add your keyword in the folder, so it appears as BillAndDeborah.com/Koromo-Koi/.

note   *Hyphen or underscore in your URL? The hyphen and underscore act like a space, so the search engines see Koi-Planet as "Koi Planet." It used to make a difference whether the URL used a hyphen or underscore, but that doesn't matter anymore.*

tip   *When you write your URL, use capital letters to mark the beginning of words. It's easier to read BillAndDeborah.com than billanddeborah.com.*

Let's now look at the HTML code. Don't worry; we'll focus only on what you need to know to modify the tags for SEO.

In the page's HTML code are two sections: the HEAD and the BODY. The HEAD section contains information about the page; the BODY section holds the text for the page.

The HEAD section contains several tags, including TITLE, DESCRIPTION, and KEYWORD. Search engines use the content of those tags to index your pages. In the following sections, we will show you how to edit a few tags.

The TITLE Tag

The TITLE tag is in the HTML's HEAD section. The text in the TITLE tag is displayed in the upper-left of the browser window. Here's an example of a TITLE tag:

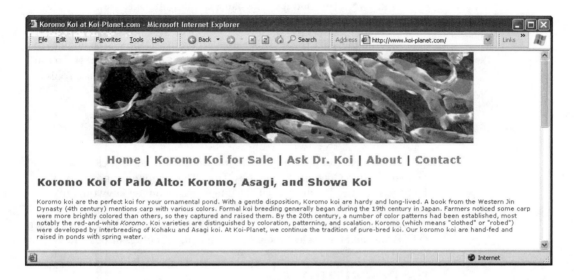

For our SEO purposes, the TITLE is also used in the heading that appears in the search engine. This is what the user sees in the search engine results list. Just as with the URL name, the point isn't to feed keywords to the search engines. It's to let visitors know that you have what they are seeking.

Here are examples of TITLE tags in a search for koi pond:

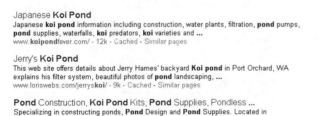

Japanese **Koi Pond**
Japanese **koi pond** information including construction, water plants, filtration, **pond** pumps, **pond** supplies, waterfalls, **koi** predators, **koi** varieties and ...
www.**koipond**fever.com/ - 12k - Cached - Similar pages

Jerry's **Koi Pond**
This web site offers details about Jerry Harnes' backyard **Koi pond** in Port Orchard, WA explains his filter system, beautiful photos of **pond** landscaping, ...
www.loriswebs.com/jerry**skoi**/ - 9k - Cached - Similar pages

Pond Construction, **Koi Pond** Kits, **Pond** Supplies, Pondless ...
Specializing in constructing ponds, **Pond** Design and **Pond** Supplies. Located in Southern California we have a large selection of hybrid **Koi Pond** ...
www.exoticwaterscapes.com/ - 57k - Cached - Similar pages

An Enquiro study found that a match between the user's search term and the text in the TITLE tag is the single most important item in attracting a click. Look at the TITLE as a short USP for your product. Here are some points to keep in mind:

- Write a TITLE tag that encourages visitors to come to your web page. The TITLE tag states the benefits and your USP. Use the keyword first and then the name of the web page.

- Search engines have a limit to the number of characters they fetch from the TITLE tag. This varies according to the search engine. In general, use no more than 66 characters (including spaces). To find the number of characters, paste the text into Word and use Tools | Word Count.

- Here's an example of a TITLE tag:

```
<TITLE>Koromo Koi at Koi-Planet.com</TITLE>
```

You can use Google Analytics to test the TITLE tags. In Google Analytics, go to Content | Content by Title. That analytics report shows the page's traffic. Try different TITLE tags, based on top keywords from analytics and PPC, and see if the traffic improves.

You can also use PPC to test the TITLE tags. Create PPC ads with different TITLE tags and then select the one with the highest click-through rate.

The DESCRIPTION Tag

The DESCRIPTION tag is also in the HEAD section.

Search engines display the content of the DESCRIPTION tag to the visitor in the search engine results page.

Let's look at those results again. The search engine fetches the content for the two lines of descriptive text from the web page's DESCRIPTION tag. In the following example, the first two entries have complete sentences. But the third description is made up of fragments of sentences.

How to choose | **Pond** filters, UV sterilizers & **Pond** Pumps
Although a backyard **pond** is a hobby for the vast majority of **pond** keepers there are of course the professional **koi pond** keepers, whose large ponds require ...
garden-**pond**-filters.com/ - 18k - Cached - Similar pages

Orlando Area **Koi** and **Pond** Club
Orlando Area **Koi** and **Pond** Club. Promoting the appreciation of **koi** and the enjoyment of **pond** keeping through educational programs and shows. ...
www.orlandokoi.org/ - 15k - Cached - Similar pages

Pond Supplies, **Pond** Kits for **Koi Pond**, Fish **Pond** and Lakes
pond supplies superstore including **pond** kits... **Pond** info for garden **pond** ...
fish **pond**, **koi pond** and lakes...
www.**pond**solutions.com/ - 29k - Cached - Similar pages

The third item has a number of ellipses (three dots). This means the search engine isn't using the DESCRIPTION tag. Either there isn't a description tag, or for some reason the search engine chose to ignore it. Instead, the search engine is fetching text from the body of the web page. It ignores superlative marketing text (such as "We're the best in the world!") and shows sentence fragments that indicate information (such as archive, news, health care, and so on).

To write your DESCRIPTION tag, follow these guidelines:

- Use your top two or three keywords and write a complete sentence. Put the top two or three keywords first, then the description, and finally the company name.

- Look at other descriptions in the search engine and notice what it considers important, such as the words *archive, FAQ, news, health care, information, tips, guide, reviews, comparisons*, and similar.

- Use up to 155 characters (including spaces) in the DESCRIPTION tag. Paste the text into Word and use Tools | Word Count to count the number of characters.

- Here's an example of a DESCRIPTION tag:

```
<meta name="DESCRIPTION" content="Koromo Koi for
Your Pond. FAQ, Tips, Advice, Information, and
More at Koi-Planet.com in Palo Alto. Call us at
800-KOI-FISH.">
```

Here's how the web page will appear in the search engine listing.

Koromo Koi at Koi-Planet.com
Koromo Koi for Your Pond. FAQ, Tips, Advice, Information, and More
at Koi-Planet.com in Palo Alto. Call us at 800-KOI-FISH.
www.**koi**-planet.com/ - 6k - Cached - Similar pages

Check Your TITLE and DESCRIPTION Tags

You can use Google's Webmaster Tools to check your TITLE and DESCRIPTION tags. If tags are missing, you can add them. If pages have duplicate tags, the search engines can't distinguish the pages. Write unique tags for each page. If tags are too long or too short, the Webmaster Tools alert you so you can write better tags. Webmaster Tool even tell you if the TITLE tags are uninformative so you can write informative, descriptive ones.

Google's Webmaster Tools are free. Go to Google Webmaster Tools at https://www .google.com/webmasters/tools/ and select Diagnostics | Content Analysis.

The KEYWORD Tag

The KEYWORD tag tells the search engine what the web page's main keywords are. Here's an example:

```
<meta name="KEYWORD" content="japanese koi, japanese
goldfish, japanese fish, koromo koi, ornamental ponds,
backyard ponds, koi planet,">
```

Use two or more words per phrase, and use up to seven phrases separated by commas.

Don't add more than seven keyword phrases. If you have too many keywords, that's seen as an attempt to spam the search engine. Your page may be ignored or your page ranking may be lowered.

Folder Names and File Names

Search engines don't really care what you call your files. But it may help your visitors if they see a web page named koromo-koi.html instead of prod-ID=3043. Whenever possible, use human-readable file names.

Should you use hyphens or underscores in file names? It used to make a difference if the file name was koi-food.html or koi_food.html. It doesn't matter anymore.

The Body Content

Let's now look at the content in the HTML page. This is what your visitors will see when they come to your page. The content includes text (both heading and body text), images, and links. Let's look at each of these.

Writing the Page

The issue is straightforward. Users are searching the Web to find information. If you offer good information, people will visit your web pages. Keep the following points in mind when creating your pages:

- The pages should be customer-centric. What are customers interested in? Describe the benefits (not the features!) of your products. Explain how to use your products. Explain how to cure fungus on koi, for example, or describe various home remedies. If this is useful information, other sites will link to your pages, which brings additional traffic.

● Write reviews and comparisons of your products and your competitors' products. You can also write articles about your industry, stories about customers and clients, trends, projections, reviews, analyses, and so on.

Regrettably, many people write a few paragraphs and hope that is enough. The search engines aren't grading you on your grammar or the number of words you use. They want to see authoritative, useful information.

To win in the content game, you have to write a page as good as the Wikipedia entry for that topic. The history of koi, the breeds of koi, how to raise koi, how to cure common diseases in koi, and so on.

Remember, useful information ranks higher than relevant keywords. If you're selling seeds, create a useful page with step-by-step instructions on how to plan and set up a backyard garden, including photos and drawings, with addresses for seeds. Go ahead and put your address at the top of the list for seeds.

The Headings

First, let's look at the page heading. Just like any magazine article, a page should have a heading. Search engines pay attention to headings because these carry information about a page. The heading should use the H1 tag (H1 = heading). Here's an example:

```
<H1>Japanese Koi for Ornamental Ponds</H1>
```

The most common problem with headings is use of the wrong tag. Web designers don't like the H1 heading because it uses a big font. They choose instead images, SPAN tags, or DIV tags. That looks nice, but by using images or SPAN, the web designer inadvertently undermines the web page's indexability. Images can't be indexed, so search engines won't see those headings. Body text that uses SPAN will be treated as body text, not as header text. Search engines want to see a heading because these contain information. To get the search engine to index the heading, use an H1 tag to mark the heading. You can still have your design. Use CSS to modify the look of the H1 tag so it renders the way you want it.

Here are two tips:

● Use your top keywords as the first word in the heading, such as "Koromo Koi Farms of Palo Alto."

● You can use H1, H2, and H3 for the headings. We recommend H1.

The Body Paragraph

The body text is the text on the page. This text should be descriptive, informational, and include the main keywords. Here are some points to keep in mind when creating body text:

- Use your keywords in the first two to three words of the body text.

- Use words that mark information, such as *news, guide,* and *summary.*

- Use the <P> tag to mark body text.

- Write naturally. Don't stuff keywords into a page. Don't use keyword-density tools. Search engines have tools to detect machine-generated text.

- Add a summary at the top of the page. This tells people that they've arrived at the right page.

If it's relevant for your company, add your street address, city, state, and telephone number on your index page and your product pages. When people look for local services, search engines will give priority to local websites.

tip *Don't open the first paragraph with a sentence that starts with a clause, such as "If you are looking for something nice to put in your pond...." People scan the first few words of the first paragraph. If it's not relevant, they go back to the search engine. Therefore, you should open the first sentence with your keywords. For example, "Koromo koi are ideal for your backyard pond."*

Cross-links within Your Site

Links on your pages let your visitors go from one page to another within your site. To get your visitors to click on the links, write text that offers useful information. Put your main keywords in the links. Here's an example:

Read <a href=koi-fungus.html>how to cure fungus in koi</a>.

Put the links within paragraphs as part of sentences. Don't put a list of links at the bottom of the page. Search engines have learned that people don't click on those long lists of links, so these don't matter.

Tags in the Images

To provide accessibility to the Web for visually impaired users, the ALT attribute can be placed in an image link. This allows descriptive text to be added to an image.

Don't put keywords into the ALT attribute in order to influence search engines. Do this only to help visually impaired users. If you add too much text to the image tag, this may be seen as an attempt to influence the search engine. Here are some points to keep in mind:

- Add your USP to the ALT tag in the image link.

- Don't put too much text into the ALT tag. The amount of text should be proportionate to the size of the image. If the image is a small button, don't add a long paragraph of text.

- Here's an example:

```
<img src="images/logo-koi.gif" width="600"
height="200" alt="Koromo Koi for Your Pond at
Koi-Planet.com in Palo Alto.">
```

Get Your Images Indexed

Google often includes images as part of the search results. You can register your site's images with Google to be indexed for inclusion in the search results. Here's how to do this:

- Set up an account with Google Webmaster Tools at https://www .google.com/webmasters/tools/.

- Select the site.

- In the left side menu, select Enhanced Image Search. Click Yes in the check box.

Google displays the same image to two random anonymous users and asks them to describe the image. If the descriptions match, Google uses those to index and display the image in Google search results. Your image will appear next to your link in the search results in Google, as shown next.

Koromo Koi at **Koi**-Planet.com
Koromo Koi for Your Pond. FAQ, Tips, Advice, Information, and More at Koi-Planet.com in Palo Alto. Call us at 800-KOI-FISH.
www.**koi**-planet.com/ - 6k - Cached - Similar pages

Sitemaps

Sitemaps list the pages at a website. There are two types of sitemaps: HTML and XML. These are for different audiences and they work in different ways. We recommend that you use both types of site maps.

HTML Sitemaps

HTML sitemaps are for people. They can get an overview of the site and find the pages they need, just like roadmaps help you find your way around town. HTML sitemaps once were important for SEO, but they have been replaced by XML sitemaps. In terms of SEO, don't worry too much about the HTML sitemap. Just make it useful for visitors. Here are some helpful tips:

- Create a plain-text sitemap that lists the significant pages at your site. You don't need to list every page, just the main pages. Place a plain-text link to the sitemap on the index page.

- Google's limit on links is 99. They've found that pages with hundreds of links have little value to users. If a page has more than 99 links, Google may lower its position. Don't push this limit. It doesn't mean that Google accepts 98 links, either. They don't like long lists of links. People generally ignore such lists, so those pages get a lower rank.

- If your sitemap needs more than 99 links, use several pages. You can divide your site maps by themes, which helps the search engine to classify your site's theme.

XML Sitemaps

XML sitemaps are also a list of files. However, the XML sitemap is written in XML format. It's not meant to be read by people. It's a long list of URLs, along with information about the files.

XML sitemaps have solved several problems. When websites began using roll-down menus, images for links, and Java, Ajax, or Flash for navigation, search engines often couldn't follow the links, so those websites weren't indexed. HTML sitemaps were fine for small sites with a few dozen pages, but it wasn't feasible to make HTML sitemaps for sites with 500,000 pages. XML solved both of these problems. Webmasters can create an XML file that contains a list of all pages and feed that directly to the search engine's index.

The major search engines agreed on a standard format for XML sitemaps. You can use the same XML sitemap for all major search engines, including Ask.com and Moreover.com.

A number of tools can be used to create XML sitemaps. If you have fewer than 500 pages, use the free tool at XML-Sitemaps.com. For larger sitemaps, try the one by Johannes Mueller (http:// gsitecrawler.com/). You can find a list of XML tools at Google Webmaster Tools.

Once you've created the XML sitemap, submit it to the search engines:

- **Google** https://www.google.com/webmasters/tools/
- **Yahoo!** https://siteexplorer.search.yahoo.com
- **Microsoft** http://webmaster.live.com

XML sitemaps can hold up to 50,000 URLs in one file (and not more than 10MB in size). That's sufficient for most sites. For very large sites, you can create an XML sitemap index file that points to subpages. The limit is 50 million URLs. And, yes, we've created sitemaps with 50 million URLs. To learn how to build sitemap index files, visit Webmaster Tools and search for "Sitemap Index File."

 note *You've seen the offer: "Have your website submitted to 600 search engines for only $20!" These are scams. If your website has good information, the search engines will find you.*

Additional Items for SEO

We have covered the main issues in SEO (architecture, keywords, USP, Meta tags, body tags, and site maps). The next few pages look at various items that affect SEO.

SEO in the Visitor's Research Phase

When consumers start the buying cycle, they first carry out research with search engines. They are looking for informative resources so they can learn about products and make decisions. That's why search engines give preference to informational pages over sales pages.

You can use SEO to fit into the visitor's research phase. Create an informational page for your target audience's searches. Use analytics to find the keywords that bring visitors. Use SEO to modify your web page's tags and content so your ideal user can find your web page in their research.

SEO in the Visitor's Purchase Phase

After consumers have learned about products and they know what they want, they begin to look for a vendor. They are in the purchase phase of the buying cycle.

SEO also works in the purchase phase. Create pages for your products. Use analytics to find the keywords that produce conversions and sales. Use SEO so your target audience can find your products when they are looking to buy. With analytics, you can track the trends in leads, conversions, and sales.

Google Pagerank: No Longer an Issue

Google used to assign a numerical Pagerank value (PR value) to every web page. The Pagerank value was based on the number of links to the page; the more links, the higher the Pagerank value, and the higher the page was ranked.

A number of tools show your page's Pagerank value. However, the displayed value can be delayed by several months. The number is also logarithmic, which means there isn't much difference between Pagerank 2.1 and 2.8, but there is a very large difference between Pagerank 5.1 and 5.8. Google only shows you a round number, so you don't know if it is 5.1 or 5.8.

For several years, people tried to increase their web page's Pagerank value by getting more links. Some sites had hundreds of thousands of links. But Google caught on to that game. Pagerank is no longer a significant factor. Google's algorithm is now generally based on the "wisdom of the crowds," which draws on billions of previous queries, which are impossible to manipulate, along with their indexing tools and ranking/rating systems.

This means Pagerank has little value. Don't worry about Pagerank. Write useful content and make sure it is indexable.

Track Your Keyword Ranking

Tools are available to track your ranking in search engines. You enter a keyword, and the tool shows your position in the various search engines. You can also add your competitors so you can see their various positions. The tool will also produce a regular report so you can track whether your ranking is increasing or falling for your top keywords.

AdvancedWebRanking.com offers a free trial on the Advanced Web Ranking tool. You can also get a free keyword-ranking tool at DigitalPoint. com/tools/keywords/.

We don't recommend these tools, however. When you start tracking your keyword rank, you'll spend time on trying to improve the page positions. SEO isn't a technical issue. It's a quality issue. Identify the pages and keywords that produce the best conversions and put your time into improving those pages.

Sitelinks

Google may display additional links within certain sites. These are called *sitelinks*. Here is an example of the sitelinks for NASA. (In some cases, Google may also add a search box for the site.)

Google does this to help people quickly go to the pages they want within the website. In the search results for NASA, you can go directly to the pages for the space shuttle, current missions, jobs, and so on.

If Google has added sitelinks for your site, you can see a list of your links in your Webmaster Tools (Links | Sitelinks). If there are links that you don't want in your Sitelinks list, you can ask Google to remove those links. However, you can't create links.

SEO for Web 2.0

Can you use SEO on Web 2.0 sites? In Web 1.0, websites and search engines belong together like shoes and socks. Because there are some ten billion web pages, search engines were created to help people find information.

But this doesn't really happen with Web 2.0. Many Web 2.0 sites are social networking sites. They allow people to connect to others within their communities. There aren't billions of pages of information. You don't search at Facebook for information. You connect and share with your friends. If you want to find your friends, you use the Facebook's internal search box. An external search engine is not the way to use these sites.

To put it another way, the Web 1.0 website owner created pages with content. In Web 2.0 sites, the website owner only provides a platform for the members. It's up to the members to create the content. In many cases, the content of Web 2.0 is the members themselves, which means their profiles and a bit of personal information. You don't search LinkedIn for information; you search for people and connect with them.

This means SEO doesn't really apply to Web 2.0 social sites. There isn't any point in making 80 million kids' pages findable in search engines, because those kids won't look for each other through an external search engine. They connect to each other personally. The vast majority of those pages have no informational or transactional value.

At best, a Web 2.0 social site can use a bit of SEO to make itself findable so investors, job applicants, and so on can find it. Navigational searches should be able to find the site. However, if the site can't get people to link to each other on their own, it won't matter whether the site is in a search engine.

This could become a problem for search engines. If the Web continues to develop toward social networking, search engines won't be at the center. The top ten sites include YouTube, MySpace, Facebook, Hi5, and Orkut. You don't use external search engines to search these because those sites have their own internal search engines.

Also, Web 2.0 sites have several technical issues. These sites aren't HTML pages with content. Web 2.0 sites are more like software. They are a tool with lots of features. For example, Google Maps and Facebook are sites where you do things, not just read pages. These sites are built with Flash or Ajax, which are very popular for Web 2.0 sites for several reasons. Ajax and Flash allow the site to offer lots of features to its members. With Ajax, the page isn't reloaded on every click, which means savings in terms of data transfer. This is all very good, but Ajax sites can't be indexed by search engines.

Every few weeks, we meet new startups that have spent tens of thousands of dollars to build all-Ajax Web 2.0 sites, and now they wonder why they don't show up in the search engines. Don't let your developers and artists build an all-Ajax site. Your developers can use these tools, but put the result in the center of the page and include traditional HTML content at the top and bottom of the page.

Get Links to Your Site from Other Sites

It used to be important to get many links to your site from other sites. Google originally used the number of links to your site to determine your page's rank: the more links, the higher you ranked. This set off a race to collect links. Webmasters used all sorts of methods to get thousands, even tens of thousands, of links. People asked for links, swapped links, and bought links.

When Google realized that people were collecting links, they changed their algorithm to downplay the number of links. However, many people continue to collect links.

With analytics, we discovered a new way to look at link building:

- *How many pages link to your website?* To slow down the links race, Google won't tell you the number of links to your site. Oh, like that will stop you? You can get this information from Yahoo!'s Site Explorer (https://siteexplorer.search.yahoo.com). Enter your URL, click Explore, and in the new screen, click Inlinks. Next, select Except from This Domain (so you see only other URLs) and Entire Site (so you see links to your website). It tells you how many links you have. For example, one of our clients has 18,836 inbound links from other sites.

- *How many of these links actually send traffic to your site?* Use analytics. In Google Analytics, select Traffic Sources | Referring Sites. For that client, only 3249 sites (17% of the 18,836 links) actually sent traffic in the last 90 days. By now, you know our next point.

- *How many of these links sent traffic that converted into leads or sales?* In the referring sites report, click on Conversions. Our client got conversions from only 54 sites, as shown next. That's not even 1% of the 18,836 links.

- *What is the value of those conversions?* Analytics will show you how many conversions and the value of those conversions. You can divide the costs of the link-building campaign by the value of those conversions to see whether it was successful.

We use the term *passive links* for the pool of all links to your site. *Active links* are the ones that actually produce visitors. *Converting links* send visitors who convert into leads or sales.

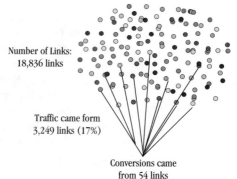

Number of Links:
18,836 links

Traffic came form
3,249 links (17%)

Conversions came
from 54 links

You can see that the value of incoming links is their ability to produce conversions. It's the 54 links, not the 18,000+ links, that are valuable. You can also see why Google downplayed the use of links in ranking sites. There isn't much value in it.

Look at those few links that produced conversions. What kind of sites are they? Perhaps you can contact these sites and place more links, texts, or pages about your site. You can use Google AdWord's Placement Targeting to place banner ads on those sites as well as look for similar sites and place ads there.

If you're thinking of engaging a back linking service, be careful. Some of these services are scams that use automated tools to create a collection of 200,000 web pages and then sell links from those pages. You buy 1000 links but because nobody actually visits those pages (mostly because the pages are blacklisted at Google), you won't get any traffic or conversions.

Legitimate link-building services are available. Pay for a few links and see if they produce traffic and conversions. Be sure to use tracking URLs so you can track the traffic and conversions. If it works, you can buy more links.

Treat link building as any other marketing campaign. When carrying out a link-building project, consider the financial value of those links. Use tracking URLs (see Chapter 4, Google Analytics) to track the campaign. You can then compare the value against other campaigns. You know your key performance indicators (KPIs) and the cost-per-lead (CPL), so you can evaluate whether the back linking is profitable.

Don't buy links in order to improve your ranking at Google. As you can see, the number of links doesn't matter very much at Google anymore. If you buy links, you do it to get traffic from those sites.

Keep Visitors at Your Site with Custom 404-Pages

In most websites, if a user searches for a page that doesn't exist (they clicked on a broken link or they mistyped a URL), they usually get a default page that says "404 Error: Page Not Found." These are called 404-pages (say *four-oh-four pages*).

When users see this, they think the site is broken and they often leave. When a search engine gets this result, the link is considered broken and the search engine leaves the site.

To fix this problem, your site should have a custom 404-page. This page is shown whenever a 404 error occurs. The custom 404-page shows a list of links, a link to the sitemap, and a search box. Thus, the visitor can stay on the site. The page also gives the search engine a link to follow back into the site, so the search engine stays in the site.

Google's Webmaster Tools will tell you if there are 404 errors at your site. Select Diagnostics | Web Crawl. This shows a list of "pages not found" at your website. You can fix the links, create the missing pages, or add redirects for those errors.

For an FAQ on 404-pages, see Insider-SEM.com.

Point Search Engines to New Pages with 301-Redirect

If you've moved or replaced a page, you need a way to point the old links to your new page. You can do this with a 301-redirect (say *three-oh-one redirect*). For the purposes of SEO, a 301-redirect tells the search engines to go to the new page and drop the old one.

This also helps your visitors. If they are at another website and click on a link to your site but you've changed the URL, they get a "page not found" error message. By using 301-redirects, you guide them to the right page. This lets you update your site without losing links from other sites.

Be careful with 301-redirects. If you are using redirects within your site (if you delete a page and add a new page), that's okay. If you are using 301-redirects to point from one domain name to another, the search engines will look at this closely to see if the redirect is legitimate. If the topic of the old page and the new page are different, the redirect may be considered to be a trick and the new page may be ignored.

You can get an FAQ on 301-redirects at our website Insider-SEM.com.

Submit Your Website to the Search Engines

If your site is already in the search engines, you don't need to submit new pages. The search engines will find your new pages. To submit a new page, use these links:

- **Google**   http://google.com/addurl/
- **Yahoo!**   https://siteexplorer.search.yahoo.com/submit
- **Microsoft**   http://search.msn.com.sg/docs/submit.aspx

If China is relevant to your website, add your site to Baidu.com, China's main search engine, at http://www.baidu.com/search/url_submit.html.

There are other ways to add pages to the search engines:

- Add the pages to your XML sitemap file.
- Use GoogleBase (http://base.google.com) to add a page into Google within hours.
- Add a link from your blog to the new page.

Keep the Search Engines Out

In some cases, you may not want a search engine to index your web page. Perhaps you have pages that are not for the public. You have two ways to keep search engines out of your site: the robots.txt file and the robots meta tag.

The robots.txt file simply lists all files that should not be indexed by a search engine. Create a text file, add a list of pages, save the file as robots .txt, and place it in the main HTML directory where your index file resides. Search engines will look for this file. Here's an example:

```
User-agent: *
Disallow: /images
Disallow: /koi/private-sale.html
```

In this example, the robots.txt file tells the search engines not to index the contents of the images folder and the private-sale.html page.

You can also use the robots meta tag. This tag is placed in the HEAD tag of each web page to be excluded. Here's an example:

```
<META NAME="ROBOTS" CONTENT="NOINDEX, NOFOLLOW">
```

NOINDEX means the page should not be indexed. NOFOLLOW means not to follow any links from the page.

Note that just because you use these items doesn't mean the page won't be indexed. There are hundreds of search engines, and not all of them follow these rules. If you have text that shouldn't appear in search engines, place it in a password-protected page.

The Google Sandbox

When Google finds a new website, they evaluate it to see whether the site is a real or spam (that is, junk pages, attempts to flood the search engine, and so on.) Many webmasters call this "The Sandbox," but it is actually the spam-review process at Google, which uses both automated filters (looking for known spam tricks and spam keywords) and human review. Google has thousands of college students who review and rate websites.

In 2006, it could take three to six months for a new site to appear in the results. Google improved the process with better filters and more reviewers. It now takes only four to six weeks.

This means if you launch your site on the first of September, your customers may not be able to find your site in Google until mid-October. To get around this, you can start a PPC campaign on September 1st so ads for your site appear in the search engines. You can also do a "silent launch" in early June and make sure the search engines start indexing the site (use XML sitemaps and analytics to track this).

Don't worry about the sandbox. Build your website, add your XML file, and your site will be added to the search engines.

When to Outsource the SEO

If your company's website is small (under 50 pages), you can use this book to manage your SEO. But analytics-based SEO can become a full-time job. You also have to keep up with changes in search engines, especially Google. They make minor changes every few weeks and major changes about every three or four months. Google doesn't explain or even announce what they do, so it's a bit of a challenge to keep up. If the website is critical to your company's revenues, we recommend you hire experienced SEOers.

Selecting an SEO Company

Be careful in selecting an SEO service. Many SEOers change the meta tags and think that is enough. Or they offer "submission to 600 search engines for $20." Worst of all, they offer tricks that make you number one. Yes, you'll be number one for five days, but when the search engines figures out the trick, you'll get blacklisted. Here are some tips for selecting an SEO company:

- Look for established SEO companies with a solid list of clients.

- Look up SEO companies or consultants in VendorRate.com and LinkedIn.com.

- Ask for several current references and talk with them.

- If the SEO company doesn't use analytics, strike them from the list.

- Make sure your project isn't handed off to a junior staffer. Ask for the name of the person who will do the SEO work. Look at their resume and ask them to explain their SEO process. They should explain how they use analytics to manage the SEO. They should also understand business issues. If relevant to your project, find out how well this person understands technical issues such as XML, problems with Ajax, and so on. If you're not satisfied, ask the company to provide another person.

- You don't need to SEO your entire site. You only need SEO work on your top entrance pages, your product pages, and so on. Use analytics to find the pages that bring the bulk of your traffic.

Good content is more important than technical SEO. Hire professional writers to write the definitive article for your products and services. Contact the editors of magazines and ask them to recommend writers. Find books on your subject and contact the authors. Hire them to write an original article that is authoritative and useful.

Be aware that this doesn't mean 300-word articles that look like school essays. Those are churned out by a number of services—and the search engines can spot them. Also, don't copy Wikipedia articles. The search engines can spot these as well.

What Not to Do in SEO

Don't focus on SEO as a technical solution. Don't spend all your time in tweaking tags, measuring keyword density, and watching your ranking in the search engines. Do just enough SEO to make your pages indexable. Spend most of your time (and money) on writing great pages. Make sure that you have a clear USP so your target audience selects your site from the list in the search engine results.

Issues in SEO

Finally, let's look at a few issues that may cause indexing problems for your website. There are two kinds of problems: using tools or methods that can't be indexed by search engines, and using methods that are banned by search engines. If your web page isn't being indexed, review these pages to see if you can find a solution. Here are details about these:

- Ajax lets web developers build interactive sites. However, search engines can't index Ajax. If you want to use Ajax, leave space on the page for content in plain HTML that is indexable by the search engines.

- Don't create a website that uses only images. Some designers do this to use unique fonts. It looks nice, but search engines can't read images and won't index them.

- Registration-required or password-protected pages will not be indexed. If you offer an FAQ but it requires registration, the content won't be indexed.

- If a link is broken, the search engine can't follow it. You can use link-validation software (available in all HTML editors) to test the links to be sure the search engine spiders can follow them to the next page.

- Frames were popular in the 90s. However, search engines can't index frames, people can't link to your framed pages, and you can't point PPC ads to framed pages. If your website uses frames, rebuild it so it doesn't use frames.

Here's what Google can index: HTML, Flash, TXT, Word, Excel, PowerPoint, Microsoft Works, Microsoft Write, RTF, Adobe PDF, Adobe PostScript, Lotus 1-2-3, Lotus WordPro, and MacWrite files. If you put these files on your website and point links to them, Google should be able to index the files.

Spammer Techniques

Search engines use tools to look for the following tricks. Your site will be blacklisted if you use them.

Doorway pages	Doorway pages drive traffic to another site. These pages conclude "... and for more, visit OurRealWebsite.com." These pages are called *doorway pages, portal sites,* or *cookie cutter sites.* They offer no informational value to users. Search engines ignore these pages.
Link farms	These are pages with hundreds of links. Spammer sites use these to bury their junk links among your valid links. Avoid offers to have your links added to link farms.
Cloaking and stealth scripts	Spammers use these scripts to mislead search engines. To the search engine, one website is shown (such as a site on how to find car rentals), but to the visitor, a porn site is shown.
Meta refresh and redirects	These can be used to mislead visitors. You can use them, but search engines don't index the source page.
JavaScript <NOSCRIPT> tag	Spammers hide keywords in the JavaScript <NOSCRIPT> tag. Because it's abused, many search engines ignore this tag.
Frames <NOFRAME> tag	Spammers can also hide keywords in the Frames <NOFRAME> tag. Because it's abused, many search engines ignore this tag.
Copied content	Spammers copy text from Wikipedia and offer it as their own. They often copy top-ranked pages. Search engines check new pages to see if they are copied from existing pages. The copies are ignored.

More spammer tricks include fake pages not related to the website's real content, keywords placed in a form's hidden field, keywords hidden with background colors, duplicate pages, and keyword stuffing. Don't use these techniques or you'll be blacklisted.

To ensure you are within the rules, see Google's information for webmasters at http://google.com/webmasters.

How Search Engines Deal with Spammers

If a website is using tricks, the website's ranking will be lowered or the website will be blacklisted. If your web page disappears from the index, you've probably been blacklisted (to see if your page is in the index, search for the page's URL). If you haven't used any tricks, contact Google and ask them to review your site. If you used tricks, remove the spam code and ask Google for reinclusion. As part of the punishment, search engines may let several months go by before they get around to looking at your urgent e-mails. Once you've been re-added, don't try any tricks because your site will be monitored.

To submit a reinclusion request, use Google Webmaster Tools at https://www.google.com/webmasters/tools/.

If one of your competitors is using spammer tricks, you can report them to the search engine to have them removed via the following URLs:

- http://www.google.com/contact/spamreport.html
- http://add.yahoo.com/fast/help/us/ysearch/cgi_reportsearchspam

Do Search Engines Really Ban Sites?

One of our clients has six websites. One day, they noticed sales stopped at two sites. With analytics, we found traffic from Google had fallen to zero. We searched in Google for the sites' URLs and saw the pages had entirely disappeared from Google.

The websites' management had been outsourced to another company. They assured us that they hadn't done anything to be banned by Google. Despite their reassurances, we downloaded all files and began going through the code, line by line.

In the middle of several long pages, we found the web company had used the DIV/absolutePosition trick, which lets you float text ten inches out in the air to the left of the monitor. The text wasn't visible to the user, but it fed spam text to the search engines. This was a common trick several years ago. However, the search engines caught onto this trick and now automatically search for it. Thus, the client's sites were blacklisted.

We removed the bad code and applied to Google for reinclusion. We had to explain what was done. Google also required us tell them who did it. In such cases, Google visits the SEO company, looks up their clients, and if there are any tricks those clients get blacklisted as well.

Within a few weeks, the sites were up again. With six weeks of lost sales, the client fired the web development company.

And then there's BMW. They hired an SEO company that added lots of hidden keywords to the pages. Google noticed, and BMW was deleted from Google worldwide. No BMW. Page Not Found. Not even a corporation the size of BMW ($80 billion in annual revenues) could get Google to answer the telephone and get around the rules. They had to apply for reinclusion, just like everyone else.

Conclusion

The search engines want to deliver the best information to their users, so you should help the search engines. Fix your site's internal architecture, clean up the HTML, and add useful, authoritative information. The search engines will find you and show your pages to people searching for your products and services.

Use analytics to manage your SEO project. With analytics, you can identify the top entrance pages. You can find the keywords that produce conversions and use those keywords for your USP as well as TITLE, DESCRIPTION, and KEYWORD tags. Analytics also lets you manage your KPIs. You can track your conversions and the value of your SEO conversions and then compare the results against other campaigns.

You can also use multivariate tools to improve your pages. The goal is to build pages that produce more conversions. You can try different headings and body text. Learn about multivariate tools in Chapter 4, Google Analytics.

Interview with Shari Thurow

Shari Thurow, author of *Search Engine Visibility*, is a leading SEO expert and well-known in the industry.

Q: Shari, let's start with an open question: Everyone wants to be number one in Google. Is that really the goal?

A: I believe website owners need to look at the big picture. Search engine visibility is a process, not a goal in itself. Part of the process is to bring traffic to a website. Another part of the process is to convert that qualified search engine traffic into buyers, subscribers, attendees, etc. Interestingly, a website's user friendliness heavily affects search engine visibility.

I have seen many web pages attain the coveted number-one position and get an initial brand impact from that top position. And I have also seen that positive brand impact instantaneously change to a negative brand impact within one mouse click. Why? Because the website owners were so obsessed in attaining that number-one position that they forgot about the people who actually use their websites. Google doesn't buy their products. End users will—they are the buyers.

Search engine positions fluctuate—all website owners need to accept this fact. A web page can have a number-one position one week and a number-15 position the following week. As long as the qualified search engine traffic is converting overall, then it really doesn't matter whether a web page is in the number-one position. To be perfectly honest, I have seen higher conversions with web pages that are not in the number-one position.

Q: What were some of your toughest projects?

A: Getting a website with over 25,000 pages of unique content unbanned in Google. Can you imagine suddenly losing almost all of your site's search engine traffic? This particular website was banned because their SEO company bought over 100 domain names, put similar content on each domain, and then added link building to each of these domains. It took me almost six months to clean up this SEO nightmare.

The result? Five years later, the site gets over 20 million unique visitors per month, and that number is continually growing. The site also does not need search engine advertising because its natural search engine traffic and conversions are saving the company millions of dollars in advertising expenses.

In my opinion, it is better to build an effective website from the outset, saving time and expenses. I find it to be far more expensive to mess up a site and then have to clean it up later.

Q: How do I convince my boss to go forward with SEO? What's the business case for SEO?

A: I believe it is easier to convince the boss to use PPC than SEO. If the company has already built a website at considerable expense, the company is not likely to rebuild the site.

If the timing is right, considerable cost savings, positive brand impact, lead generation, closed sales, and other conversions are waiting to happen. Believe it or not, most of my clients do not utilize search engine advertising because it is not necessary for the success of their businesses. Their sites get consistent, qualified search engine traffic over time—traffic that converts.

Q: The CEO wants results. How do I track the leads, sales, exposure, branding?

A: Web analytics software can help all website owners pinpoint the exact reasons for conversions and failures to convert. It can show the time of day when site visitors tend to purchase products and services. It can help pinpoint lifetime-value customers. It can help web developers identify pages that need improvement and pages that are working extremely well. I look at web analytics data almost every day.

Web analytics software has improved so much in the past ten years, and it continues to improve. There are more players in the industry, too, which is refreshing.

Q: Do you see SEO as a one-time project or is it ongoing?

A: SEO is always ongoing. Web pages are continually added, deleted, and updated on individual websites; therefore, search engines are constantly updating their databases.

Web analytics and usability testing also show searcher behavior, which continually changes. In my opinion, a website is always a work in progress, always evolving. I do not know any marketer or advertiser who shows the same ads or does the same marketing campaigns year after year.

Q: What are your tips for SEO?

A: First, the web pages must use the users' language. They must contain the words and phrases that their target audience types into search queries. These pages should be focused on specific keyword phrases.

Also, search engines and site visitors should have easy access to web page content. This is done through an effective information architecture that uses the users' language and corresponding interface. The interface design should communicate "you are here" cues because site visitors do not always enter a site from the home page. In the event that site visitors do not land on a page that contains desired information, web pages should also contain an accurate "scent of information" (a phrase coined by usability expert Jared Spool) to guide them to desired information. Finally, link development is the number and quality of links pointing to a website. Quality is far more important than quantity. I see external links as validation. Other people validate what you say about your own products, services, and information.

Books on SEO and PPC

Several good books on SEO are available, the authors of which understand the technical issues in SEO. The following recommended books are listed alphabetically by author:

- *Search Engine Optimization for Dummies, Second Edition,* by Peter Kent (Wiley, 2006). A straightforward "what to do" list for SEO. Peter Kent covers the technical points.

- *Search Engine Marketing, Inc.: Driving Search Traffic to Your Company's Web Site,* by Mike Moran and Bill Hunt (IBM Press, 2006). Mike Moran is an IBM Distinguished Engineer. Bill Hunt is CEO of an SEO company that services Fortune 500 clients. Their 560-page book is a solid presentation on how to create and manage SEM strategies for large corporate websites. It includes chapters on how to successfully present SEM campaigns to upper management.

- *Search Engine Visibility,* by Shari Thurow (New Riders Press, 2003). Shari approaches SEO as a complete strategy. She explains how to build a website that will have high visibility in the search engines. It's not just a matter of tweaks to the code. The overall design of the website combines usability, search engine compatibility, and useful content.

Enquiro's studies are also interesting. See the "Eyetracking Study" (2005) and "Inside the Mind of the Searcher" (2004) at http:// www .enquiroresearch.com/.

We've reviewed more books on SEM and SEO. See Insider-SEM.com for these reviews.

Chapter 6
PPC

This chapter covers the pay-per-click (PPC) services that allow you to place your ad in a search engine. We discuss strategies and tips for managing your PPC accounts, including the use of analytics with PPC. We show you how to evaluate the different channels to get the best results.

What Is Pay-per-Click?

Pay-per-click (PPC) started out as the placement of small text ads in the search engines, beginning with GoTo.com and Yahoo! In 2002, Google added PPC to their search engine, and Microsoft added PPC to their search engine a few years later.

PPC became an interesting form of advertising because for the first time, you could track the displays, clicks, and conversions. Better yet, you could keep track of these down to the penny. You knew precisely how much each click cost and how much you had spent to get a conversion.

PPC grew up among technical users who were good at the technical issues, but knew little about general business methods. Even today, many PPC users and agencies don't know how to calculate cost-per-lead (CPL) or cost-per-acquisition (CPA). PPC is moving beyond that initial phase and turning into an essential business tool, which means business people and MBAs are applying their financial methods to PPC.

Because PPC shows you the number of ad displays and clicks on your ads, you can use it for research. For only a few hundred dollars, you can test to find the headings for e-mails and slogans for ad campaigns that produce the best response. You can test a list of keywords and find which ones get the most traffic. You can use A/B split testing and quickly find the optimal selling price for your products.

Because PPC lets you place your ad at the top of the search engines, you can compete against established, large corporations. You can launch campaigns literally in minutes as markets change. You can place ads to counteract negative publicity. You can create ads for product recalls.

In spring 2007, Google released a useful version of analytics. Using analytics you can find keywords that produce sales via search engine optimization (SEO) and add them to PPC; you can find successful keywords and ads in PPC and use them for SEO. Analytics lets you use PPC as another channel, alongside traditional advertising channels, and compare the costs and results. Analytics lets you tie PPC and SEO together.

The widespread consensus among the leaders in the analytics industry is that things have only just begun. Omniture turned their analytics tool into a platform that can manage the PPC. It will eventually manage all other forms of advertising. Unica offers a complete marketing management platform.

Google Analytics and Google AdWords will evolve into a unified tool, where you can add, delete, and manage bids in the analytics. In mid-2007, Google began to turn into an ad delivery platform, which uses its methods from PPC to deliver advertising in other media, including radio, TV, newspaper, and mobile devices. This becomes possible because media is turning into IP-based digital media. The next ten years will see revolutionary changes in advertising.

Paid Placement vs. Unpaid Links

First of all, there are two kinds of links in search engines. The links are either unpaid (the ones on the left side that the search engine finds and ranks) or paid (the links on the right side), as shown next. The paid links are the PPC ads. You pay to place these ads in search engines.

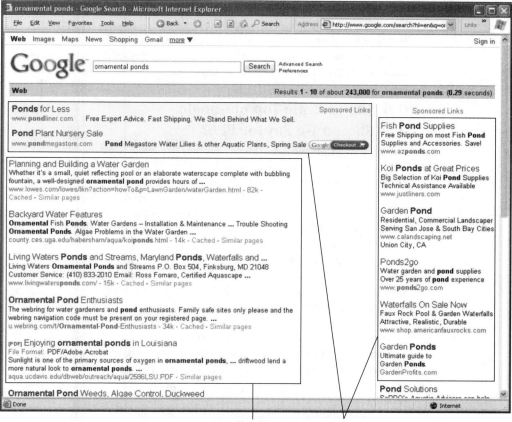

Unpaid   Paid

As the name suggests, you pay when someone clicks on your ad. There is no charge for showing your ad. Your ads can appear in a search engine thousands of times, but you pay only when someone clicks.

You can't use paid listings to affect your unpaid listing. Paid listings won't get you into the unpaid listings or have any effect on your unpaid listing's ranking.

Before that click happened, the visitors took several steps: They searched for your products and services in a search engine, they saw that your keywords matched theirs, and they clicked on your ad.

When the customers click the ad, they may come to a landing page, where they are assured they have found the product they are seeking and can buy it. You use analytics tools to study the results and adjust the campaigns to improve the results. You place bids on your keywords to affect your ad's position. In general, the more you bid, the higher your ad will rank (we will discuss the details later). PPC campaigns can be targeted to countries, states, or cities. You can even target neighborhoods and parts of cities. Analytics lets you see where your customers are, so you can target your advertising to where it works. Because you don't pay if the visitors don't click, you can test new keywords and ads for free. The tracking tools show which keywords work, along with statistics on those keywords.

Our Site Is at the Top of Google: Why Should We Pay for PPC?

We often meet people who tell us that they are already number one in Google. So why should they spend money in PPC? Won't they just be paying for clicks that they already get for free?

In many cases, they are indeed at the top of Google, but only for their company name. If someone searches for the company name, they should be the first listing. However, if customers search for products, the company generally isn't at the top or even on the first page. By using PPC, they can be on the first page for their products and services. It's like Koi-Planet.com, which is number one for its own name. Google nearly always will rank a website as number one on a search for the site. But if you search for koi, the website isn't on the first ten pages. So Koi-Planet.com should use PPC to sell koi.

Look in your analytics and see what your customers are using to find your site. If all your search terms are just your company name, but not the names of your products, that means your company is only getting the visitors who already know you. You're not getting the customers who are looking for your category of products.

There is also the business case. By using PPC, you'll make additional sales. If you keep the cost of PPC within your CPA, you make extra profitable sales.

More revenues and profits will help you reach your breakeven point quicker. Once you've passed the breakeven costs point, your profit margin becomes much larger.

Although you should add PPC, that's not all. You'll learn in this chapter that you should add all additional advertising media that are appropriate for your business. If radio, TV, newspapers, and PDAs can help your company be more easily found by your audience, you should use those outlets—if you can do so profitably. You make more sales, reach your breakeven costs quicker, and reap greater profits. Thus, you can invest the profits into your company and grow faster.

PPC at Google, Yahoo!, and Microsoft: Similarity and Differences

Google, Yahoo!, and Microsoft offer PPC advertising. All three PPC services are the same in principle. When you understand one of these, you can easily pick up the other two.

One of the reasons for the similarity is the job switching that goes on among them. People from Yahoo! go to Google. Google people go to Microsoft. Microsoft gets people from Yahoo! A number of top engineers and directors have switched from one to the other, bringing information and experiences. They also all meet at conferences and events.

The practical differences are cost and results. Google AdWords has overwhelming market share, which means lots of competition from other advertisers, so the bids are higher. The clicks in Yahoo! Search Marketing and Microsoft adCenter are generally cheaper and they tend to convert better. Regrettably, Yahoo! and Microsoft have low traffic volume compared to Google AdWords. We strongly recommend you try all three PPC services. Compare the campaigns and use the ones that produce profits.

Do People Really Click the Ads?

We are often asked if people really click those ads. In general, 85% of clicks are on the left side. That reflects the fact that most people are researching. But that doesn't mean they are researching in order to buy. They are looking for tips on how to get rid of ants in the kitchen, the history of the fall of the Berlin Wall, notes for their school homework, names for their new puppy, and so on. They don't pay attention to the ads, and there's a reason for this.

When you drive down the street, you see ads on billboards, storefronts, the sides of buildings, buses, and taxis, and bus stops. There are more ads on the car radio. When you walk into a supermarket, every one of the 35,000 products uses its packaging to advertise itself. We see perhaps 10,000 ads every day, so we've learned to ignore them. This is called "ad blindness."

This doesn't mean people ignore all advertising. They ignore the ads that aren't relevant to them. If they're looking to buy car insurance, they will notice ads for car insurance. It's your job to create ads that are easily found and noticed by people who are looking for your product or service.

The Benefits of PPC in the Purchase Phase

After consumers have finished the research phase of the buying cycle (see Chapter 1), they search for a vendor. They have decided what they want, and now they are looking for a company that can deliver.

PPC lets you place your ad with your product's name and price in front of the consumer. You write ads to catch the buyer's eye. Best of all, you can place your ad at the top of the search engines. The people who click on these ads are highly qualified customers; they want to buy.

Using PPC for the Three Basic Types of Searches

For Google, there are three types of searches:

- **Searches for the official site**   Someone is searching for the official website for a country, a government office, an organization, a company, a city, or a person.

- **Informational searches**   Someone is searching for information, such as how to make chicken soup, how to use the Paris Metro, where Cubbon Park is in Bangalore, how to configure Adobe PDF, and so on.

- **Transactional searches**   Someone wants to carry out a transaction. They want to get something. They want a product, a service, a download (software or PDF), and so on. This includes entertainment, such as watching a video or listening to music. The category is broad: They aren't looking for information, they are looking for something.

You can use PPC for the three types of searches:

- **Using PPC for searches for the official site**   If people use variations of your name, you can add all these versions to your PPC keywords list, so they can find your site, no matter how they spell (or misspell) your name. For your company or organization, add the names of key people. Look in your analytics to see the keywords people use to find your site. Create a campaign for your name and add those keywords.

- **Using PPC for informational searches**   People in the research phase of the buying cycle are looking for information. Create pages with information, comparisons, reviews, and so on, which will be useful information for potential customers. This also includes sites with manuals, support, and FAQs. Use PPC to place ads for those informational pages at the top of the search engines. For example, people will click a PPC ad that states "12 Type of Koi: What's the Difference?" and points to a comparison page. Sites that offer news or magazine articles can use PPC to reach their target audience. For example, a magazine can use PPC ads for topics, authors, and articles of note.

- **Using PPC for transactional searches**   Use PPC to advertise your products and services to people in the purchase phase. Google gives ranking priority to the manufacturer of a product, so if you're a reseller, you'll have to use PPC to place your ad at the top. Put the product names in the PPC keywords and ads. Offer free shipping, no sales tax, and so on.

What Kind of E-commerce Site?

Before we get into PPC, let's talk about your e-commerce tools. If you're selling online, you may be using e-commerce tools to process payments. If your pages are affiliate sites, you're redirecting customers to the company's site for the actual transaction.

Google evaluates e-commerce sites by their credibility and the level of transaction. They give preference to companies that actually sell a product. Affiliate sites get lower preference.

Affiliate sites are pages that find customers and collect a small fee. For example, you want to buy a book by Pankaj Mishra. You search, find PankajBooks.com (a web page that offers his books), and you click to buy. The book is actually sold by Amazon.com. The PankajBooks.com page was only a pass-through page. They earned 2%–3% from Amazon.com.

Google doesn't like affiliate pages. People create millions of these pages to collect small fees from users. It doesn't improve the user's experience; they could have gone directly to Amazon to buy the book.

When Google sees that a site is an affiliate that points to Amazon, eBay, or a similar site, they lower the page's ranking. Google also lowers the page's Quality Score (more on this later).

If you are offering products and services on the Web, your site should appear to be a reputable merchant. That means your website has

the features and services of a real company. For companies such as
Eddie Bauer, Pottery Barn, and so on, this isn't a problem. If you have
a small company, you need to build a website that works like an established
company. This includes the following aspects:

- Products have descriptions and clearly stated prices.

- Customers are allowed to view the contents of their shopping cart.

- Customers can calculate shipping fees and can access FedEx tracking
  information.

- Complete contact information is provided (street address, telephone
  numbers, fax numbers, and so on).

- Return policy provides details on how to return or exchange products,
  along with any fees.

- Privacy policy states how you protect your visitor's information.

Google also likes to see wish lists, gift registries, and forums or chat
lists for user feedback.

For small merchants, you can use the Yahoo! Stores service. Google
accepts these merchants as real merchants.

In Chapter 5 on SEO, you learned that Google gives preference to the
manufacturer. If you are a reseller, you're competing against other resellers,
and this can become difficult. We suggest two approaches:

- *Hire a professional writer to write the definitive guide to your product
  or service.* This means a document as good or better than a Wikipedia
  article. Include a comparison of companies for your field and put your
  company at the top of the list.

- *Develop your own brand and products.* Contact your manufacturer
  and see if they have a white-label service (that means they put
  your name on their product). If they won't do this, see if other
  manufacturers will produce products for you with your brand label.
  Talk to manufacturers at trade shows and so on.

Neither of these will be easy or inexpensive. It will be difficult to build
a brand against larger brands. But in general, you'll be competing with
only a few large-brand companies, which is easier than competing against
hundreds or thousands of resellers.

Overview of a PPC Campaign

Let's first go through an overview of a PPC campaign in Google AdWords. This is just a quick summary. We'll go into the details later in this chapter.

1. You sign up for an account at Google AdWords.

2. You create a small AdWords ad with a title, two lines of text, and a URL. When someone searches for your keywords, your ads show up. Your ad can be text, images, video, or a widget.

3. You add a list of keywords that are relevant to your product. These are the search terms that people type into search engines to find you. Start with a wide collection of keywords and narrow this down to find the best keywords for your product. These keywords are customer-centric: This is how the customer defines your product, not how you see your product.

4. You set the daily maximum for your budget. If you set this at $20 per day, then Google AdWords will display your ads until you reach $20 in clicks and then it stops for the day. Google spreads the ads across the day, so you won't use up your entire budget in the morning.

5. You place a bid for your keyword (for example, 12¢). If your competitor is number two and you are number three, you increase your bid until your ad appears above your competitor's. This is an auction: the more you bid, the higher your ad appears. If you want to be number one, increase your bid.

6. When someone types a search that matches your keyword, Google displays your ad in the results. They search for "koi" and Google shows ads about koi.

7. Google AdWords displays eight ads per page. If you go to the second page, you'll see eight more ads.

8. When a visitor clicks your ad, your landing page comes up. For example, the landing page shows a picture of the koi they want and describes the koi. The purpose of your landing page is to convert the visitor—for example, subscribing to a newsletter, filling out a form, downloading a PDF, or buying a product. When the visitor clicks Submit or Buy, a thank-you page is displayed. PPC conversion code is added to the landing page, which allows PPC to confirm the conversion.

9. Google AdWords charges you for the click. If you bid 12¢, Google charges you 12¢ for the click. (We explain the details later.) You pay for the click, which is why this process is called "pay-per-click." If nobody clicks on your ad, it was shown for free.

10. The account is linked to your credit card. Google AdWords charges your credit card at the end of the month.

11. You use analytics tools to manage the campaign so you can improve the results. The analytics tools show you the keywords that produced conversions, the value of the conversions, and so on.

The rest of this chapter covers the details.

AdWords Acronyms

PPC adds several more acronyms to your life, as detailed here.

Acronym	Explanation
Impr	Impression. When the ad is displayed to someone, that's an impression. It doesn't mean they saw it. It only means they had the opportunity to see it. When you're browsing through a magazine and see an advertisement for Honda, that's an impression.
CTR	Click-through rate. This is the number of people who clicked the ad in comparison to the number of impressions. If the ad was displayed 100 times and 25 people clicked it, that's a 25% CTR.
CPC	Cost-per-click. What you pay for a click.
Avg CPC	The average cost-per-click.
Conv. Rate	If you set up conversion tracking, this column reports on the percentage of visitors who bought a product.
Cost/Conv	This shows the cost of each conversion. If the overall cost is $12 and you made two sales, it cost you $6 per conversion. This is the most significant number on the page: Your Cost/Conv should be within the range that you're willing to pay for advertising the product. If this number is greater than your profits, you're losing money on the sale.
KW and KWP	Keyword and keyword phrase.
AG	Ad group.
GAW	Google AdWords.
MAC	Microsoft adCenter.
CPL	Cost-per-lead. This is what it costs to get a lead. If ten people filled out a form yesterday and your total ad spend was $50, the cost-per-lead was $5.
CPA	Cost-per-acquisition. What it costs to acquire a conversion. If you spent $50 yesterday and you got one customer, your CPA is $50.

How Your Ads Are Distributed:
Search Network vs. Content Network

Your ads are distributed in two different ad networks at Google AdWords:

- **Search Network** The ads are shown in Google.com's search results. The ads are text only (you can't use image ads).

- **Content Network** The ads are shown on websites that have signed up to show Google's ads. These websites include *The New York Times* and millions of other sites. These ads can be text or image ads, depending on the site.

There are several additional Google networks, including radio, TV, print, and mobile devices. For these, the ads are in the appropriate formats (for example, audio ads for radio and video ads for TV).

When you set up a campaign, you can choose to have your ads displayed in Search Network, Content Network, or both. By default, the campaign uses both. You shouldn't use both in the same campaign because they will perform poorly. The Search Network and the Content Network appear to be similar, but they are based on different technologies. If you structure your campaign for the Search Network, it will perform poorly in the Content Network (and vice versa). Most advertisers don't realize this, which is why they get inefficient results and lose money.

You have to create two campaigns, one for the Search Network and another for Content Network, and manage them separately, with different strategies.

In the next few pages, we will discuss the Search Network and then the Content Network. We show you how to set up and manage each one.

Set Up the Search and Content Networks

You create two campaigns, where one uses the Search Network and the other uses the Content Network. We usually identify these by adding an S (for Search) or C (for Content) to the campaign name. For example, we set up two campaigns named S-Koromo Koi and C-Koromo Koi.

Select the campaign that will be for the Search Network and click Edit Settings. Turn off Content Network and save your settings. Select the campaign for the Content Network and click Edit Settings. Turn off Google Search and Search Network. Turn on Content Bids and save your settings,

as shown next. When you save, Google will ask you if you want to set the
content bids. Set this to $1 to start.

Overview of the Search Network

Here is a quick overview of the Search Network. The next few pages will
cover the Search Network in detail.

- Search Network uses keywords and text ads. You create a list of
  keywords that match what your target audience is searching for. If
  their search term matches your keyword, your text ad shows up. You
  manage the bids for each keyword. In general, the more you bid, the
  higher your keyword will be ranked.

- With Search Network, your ads show in Google's search engine. Just
  place high bids and, yes, you can be number one.

- Your ads also appear in several search engines that get their ads from
  Google AdWords or license Google's technology. This includes
  AOL, Ask.com, Amazon, Netscape, CompuServe, Earthlink, AT&T,
  Shopping.com, and others.

- The ads in Search Network are text-only (Google doesn't allow
  images or video).

Keyword Research

Select your keywords generally the same way you do in SEO (see Keyword
Research in Chapter 5, SEO). For PPC, build the widest possible set of
keywords. Use the keyword tools and look at the analytics. Start with
hundreds of keywords. Group them into clusters of similar keywords and
put each cluster in its own ad group.

A common question is, How many keywords should I use? This depends on your product or services. For specific products or narrow markets, there just aren't many keywords. How many different words can there be for koi? Advertisers with many products such as Target may need tens of thousands of keywords.

We usually test several thousand keywords. For some clients, we've tested over 100,000 keywords. After several months, we end up with the keywords that produce good conversions and profits.

Let a keyword run until it has 1000 impressions and look at its Quality Score and conversions. Keep keywords with a good Quality Score (explained later) and conversions.

> **tip** *There's a way to quickly find high-traffic keywords. Open an ad group and click Keyword Tool. In the Show Columns dropdown menu, select Search Volume. This shows the search volume for each keyword. Click Search Volume to sort by the amount of traffic. Look for keywords with high volume.*

Types of Matching

Google AdWords uses four types of matching, described next.

Name	How to Use	Example	Explanation
Broad match	Type your keywords.	koromo koi	Your ad shows when users search for *koromo* and *koi* in any order, even if the query includes other terms, such as *pond* or *pool*. Google also shows your ad for related keywords (such as *ornamental fish*).
Phrase match	Place quotes around your keywords.	"koromo koi"	Your ad shows when users search for *koromo koi* in that order and with other search terms. Your ad will show for *red koromo koi for sale* but not *koi for sale.*
Exact match	Place square brackets around your keywords.	[koromo koi]	Your ad shows when users search only for *koromo koi* in that order without other terms. Your ad won't show if someone searches for *red koromo koi* or *koromo and asagi koi.*
Negative keyword	Put a dash before the keyword.	-cheap	Your ad will not show if a user searches for *cheap koromo koi.*

Try the three match modes. These will have different CPCs and Quality Scores. Let these build up data and keep the ones that work best.

Trademarks and Keywords

Here's another common question: Can I use my competitor's trademarked name as a keyword? Can I put their name in an ad? For example, can you use *Porsche Boxster* in your keywords and your ads? A lawsuit was brought against Google (GEICO vs. Google) and federal courts have ruled on this, as follows:

- If the company has registered their trademark and have filled out a form at Google, then Google will block the use of their trademark term in your ad within the U.S. and Canada. You can't use their trademarked terms in your ads. However, you may use your competitors' trademarked terms as keywords.

- If the company has not registered with Google, you can use their trademarks in your ads and keywords.

- If you're the holder of trademarked terms, contact Google and submit the forms. Google will block the use of your trademarks by others in their ads. However, you can't block the use of your trademark as keywords.

If you're using a term as a keyword and someone tells you to stop, tell them to contact Google.

In general, Google discourages the use of trademarked names by asking for high minimum bids. If you use words that are trademarked by other companies, Google often sets the minimum bid at $5 or $10.

 tip *If others are using your product's name, use "Official Site" in your ad's headline. That distinguishes your ad from other ads.*

Negative Keywords

Use *negative keywords* to prevent ad displays to irrelevant searches. If you're selling a $100 koi, you don't want the ad to appear when someone searches for free koi. To block that search, add a minus sign before the keyword (-free, -cheap) and add that to your keyword list. You can also add global negative keywords for all Ad Groups within a campaign.

Look in your analytics account for keywords that produced traffic but no conversions. See if these should be added as negative keywords.

How Many Keywords Can You Have?

Google AdWords has limits. You can have up to 2000 keywords per ad group, 100 ad groups per campaign, and 25 campaigns per account. This works out to 200,000 keywords per campaign and five million keywords per account.

We generally start with several thousand keywords to find several dozen that work well. This depends on the client. For some clients, we use 75,000 to 100,000 active keywords with high conversion rates.

Creating the Ad Groups

You should try several types of ad groups, based on the buying cycle and your competitors, as detailed here.

Ad Groups	Purpose	Suggestions for Your Ad's Headlines and Text
Informational ad groups	Create an ad group for visitors who are in the research phase. Use keywords such as *research, learn about products, types of products,* and so on. In the ads, offer white papers, FAQs, comparisons, and so on.	Learn about Koi. Guides & FAQs to Raising Koi in Your Pond. Which Koi Is Right for You? Compare Pumps for Your Pond. Free Koi Breeder's Guide.
Product ad groups	Create ad groups for visitors in the purchase phase. Use specific keywords with names of products or services. Create ads that offer the product *(Buy Healthy Koi Now)* and include extras in the ad, such as *No Sales Tax & Free Shipping.* Create a sense of exclusivity or urgency. State your USP.	First-Year Koromo Koi. New Litter of Koromo Koi. Buy Six Koromo Koi. All 12 Breeds of Koi. Easter Special: No Sales Tax & Free Shipping. Year-end Clearance. Last in Stock. Certified Koi Breeder. Only Supplier of Koromo Koi in Northern California.
Your company	Create an ad group that uses your company's name. Look at your analytics and see all the different ways your customers search for your company *(koi-planet, koiplanet, planetkoi, koiplanet.com,* and so on). Add these as keywords. We also add the names of main people in the company, such as the CEO, members of the board, VPs, and directors. Your customers may know these people by name and will search for them.	Koi from Koi-Planet.com Maggie Xin Guan at Koi-Planet.com Koi-Planet.com in Palo Alto
Competitors' products and companies	Put your competitors' companies and product names in the keywords. In the displayed ad, use your company name and products. Point the ad to your website.	Koi at Koi-Planet.com

Naming the Ad Groups

The ad groups should have relevant names. This helps Google AdWords to identify the theme of the ad groups so they can place the ads in the right market. Here are some tips for naming your ad groups:

- Don't use names such as Campaign-27 or Ad-Group-Test.

- Use descriptive names, such as *Koi* for the campaign and *Koromo Koi* for the ad group.

Writing the Ads

Review the USPs you wrote for SEO (see Writing Your Unique Selling Proposition in Chapter 5, SEO). You'll use these to write your ads. Here are some helpful tips:

- Put your top keywords or product's name in the ad's headline.

- The ad has two lines of body text. Put your top keywords at the beginning.

- The display URL is shown to users. The folder may be different from the target URL. Skip the "www." part, which saves you four characters (including the period). Use capitalization in the display URL. Instead of writing *www.koi-planet.com*, use *Koi-Planet.com*, which is easier to read. You can also add keywords into the display URL's folder path, such as *Koi-Planet.com/Koromo-Koi*.

- Point the destination URL to your product's landing page, not the website's front page. Visitors are looking for products, not companies.

The ad editor lets you enter the text for the headline, description lines, the display URL, and the destination URL. You can also see the resulting ad, as shown next.

Headline:	Koromo Koi	Max 25 characters
Description line 1:	Koromo Koi for Your Pond.	Max 35 characters
Description line 2:	Free Shipping. No Sales Tax	Max 35 characters
Display URL:	http:// Koi-Planet.com/Koromo-Koi	Max 35 characters
Destination URL:	http:// [v] www.koi-planet.com/koromo-koi.html	Max 1024 characters

Koromo Koi
Koromo Koi for Your Pond.
Free Shipping. No Sales Tax
Koi-Planet.com/Koromo-Koi

Here are additional tips for writing your ads:

● Your ads should be customer-centric and benefits-centric. Remember, your buyers will click your ad if you have what they want. Provide the solution to their quest.

● If appropriate, include your price in the ad. This reduces unqualified buyers. If you say your koi are $500, buyers looking for $20 koi will go elsewhere. You save money if they don't click on your ad.

● Add extras, such as *In Stock. Free Shipping. No Sales Tax. Worldwide Delivery. $200 Coupon.*

● Use phrases with a call-to-action. Examples include *Buy today, save 50%. Download free trial now. Sale ends Friday. Sale-priced, special offer, limited offer.*

● Use words that evoke positive emotions, such as *tips, learn, discover, fast, easy, convenient, quick, fun, instantly, save time, powerful, save money,* and *popular.*

● Don't use negative words. Words that evoke fear or worry have lower results than positive ads. Negative phrases include *avoid, worried about, bankruptcy,* and *don't get caught.*

● Don't mislead. Users strongly dislike deceptive or misleading links. They will instantly back out and return to the search engine. You'll still be charged for the click. If Google notices that users press Backspace and return within a few seconds, the ad's ranking will be lowered.

Run your ads until you get about 1000 clicks. Sort the list by clicks and write down the top three to five keywords. Now sort the list by CTR and write down the top three to five keywords. Finally, sort by conversions and write down the keywords that brought conversions. These are your best keywords. Create ads that use these keywords in the headline and the body text. Work with these until you find the keywords and ads that produce profits. If there are keywords with high clicks but don't produce conversions, try different landing pages.

How to Use Dynamic Insertion

The PPC tools include a little-known-but-useful feature. Known as *dynamic insertion,* it inserts the user's search terms into the ad. Because the user sees their own keywords, the ad becomes more relevant. These ads get higher conversions.

To use this, you first create your list of keywords. You then create a new ad with a special headline. In the ad's headline, you use curly brackets around the headline's text. Add the word "keyword" and a default keyword.

For example, your list contains the following keywords:

- koromo koi

- asagi koi

- kohaku koi

The ad's headline is in curly brackets:

```
{KeyWord: Healthy Koi}
```

If the user searches for *koromo koi,* the keyword *koromo koi* is inserted into the headline and the ad appears as:

Koromo Koi
Get Your Koromo Koi from
Koi-Planet. Free Shipping.
Koi-Planet.Com/Koi

Because the visitor's search matches our keyword, dynamic insertion inserts the keyword *koromo koi* from our list into the ad.

If the visitor searches for *where do i find healthy koi for my pond* (which has more than 25 characters), the ad uses the default headline (*Healthy Koi*) and appears as follows:

Healthy Koi
Get Your Koromo Koi from
Koi-Planet. Free Shipping.
Koi-Planet.Com/Koi

By capitalizing the word *keyword* in the dynamic insertion code, you can vary the keyword's capitalization. In the following table, see how *keyword* is capitalized. The *K* or *W* can be uppercase or lowercase.

Capitalization of Keyword	How the Result Is Capitalized
{keyword: Healthy Koi}	koromo koi
{Keyword: Healthy Koi}	Koromo koi
{KeyWord: Healthy Koi}	Koromo Koi

There is no reason to use lowercase. We always capitalize the headlines because it gets better results.

You can also use dynamic insertion in the body of the ad. Dynamic insertion works only with ads in the Search Network. Google doesn't use this feature for ads in the Content Network.

Ads with dynamic insertion will generally be your top-performing ads. Why? Because these ads show the visitor the keywords for which they are searching. All three search engines (Google, Yahoo!, and Microsoft) offer dynamic insertion, so be sure to use this feature.

Use A/B Split Testing to Write Better Ads

You can quickly learn how to write ads with high conversion rates by using a marketing method called *A/B split testing*. You create two ads (A and B) and see which one gets better results. You delete the weak ad, create a new ad that's based on the successful ad, and test again to find the best one. You repeat this over and over, and gradually you will get higher conversion rates. A/B testing is Darwinian evolution in action. Here are some points to keep in mind when using A/B split testing:

- In each ad group, create three or four ads.

- Run an ad until it gets 1000 impressions and then look at the ad's conversion rate.

- Delete the weaker ads. Create new ads based on the top ads. You can also look at your list of keywords from analytics or PPC with the highest CTR or conversion rate. Use those keywords in the ad's headline, as the first two words in the ad text, and in the ad's display URL.

- Try different ads. Switch two words. Write clever ads. Write boring ads. Write ads without thinking about it. Test them all and find the ones with the best results.

It's always surprising to see which ad is the winner. You can't predict this. Sometimes, poorly written ads work better. Sometimes, a simple reversal of two words gets a substantial improvement.

Note that many advertisers think Google matches the ad to the keyword. For example, suppose you have a keyword for koi and you have two ads, one for koi and another for turtles. Many advertisers think Google will show the koi ad whenever someone searches for koi. However, it doesn't work like that. Google cycles through the ads, one by one, over and over. If you have two different products and two different ads, every other display will show the wrong ad to your customers. The koi customer will see an ad for turtles.

To make sure your visitor sees the right ad, don't mix different products in the same ad group. Set up an ad group for each product, and use two different ad groups.

Ads in the Blue Box

Sometimes, Google places a few ads in a blue or tan box at the top of the page above the search results, as shown next. This is called the "blue box." If your ad gets into the blue box, it's bonus day. You'll get more clicks because many users don't realize these are ads. They think these are the top listings. Here are some tips on how to get your ad in the Blue Box:

- First, your ad needs to have a high Quality Score. (More in the section on Quality Score later in the chapter.)

- The blue box doesn't appear every time. People have learned to ignore ads. To prevent "ad blindness," Google shows the blue box only every once in a while.

Setting the Ad Timeframe

When you use AdWords, your ads show up in Google within minutes. Here are some points to keep in mind:

- You can set up an AdWords campaign ahead of time and have it ready to start on the product release date. Create the campaign, select the keywords, and write the ads. You can then use campaign settings to set the start and end dates. If you set the campaign to start Sept. 13 and end on Sept. 23, then it starts at one minute after midnight, between Sept. 12 and Sept. 13, and shuts off at the end of the day (11:59 P.M.) of Sept. 23.

- You can also put campaigns, ad groups, or ads on pause. These can be turned off until you need them.

We built a website for a client who was about to release a new product. While we were building and testing the landing pages, we prepared the AdWords campaign and put it on pause. When everything was finally ready, we turned on the AdWords campaign. Within minutes, he had his first customer lead.

> **tip** *When preparing a product release, you may need to consider the time zones. Remember that your account is set to your time zone. If you're rolling out a product for the U.S. market, the advertising should be available at 9 A.M. in New York City. If your market is in Germany, make sure your ads will be available at 9 A.M. in Europe.*

AdWords Bidding: Minimum Bids

Google AdWords uses the Minimum Bids system (which we usually call *min bid*). Here's how it works:

- Google AdWords shows you the minimum bid that is required for a keyword to show.

- If AdWords considers your bid to be too low, the keyword becomes inactive. If the keyword is inactive, it won't trigger an ad when someone searches for that keyword. Change the keyword to an active status as soon as possible by raising the bid or changing the keyword's match type (phrase or exact). Inactive keywords do not affect your ad group's Quality Score. They are ignored.

- If you raise the bid to the min bid amount (or higher), the keyword becomes active.

It can happen that you raise a bid to match the min bid and a few days later, Google makes it inactive once more. In that case, just raise your bid again.

You can also improve the keyword to lower the required min bid. If your keyword is in broad match, try it in phrase match or exact match. Those may have lower min bids.

Min bid lets you use any keyword. If Google thinks the keywords aren't relevant to your ad groups, ads, or landing pages, they will raise the min bid to punitive levels, such as $5 or $10. If this happens, move the inactive keywords into a new ad group, write ads that use the keywords, and create landing pages that use the keywords.

Min bids are based on your account's history. The better the overall CTR and relevancy of ads and landing pages, the lower your min bids. Google looks at the total CTR of all keywords, all ads, and all ad groups.

Min bid lets you bid on keywords, even if these get no conversions. If Google thinks the keyword isn't relevant to your ad group or ad, you will get a low Quality Score. This hurts your ad group. Just because you can bid on a keyword doesn't mean you should. Delete the keywords with a low Quality Score.

There is no standard min bid for a keyword. A keyword's min bid will be different for each advertiser. The min bid may be $1 for me and 20¢ for you. It depends on your Quality Score, which is based on the relevancy of the keyword, the ads, and the landing pages in your account. You can sometimes get a lower min bid by moving the keyword into its own ad group and writing an ad that uses the keyword in the header.

tip *When you add new keywords, Google often sets a high min bid (such as $0.50) and sets the Quality Score to Poor. The easy thing to do is to increase the bid to $0.50. But we found that if you wait a day, the min bid often drops to $0.10 and the Quality Score goes up to Okay.*

What about Your Competitors' Bids?

You calculated your key performance indicators (KPIs) and you know that the maximum profitable CPA for your product is $17.25. Yet some competitors rank higher. Are they outbidding you? What's going on?

Very likely, they have high Quality Scores. If you improve your keywords, ads, and landing pages, your Quality Score will go up and your ads will rank higher.

A few competitors may have irrationally high bids. In general, most competitors tend to bid too low because they don't calculate their KPIs. For example, $3 for a click sounds high, so they won't bid $3. Because you've calculated the CPL and CPA, you know that you can afford a higher bid.

It may sound odd, but it's not good business to bid too low. The advertiser misses out on opportunities to make more sales, and the few sales only cover the basic costs (rent, salaries, supplies, and so on), which means less money to invest in growing the business.

Other competitors may bid too high. Google lets you bid up to $100 for a keyword. If they haven't calculated their maximum profitable CPA, they are losing money in their campaign. Don't worry about them. After a few months, they'll blog that Google doesn't work and they'll quit.

What You Actually Pay

You bid for a keyword, but what you actually pay is a different amount. Sometimes, it's very different. The actual amount you'll pay depends on your ad group's Quality Score and the bids from other advertisers. By understanding this, you can reduce the amount you pay and get more clicks for the same budget.

First, let's review the formula for calculating the CPC, which is what you actually pay when someone clicks your ad. This formula includes an Ad Rank score, which is your bid multiplied by your keyword's Quality Score (QS). The CPC is your QS divided by the next-lowest ad's Ad Rank, plus 1¢.

Let's use an example to explain this formula. Let's say there are only three companies using AdWords in the koi market. Apricot bids $2, Berry bids $5, and Cherry bids $1. Laura clicks on all three ads. What does each company pay for these clicks? The following table shows the bid, the Quality Score, the Ad Rank, and the CPC. It also explains how the ads were ranked and what the advertisers paid.

Company	Their Bid	Quality Score (QS)	Ad Rank Value	What They Pay (CPC)	Why They Pay That Amount
Apricot	$2.00	40	80	$0.27	Multiply the bid ($2) by the QS (QS 40) to get the Ad Rank (80). Apricot's QS (40) divided by Berry's Ad Rank (15), plus 1¢ means Apricot pays $0.27.
Berry	$5.00	3	15	$1.51	Multiply the bid ($5) by the QS (QS 3) to get the Ad Rank (15). Berry's QS (3) is divided by Cherry's Ad Rank (2), plus 1¢, so Berry pays $1.51.
Cherry	$1.00	2	2	$0.05	The min bid is 5¢, so Cherry pays 5¢.

Apricot bids $2 but ranks higher than Berry, who bid $5, because Apricot has a much better Quality Score (40). He also pays only $0.27 instead of his $2 bid. Berry is number two yet pays more ($1.51) than number one (who pays only $0.27).

If the three advertisers each have a $200 daily budget, Apricot will get 741 clicks ($200 divided by $0.27 = 741 clicks), but Berry will get only 132 clicks ($200 divided by $1.51 = 132 clicks), even though he is bidding more than twice per click. If we assume both have the same conversion rate, Apricot is bidding less than Berry but he will sell five times as many koi.

Because the Quality Score is based on a number of factors, it may be higher than 40 points. Let's see how Quality Scores are calculated.

The Quality Score

Google AdWords uses a Quality Score (QS) to rank your keywords and ads. The higher the QS, the higher your ad will rank and the less you'll pay for the click.

The QS Score is based on a number of factors. Here are the factors and our tips on how to improve your QS.

Factor	How to Improve Quality Score
The keyword's relevancy to the ad group	Create ad groups and landing pages with a common theme, and add keywords that match the ad group's theme and the landing page.
The keyword's CTR	Use the three match formats (broad, phrase, exact). Find the versions that have the highest CTR.
The ad's relevancy	Make sure the ad is related to your keyword and ad group. If your keyword is *koromo koi,* use the words *koromo koi* in your ad. Don't use *immersible pumps* and so on.
The ad's CTR	Use A/B split testing to develop ads with a higher CTR. Delete ads with a low CTR or conversion rate.
The ad group's cumulative QS	Look at the displayed Quality Score for your keywords. If it's just OK or poor, move those keywords to another ad group.
Landing page relevancy	Write landing pages that match your keyword, ad, and ad group's theme. If Google sees that people return within seconds from your page, Google figures your page isn't relevant. Use analytics to look at your landing page's bounce rate. If it is higher than 30%–40%, use multivariate tools to lower the bounce rate.
Landing page load speed	The faster your landing page opens, the more Quality Score points you get. Fast pages are a better experience for visitors.
Age of the account	The older your AdWords account, the more points you get. We manage accounts that were created in 2002. The ads are at the top and CPCs are just pennies. Google rewards the early birds.

Factor	How to Improve Quality Score
Activity in the account	We suspect Google rewards accounts that are actively managed.
Location	Google looks at the location of the user and advertisers. If Laura is in Denver and she searches for a dentist, a local dentist is going to rank higher than a dentist in Miami.
"Other factors"	Google's reviewers look at your page and rank it on credibility as a merchant page. If the site doesn't appear to be a credible merchant or it is an Amazon or eBay affiliate or some other sort of light affiliate, it loses points. Build a merchant site that has the features of a real merchant, such as EddieBauer.com. Offer comparisons, reviews, and additional information.

Overall, the account should have a high general quality. This means ad groups with high cumulative CTR. Each ad group should be focused with a clear theme. The keywords, ads, and the landing page form a consistent theme. Later in this chapter, we will look at landing pages.

Don't create ad groups with hundreds of keywords (if there are too many keywords, the theme will be unclear). Also, don't create ad groups with only one keyword (the theme won't be clearly established).

Now that you know about the QS, you'll want to know the numbers. Regrettably, Google AdWords won't tell you this. In your ad group, you can turn on the QS display (select Customize Columns), but this only tells you Great, Good, OK, or Poor.

You can guess at your QS by looking at your minimum bids. The lower your min bids, the better your QS. Look also at the difference between your min bid and the CPC. The greater the difference between your bid and the CPC, the higher your QS. If you're paying about the same as your bid, your QS is low. If you bid $3.50 and pay only $0.14 (that's 4% of the bid amount), you have a very good QS (that's an actual example).

This doesn't mean you can always set your bids to the minimum. You need to bid enough to get your ads on the first six positions of the first page. If your ads are in position 34 (the third page), very few people will see your ads. Set the ad group display to the last business day (usually, yesterday) and sort the table by Avg. Pos. (average position). If keywords are at positions lower than 6 or 7, the ads are appearing below the fold. Increase the bids to bring the ads up on the page.

Are you baffled yet? That's quite a formula. Don't worry, though. Just remember this: The higher your QS, the higher your ads will rank and the less you'll pay. In fact, a high QS is much better than a high bid. So work on improving your QS.

The Ad Rank Score

Another important number is the Ad Rank. This determines the position of your ad. The higher the Ad Rank value, the higher your ad will appear on the page.

Ad Rank is your bid multiplied by the keyword's QS. If you bid $2 and your QS is 10, then $2 × 10 QS = 20 Ad Rank.

To raise the Ad Rank, you place a higher bid or you improve the QS. You can see that Google gives preference to the QS, not the bid. If you bid $50 but you have a poor QS, you're basically sending lots of money to Google but you'll have a poor ranking. Work on your QS.

Why Is Google Doing This?

Why does Google AdWords use such a complex system? The Quality Score and Ad Rank are some of the most important ways to manage your account, but it's safe to say very few people have even heard of these. It doesn't help that Google is unnecessarily secretive.

Google didn't invent PPC. That started at GoTo.com (later bought by Yahoo!). Google's innovation was the use of CTR, QS, and Ad Rank to rank ads. These had the following far-reaching effects:

- **Great for consumers**   When consumers search for products, Google shows the most relevant ads at the top.

- **Good for advertisers**   CTR and QS reward advertisers who improve their campaigns. They get a higher ranking and lower CPCs. Well-managed accounts will substantially outperform competitors and be very profitable.

- **Good for Google**   They earn more if 50 people click on a well-written $1 ad instead of two people clicking on a poorly written $10 ad.

- **Very bad for lazy advertisers**   If advertisers ignore the QS, have poor ads, and don't have a dedicated landing page, their ads will get a lower position and won't be shown as frequently, and Google will charge them more for the click. They are literally pushed to the bottom. A large corporation with an unlimited budget but a poor strategy will not be successful in PPC. We know several cases where large corporations rank lower than small companies with daily budgets that wouldn't even buy a round of coffee at Starbucks. The little guys did a great job at optimizing their ad groups and landing pages.

Google's QS system means that PPC is not an issue of bid management. Many PPC companies tell you they will manage your bids. That's nice, but you will get better results if you improve your QS.

This system rewards agile companies that take advantage of Google's strategies and technologies. With modest budgets and highly optimized accounts, they can beat large corporations with unlimited budgets. Google is pushing its PPC methods into all forms of advertising, which may end up restructuring the way companies do marketing.

This is similar to the so-called "Walmart effect." Every week, about half of the U.S. population shops at Walmart. With such a large share of consumer retail, Walmart can dictate to manufacturers how they will package and price their products. If a manufacturer doesn't comply, Walmart won't carry their products.

Google is putting a similar pressure on companies. If companies want to sell via search engines, they must write and manage their ad campaigns according to Google's formulas and they must build their web pages according to Google's criteria for relevancy. Just as with Walmart, companies can certainly do whatever they like, but they won't be on the shelves at Walmart—or at the top of Google. It's their choice not to be available to the bulk of consumers.

The X-Charts: How to Tell When Your Optimization Works

When you optimize your ad groups, a curious thing happens. As you improve an ad group, Google AdWords lowers your CPC. If your budget stays the same and your clicks are cheaper, you'll get more clicks, which means the number of conversions will increase. The result produces what we call *X-charts*.

This X-chart shows the CPC and number of conversions. The CPC falls, and the number of conversions increases. The lines cross to create an "X" in the chart.

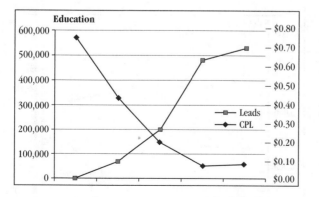

We see these X-charts in many types of accounts. By using Reports in AdWords, we can create graphics of CPC and conversions. Here are X-charts for social networking sites, finance services, and software, respectively.

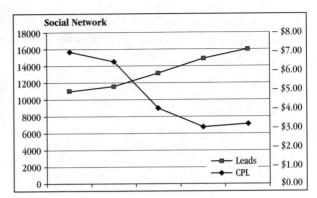

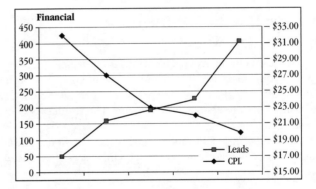

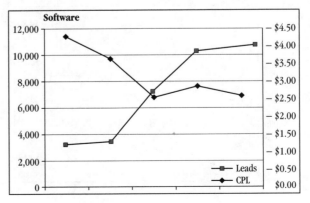

How long can this improvement continue? At some point, you begin to reach the limits of optimization.

For example, we manage the PPC for MIT's OpenCourseWare project. When we took over the account, the average CPC was $0.70. Within several months, we brought that average down to 7¢ per click (for more than 70,000 keywords). It can't really go down much further than 7¢, so the trend flattened out. The ad group reached the limit of optimization. We call this "Stephanie's Limit" after the person who first noticed it. We work on an account until it reaches Stephanie's Limit, and then we expand into additional campaigns, ad groups, and ad types. This generally takes about 40–60 days (your mileage may vary).

Manual Bid Management: Do It by Hand

You can manage bids by hand. But as you've seen, the QS matters more than the bid. It's better to spend time on improving your QS than fussing around with bids. Still, you shouldn't overbid or underbid. Here's how to manage your bids by hand.

Go to Google Analytics and select Traffic Sources | AdWords | Keyword Positions and set the time span to get sufficient data. At the left is a list of keywords from AdWords. At the right is a blank screen. Click a keyword on the left side. The right side now shows you a Google search page; your keyword showed up in Google in those positions. It shows you the number of visits (clicks). Click on the dropdown menus to display conversions. This shows you which positions brought conversions. It may well be that position 3 works better than position 1. Write down these optimal positions and then lower or raise your bids to get your ads in these positions.

Automated Bid Management: Let the Machine Do It

Adjusting the bids every day for your account can become a chore, especially if you have several hundred keywords. Is there a way to automate the PPC?

Automated Bid Management (ABM) tools handle the bidding. If a keyword is producing good results, bids are increased. If a keyword has low results, bids are decreased or the keyword is deleted altogether. These tools can adjust bids several times per day.

ABM companies often charge a substantial percentage (5%–10% or more) of your ad spend. Atlas Search, Omniture, MarinSoftware, and Efficient Frontier offer ABM tools. To find ABM tools, search for "Automated Bid Management."

Let's look at Omniture Search Center. Their enterprise ABM tool unifies analytics and PPC so you can use the analytics to manage the PPC. You use one interface to manage all of your PPC accounts, including Google, Yahoo!, and Microsoft adCenter, plus other PPC services. You can easily copy and move keywords, ads, ad groups, and campaigns among Google, Yahoo!, and Microsoft adCenter, so whatever works in one, you can try in the others. It includes a library of automated best-practice strategies, and you can create custom rules. It's integrated with Excel, so you can use Excel spreadsheets to manage your campaigns according to business goals.

All this highlights the limits of Google Analytics. Google offers an ABM tool, which works well because Google has full access to their data about market activity. However, you don't know the bidding rules because Google won't tell you, and there isn't a way to customize or create rules. Also, Google's support is minimal. Google Analytics won't allow companies to use lookup tables. Raw data can't be downloaded for BI data analysis or rollup reports by site, site group, or across a large networks of sites, such as distributed partner and resource sites.

Google's ABM Tools

Google offers two basic ABM tools that are both free in Google AdWords:

- **Budget Optimizer**   This tool maximizes the number of clicks within your budget. If your campaign is based on driving traffic to your site (but you don't measure conversions), you will get more clicks. Be careful: This tool ignores conversions and profits. You should focus on conversions and profits, not clicks.

- **Conversion Optimizer**   This tool maximizes the number of conversions. You set the maximum CPA for a conversion, and this tool uses portfolio management to manage the bids within the ad group. For you to use Conversion Optimizer, Google requires at least 100 conversions per month.

To use either one of these tools, go to a campaign's settings and select Keyword Bidding options.

You can use Budget Optimizer in campaigns where conversion tracking is not possible. For example, realtors and companies with long (and untrackable) sales cycles might use the Budget Optimizer. When a company sells a $500,000 transmogrifier, it's often not clear which action caused the sale. They're using PPC, booths at trade shows, technical sales teams, and so on. In such cases, the company would just want to drive qualified traffic to the site.

When Budget Optimizer is turned on, some keywords become inactive. Google is trying to get you the most clicks, so they ignore keywords they consider "low value." If you want those keywords to be active, go to Campaign Settings and increase the budget or the maximum bid. You can also move the keywords into another ad group or another campaign. You may also leave the keywords in Inactive status; this won't affect the ad group's QS.

Budget Optimizer will spend your budget. If you set high budgets, Google will reach those limits. Therefore, set an ad budget that you can afford to pay.

Google's ABM tool adjusts bids by location, depending on local results. Google can bid lower in Austin and higher in Pittsburgh, for example. The Google ABM tools also adjust by time of day and day of week.

It's tempting to set up ABM and let it manage your PPC. However, this is a bad idea. You need to focus on strategy and campaigns. You must test new keywords, create new ads, and continually improve the QS.

 note
Be sure to carefully test Google's ABM tools. Run them for a few weeks and see how they affect conversions. For most of our clients, the results tripled or quadrupled. However, for a few campaigns, the traffic crashed. In some cases, it stayed at near-zero for a few days and then climbed to a much higher level than before. For other campaigns, the traffic crashed and never recovered; we had to turn off the ABM tools to restore the traffic. You can monitor these tools with Account Snapshot. Select the campaign, set the time-frame for the last few months, and look at clicks and conversion rates. We recommend you monitor this daily for a few weeks.

What Is the Best Position for Your Ads?

The first page in Google shows eight ads. If there are more ads, they appear on subsequent pages.

So where should your ads be? Position 1? Position 4? Position 7? Although theory and studies say that number one gets most of the clicks, we've found ads often get more conversions in lower positions.

Why does that happen? We think if the same product is offered by multiple vendors, the visitor clicks on the first ad, sees the price, and then clicks on the second, third, and fourth ads to see if the price is lower. By the time they reach the fifth ad and the price is the same, they buy from the fifth vendor.

You can see this in analytics. Go to Google Analytics | Traffic Sources | AdWords | Keyword Positions and compare the positions and conversions. You'll find that the lower positions often produced more clicks and conversions.

If your budget is too low, you'll notice that your campaign will max out its budget early in the morning and your ads won't show for the rest of the day. We recommend you improve the QS, which lowers your click costs and gives you more ads and clicks with the same budget. Calculate your CPA and CPL. If the account is profitable, you'll be able to increase the budget with confidence.

Why Isn't My Ad on Google?

This is one of the most common questions from our clients. They search in Google for their top keywords and don't see their ad. There are several reasons for this:

- Go to your AdWords account and look at the number of impressions for the last business day. If a keyword is getting impressions, it is being displayed to other people, even if you don't see your ad.

- Click the Tools tab and select Ads Diagnostic Tool. If the ad isn't being displayed, it gives the reason.

- If the daily budget is too low, AdWords will display the ad intermittently. If you want the ad to appear all the time, increase the daily budget.

- Google displays ads according to location. If Google sees that koi ads get clicks in Los Angeles and Chicago, but not in New York, then Google won't show the ads in New York. If you happen to be in New York, you may never see your own ads. Google also adjusts to the time of day. If late afternoon works better, your ads won't show up in the morning.

 tip　*If your CEO really wants to see his ads, here's what you can do. Create an ad campaign, assign a $20 budget, and set the location to two miles around his office address or home address. When he searches Google every 30 minutes, he'll see his ads!*

Using Campaigns and Ad Groups

AdWords has campaigns and ad groups. The following table looks at these in more detail.

Category	Description	How to Use This
Campaign	Use a campaign for each product. In the campaign's settings, set the daily budget. For example, set the maximum at $100 per day. You can also set geographical targeting and language.	If you're selling koi, turtles, and ducks, then create three campaigns named Koi, Turtles, and Ducks, respectively.
Ad Group	Within the campaign, create ad groups for each product version.	In the Koi campaign, create three ad groups named Koromo Koi, Asagi Koi, and Kohaku Koi.
Keyword	Within each ad group, you add the keywords and ads.	Within the Koromo Koi ad group, use keywords such as *koromo koi* and *young koromo koi*.

note *Some people create dozens of ad groups with a single keyword in each one. That isn't sufficient for the search engine to know your ad group's theme. Others put all the keywords in one ad group. Thus, the theme is unfocused. Don't make either of these mistakes. Your campaigns and ad groups should reflect your products.*

Use the Content Network

Let's now look at how to use the Content Network. This appears to be like the Search Network, but the rules are different.

First of all, why bother with the Content Network? The simple reason: The clicks and CPAs are generally cheaper. If clicks cost $0.75 in Search Network, they may cost only $0.12 in the Content Network. It is a bit more complex to set up Content Network ads; however, that also means fewer advertisers understand it, so we suspect there is less serious competition.

The Content Network displays your ads in websites that sponsor Google's ads, such as *The New York Times,* Yahoo!, USNews.com, *Forbes,* ABC, Economist.com, Fox, TheStreet.com, *National Geographic,* About.com, Business.com, HGTV, iVillage.com, and several million more websites. These reach 86% of all web users.

Your ads also appear in Google's various services, such as Gmail, Blogger, Google Maps, AdSense, and YouTube. For example, Google looks for keywords in Gmail e-mails and then inserts related advertising into the e-mail. If you and your friends start e-mailing about plans to go trout fishing in Wyoming, Gmail might insert Google AdWords advertising for Wyoming fishing resorts. Gmail includes Google search, so when people search their emails, more Google AdWords ads are displayed.

Here is the main difference between the Content Network and Search Network:

- For the Search Network, AdWords matches the user's query and the keyword. If there is a match, an ad is displayed.

- For the Content Network, AdWords matches the theme of the ad group with the theme of the web page. Google matches the themes, not the keywords. The ad group should have enough keywords for AdWords to establish the theme, which means about 15 to 30 keywords. You can use keywords in singular and plural.

In the Content Network, don't use "Phrase Match," [Exact Match], or Keyword Insertion. These have no effect in the Content Network. Also, don't put hundreds of keywords in an ad group.

Because Google doesn't use the keyword to match, it doesn't report clicks or conversions for keywords. Don't worry about impressions, clicks, or CTR. Google's algorithm takes care of that for you; Google wants to get the highest CTR, so they eliminate sites with high impressions and low clicks. However, Google doesn't know your target CPA, so you have to manage that.

Instead of managing the bids for each keyword, you manage the bids to control the average ad position for the whole ad group. Manage content ads in the following way:

1. In AdWords, select Campaign Management | Account Spanshot.

2. Select the Content Campaign.

3. Set the date range to the last 60–90 days.

4. Set the chart to Cost Per Conversion.

5. Add a second metric chart and set it to Conversions.

6. If Cost Per Conversion is greater than your profitable CPA, lower your bids until the actual CPA is within your profitable CPA.

7. If the Cost Per Conversion is lower than your calculated CPA, increase your bids. Wait several days and check the graphics again to see if conversions increased.

Create ad groups with themes that match the theme of the target pages. In each ad group, write ads that describe the theme. In the Search Network, you can only use text ads. In the Content Network, you can use text ads, image ads, video ads, and widgets. This provides greater opportunity for you to show your products to your audience.

tip *You can see where your ads are showing. Use the Placement Performance report (a report in Google AdWords) to see the URLs that host your ads, along with the number of displays, clicks, conversions, CTR, and CPA. If the cumulative CPA is within your target CPA, then allow the campaign to continue. If the cumulative CPA exceeds your target CPA, sort the table by CPA (click on Cost/Conversion) and look at the sites with the highest CPA. If the CPA exceeds your target CPA, use Site Exclusion to block those URLs. By deleting those, you free up budget for other sites. To block sites, return to the campaign view and click No Excluded Sites: Add, and then enter the domain names of the sites to exclude.*

Use Image Ads in the Content Network

The Content Network includes both text and image ads. The image ads can be horizontal, vertical, or square.

Your image ads should show a product shot and your USP. Image ads convert better. We think this is because if your customers are looking for a product, they will select an ad that shows the product. Someone looking for koi is more likely to click on ads that show koi instead of ads that have only text. Many advertisers lack the resources to create a set of image ads with professional photographs and layout. There is also the expense. Professionally produced image ads can cost several hundred dollars. However, this is good news; you'll have fewer competitors, so the clicks will be cheaper.

To get a very sharp and clear image, use PNG format (not JPG or GIF). The maximum file size is 50KB. If the PNG file is too large, save it once as a JPG. Ads may include 15 seconds of animation if it's not looped. You can add a sparkle to the logo, and so on.

We strongly recommend animated Flash ads. These generally perform better than still images.

You can also use video ads. Video ads appear first as a static image. When the visitor clicks, the video opens in a pop-up window. Video ads use the same sizes as image ads.

Image ads are reviewed by the search engines to make sure they are family-friendly. This review can take up to five workdays. If you have an account representative, ask them to approve your ads.

You must create ads in all eight sizes shown here. Sites select the format that fits into their design. Because you don't know which size that will be, you have to offer all formats. Some sites may also choose to show text ads, so you should include at least one text ad.

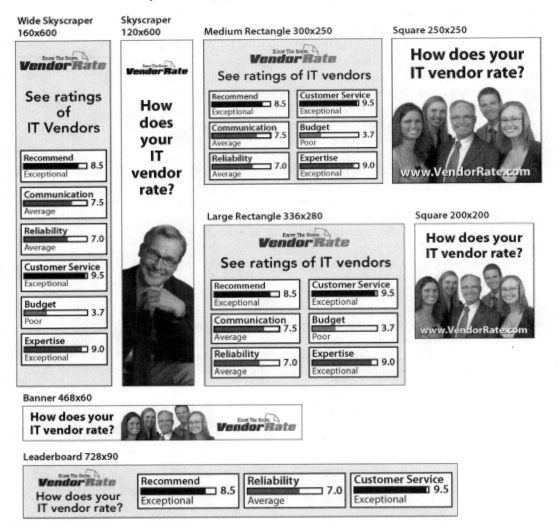

Google Gadget Ads

Gadget ads are yet another format for ads at Google. A gadget ad is a small box that can contain software such as a mortgage calculator, a game, or a mini-website of your site. You can create widgets in the various Google image ad sizes. You can see examples and learn more about gadget ads at www.google.com/adwords/gadgetads.

Placement Targeting

Another way to place your ads is to use *placement targeting,* which enables you to select the websites where your ads will be displayed. You can use text ads, image ads, and video ads. You can select sites by categories, related topics, URLs, or demographics. This lets you place your ads in front of a highly targeted audience. In the following example, you can see that Animal-World gets 10,000 to 100,000 page views per day, but AquaBid.com gets up to 500,000 views per day.

Results related to: koi fish	Ad Formats Choose Formats »	Impressions per day ⓘ	Add all »
Placements			
animal-world.com	▤ ▦ ▨	10k-100k	Add »
View all animal-world.com placements (4)			
aqua-fish.net	▤ ▦ ▨	0k-10k	Add »
View all aqua-fish.net placements (2)			
aquabid.com	▤ ▦ ▨	100k-500k	Add »
— Homepage,Top right	▤ ▦ ▨	10k-100k	Add »
View all aquabid.com placements (1)			
planetcatfish.com	▤ ▦ ▨	0k-10k	Add »
— All Planet Catfish,Multiple locations	▤ ▦ ▨	0k-10k	Add »
View all planetcatfish.com placements (1)			

Your ads will appear only on these sites. This lets you target the advertising to highly relevant websites. For example, you can place your koi ads in Koi-Magazine.com, but not Gourmet.com.

Many high-traffic magazine websites carry Google's ads. To sell our koi, we can advertise in RobbReport.com and *The New York Times* website. Enter the sites you want, and similar sites will be shown.

You can pay either by CPC or CPM (you pay for every 1000 displays of your ad):

- Use CPC if your goal is conversions (such as sales, leads, downloads, and so on).

- Use CPM if your purpose is to increase brand awareness among your target audience. You set the amount that you'll pay for 1000 impressions.

You can also bid according to demographics. If your target audience is women 22–35, you can bid higher when your ad shows to this group.

To manage your costs in placement advertising, use placement reports. Find the sites that have poor CPL or CPA. You can block them from your ad distribution by adding them to your campaign's Excluded Sites list. You can also block sites by category. If you find that a site doesn't convert well for you, you can block that site and similar sites with the Category Exclusion tool.

The Strategy for Landing Pages with High Conversions

Let's now look at what happens after the click. Suppose Laura, a potential customer, has clicked on your ad at Google. Instead of sending her to your general website, you should send her to a page that shows her the product she wants. The landing page must be highly relevant to Laura's search. If the landing page is not relevant, she will return to Google and go to the next website. This will lower your QS. The landing page must reassure Laura that you will deliver what she orders. She should feel comfortable with her decision to buy from you. Here are some points to keep in mind:

- The purpose of the landing page is to get visitors to convert. They should fill out a form, buy a product, download a PDF, and so on.

- The ad group, keywords, ad, landing page, and thank-you page should form a seamless customer-centric whole.

- If you're selling koromo koi, then create an ad group just for koromo koi and put *koromo* in your keyword list. Write an ad with *koromo* in the headline, in the first line of body text, and in the display URL, and then point the ad to a unique landing page, such as Koi-Planet.com/koromo-koi.html, where visitors can see a photo of a koromo, read about koromo, and can fill out their name and credit card information on the same page.

- The landing page should be short and simple. The more steps involved, the more buyers you will lose. The best landing pages are those of the everything-on-one-page variety.

Landing pages move the emphasis away from websites. From 1995 to 2004, the focus of e-commerce was on websites as a set of pages with product, company, help, and contact information, among other things. This classical approach presented the company's perception of itself to the customer.

That theory doesn't work anymore because search engines allow people to shop anonymously, gathering information and evaluating suppliers. People don't search for websites. They search for information and products.

People in the buying cycle are either gathering information (so they ignore ads) or are ready to buy (so they have decided on the product and are evaluating suppliers). Laura does research to learn about *her* interests. When she is ready to buy, she looks for "Mr. Right," the supplier who delivers what she wants. She types her search and looks at the top results in both the left and right sides of the screen. She eventually comes to a landing page that is highly relevant to her search. Google's use of landing page relevancy as part of the QS reduces the traditional emphasis on the general website.

tip *Many PPC campaigns ignore landing pages. They point the traffic to the website's front page. With good landing pages, you can get very high conversions. Use multivariate tools to find the best landing page design. Just so you know what's possible, we've built landing pages with 50%–70% conversion rates.*

How to Build Landing Pages for High Conversions

Here are tips for a successful landing page:

- A heading that includes the visitor's search terms.

- A color photo of the product. Use professional photographs, and add a caption.

- A selection of models, colors, and features. Offer comparisons and explain the advantages and disadvantages. State the price on the page. If you write "Click here to learn about our prices," visitors generally go back to the search engine. You can also offer discounts, free shipping, no sales tax, a money-back guarantee, and similar.

- A professional layout. A professional layout works better than amateur design.

Here are some other tips for creating a landing page:

- Keep it to one or two pages. If visitors find a long series of forms, they often quit and go back to the search engine.

- Remove links that lead your visitors away from your message and conversion goal.

- Include reviews from trusted information sources, such as reputable newspapers or magazines. To create a sense of confidence, add a list of trusted name brands and vendors. Use logos, including credit card logos.

- Include your business location (if it is applicable), complete with street address, city, state, and telephone number.

The landing page's content also affects your ad group's QS. If the content of the landing page matches the keywords and ads, the QS will improve.

That's what visitors want to see. But what about Google? What do they want to see on your landing page? They give higher ranking to merchants who have credible sites. Here are some points to keep in mind:

- Google prefers a landing page with one product instead of pages with multiple offers. Put only one product on each landing page.

- Clearly identify your business. There are too many scam websites. Google prefers websites that state their contact information. This means your name, address, e-mail, telephone, and fax number.

- If your landing page use a shopping cart, include useful features. Allow customers to view the contents of their shopping cart as well as calculate the shipping fees. Add FedEx tracking. Good e-commerce packages include Yahoo! Stores and Volusion.com. Google accepts these as real stores.

- If you ask for personal information, state your privacy policy. Add a privacy policy to your site and link your landing page to your privacy policy. If you need a privacy policy, look at Koi-Planet .com's privacy, statements, copy that, and modify it for your site.

- State your return policy, with details on how to return or exchange products, along with any fees.

- Don't build affiliate sites that point to Amazon, eBay, or similar sites.

- The landing page should open quickly. Google deducts points if your page takes too long to open. This is bad news for many corporate sites that use lots of Flash on their home pages.

The keywords, ads, and landing pages should be in the same language. If you use French keywords and write your ads in French, the landing pages should be in French. Don't mix languages. You can always use English as the universal language for any country, but preference will be given to ads in that country's language. We often create landing pages that include both English and Chinese side by side on the page, so everyone can read the page. To develop the best landing pages, see the upcoming section on multivariate testing.

As shown next, by placing information in tabs on the left side of the page, you can add more information to the page without having the visitor go to another page. Tabs can include benefits, options, comparisons, testimonials, and so on. You also keep information above the fold where they will see it. At right side of the page is a simple form with a strong Submit button. It includes a free offer to encourage visitors to send their contact information.

In your order form, always ask for a telephone number. If you ask only for an e-mail address, you'll get many leads with invalid e-mail addresses. For several clients, as much as 20% of the e-mails have been invalid. People often mistype their e-mail address, but they always remember their telephone number.

Use a Thank-You Page

After the customer completes the form, they are sent to a thank-you page. This confirmation page usually says something like, "Thank you for buying our koi. Your koromo koi will arrive by FedEx Overnight."

The thank-you page is a good opportunity to interact further with your customers. They just purchased from you, so they will look at whatever you offer. Use the thank-you page to make additional offers, such as newsletters, another product, coupons for additional products, a case study, a feedback form, or the opportunity to refer a friend. Use the thank-you page to cross-sell and up-sell.

Multivariate Testing

Tools are available to help you create the optimal landing page. These are called *multivariate testing* (MVT) tools.

Let's say your page has a heading, a photo, and a block of body text. Maybe a different heading would work better, so you write five headings. You could also try different product photographs: small, large, and one of the product with a person. What's more, you could try three different sets of body text. In total, that's five headings, three photos, and three sets of body text. If you multiply these ($5 \times 3 \times 3 = 45$), you'll find there are 45 possible combinations for your page.

You feed the different parts (the headings, photos, and body text) into the multivariate tool, it creates the 45 combinations, and then it tries them out and compares the results. Within days, you'll see that, for example, combination number 12 outperforms the original with 64% more conversions.

A number of companies either sell MVT software or offer MVT services. One of the best-known tools is Omniture's Offermatica. Google also has an MVT tool called Website Optimizer, which is free.

Two types of MVT tools are available. If you have 45 combinations for your page, the first type of MVT tool will test all 45 versions. With the second type of MVT tool, it's possible to show that a test of seven of the 45 combinations will produce the same result. This allows you to test much larger combinations (literally tens of thousands of combinations). This type of MVT tool uses the *fractional factorial* or *Taguchi Method,* which was developed by Genichi Taguchi, a Japanese quality engineer. Google's MVT tool does not use the Taguchi Method, which means you are limited to the number of combinations based on your traffic volume. You need five conversions per page to make a conclusion about that page, so if you have 1000 conversions or sales per month, you can test 200 combinations in a month.

You can also use multivariate testing to improve many pages at your website, not just the landing page. Look at your analytics and identify the top entrance pages. The tool shows you which combinations produce the best performance. For example, combination 11 converts 24.9% better than the original, as shown next.

		Combinations	Page Sections				

Combination	Estimated Conversion Rate Range [?]	Chance to Beat Orig. [?]	Chance to Beat All [?]	Observed Improvement [?]	Conversions / Impressions [?]
Original	31.2% ± 3.0%	—	0.41%	—	125 / 401
Combination 11	38.9% ± 3.1%	99.0%	85.4%	24.9%	160 / 411
Combination 4	33.6% ± 3.0%	76.8%	4.12%	7.74%	133 / 396
Combination 23	33.4% ± 2.8%	75.9%	2.82%	7.17%	153 / 458
Combination 16	32.7% ± 2.9%	67.8%	1.56%	4.75%	144 / 441
Combination 10	32.6% ± 2.9%	67.5%	1.69%	4.67%	139 / 426
Combination 8	32.4% ± 2.9%	64.6%	1.30%	3.90%	137 / 423
Combination 22	32.0% ± 3.0%	60.0%	1.03%	2.69%	129 / 403
Combination 7	31.6% ± 2.8%	55.1%	0.45%	1.27%	143 / 453
Combination 14	31.4% ± 2.8%	52.2%	0.41%	0.57%	137 / 437
Combination 21	31.1% ± 2.9%	49.1%	0.40%	-0.20%	126 / 405
Combination 18	30.3% ± 2.8%	39.1%	0.11%	-2.79%	130 / 429

Analysis for: Aug 21 2006 - Aug 21 2006. View: Best 23 Combinations / Worst 23 Combinations. Download: T. Print. Preview.

The optimizer report shows you the pages ranked by success. The next seven combinations will also outperform the original page. When you start the testing, you'll quickly see that some combinations don't work. You can delete those from the test. When you end up with the best version, you can use that one. Better yet, use the best one as your standard and create more combinations. Do this over and over to get high conversion rates.

Geotargeting: Advertising by City or State

You can have your ads appear in the markets you want. This is called *local targeting* or *geotargeting*.

For example, suppose a dentist in Seattle wants to advertise. People in Miami will never come to her office, so that would be a waste of advertising. She can use local targeting so her ads are shown only in her city.

To use local targeting, check mark the campaign and click Edit Settings. In the targeting page, select Custom and use the Map Point tab.

The dentist can set a radius, such as 16 miles, and thus create a circle around her office. The ads will be shown only to users who live within that circle and search for a dentist. The dentist should consider how far a patient will drive to get to her office and set the radius accordingly. To do this, she could enter her address and city, or she could use the map to find her city, double-click to set the point, enter the radius in miles or in kilometers, and click View on Map to see the size of the area, as shown next.

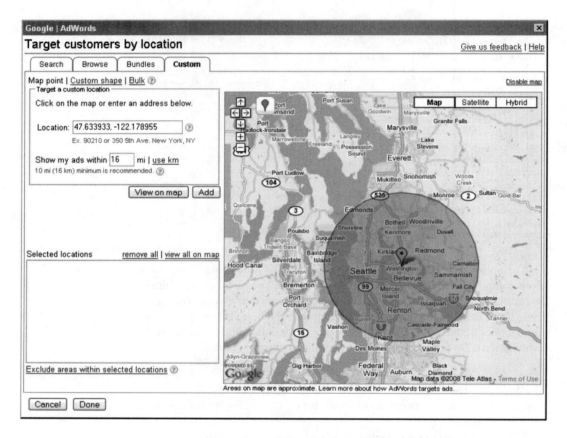

There is also a feature called *multipoint targeting*. Suppose a cabinet maker wants to work with clients only within five miles on either side of the freeway from Sacramento to San Francisco. To do this, he can set a series of points to create a long rectangle (or an irregular shape) that encloses the area along the freeway. To use multipoint targeting, the cabinet maker would check mark the campaign and click Edit Settings. In the targeting page, he would select Custom and use the Custom Shape tab. Finally, he would zoom in on the map until he sees the area to mark and then would click a series of dots to create the target zone, as shown next.

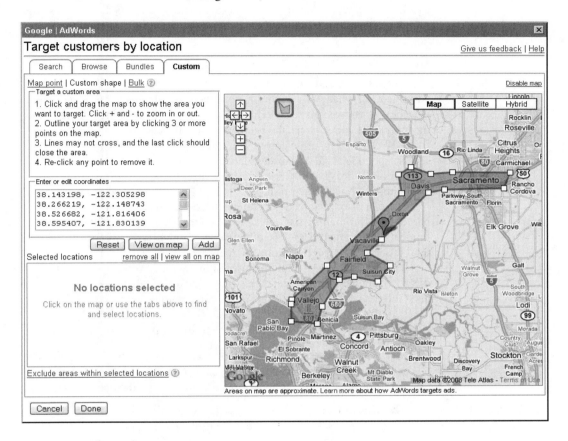

In early 2005, we came up with the idea for multipoint targeting. Based on gerrymandering in politics, we thought it'd be useful for targeting ads for several of our clients. We wrote a description of this, along with examples of how this would work, and gave it to people we knew at Google. A few months later, they added this feature.

The bulk map feature lets you target up to 100 cities or areas that aren't connected to each other. From your analytics, you can find the cities that produce the most conversions. Upload this list and target your advertising to only those cites.

You can use this for testing products by DMAs (direct marketing areas), specific communities, parts of cities, regions, and so on.

These tools use the searcher's location. When you use a browser, your computer sends its IP address to the server. The IP address can be matched to a ZIP code, which lets the server know where you are located. That's how search engines know someone's location when they click on an ad.

Conversion Tracking

One of the best features in AdWords is conversion tracking. A click on your ad is nice, but what really counts is when the visitor buys your product. This is a conversion from visitor into buyer. The conversion tracking feature shows the number of conversions, the percentage, and the cost-per-conversion.

AdWords offers a free conversion tracking tool. You fetch a bit of JavaScript code at AdWords and place it in your website's thank-you page. This lets AdWords know that the visitor clicked on the AdWord, came to your site, and bought the product.

You can also track lead generation. If you use the website to capture names for your mailing list, the conversion tracking feature will show the number of generated leads, the effectiveness of the lead conversion, and the total costs of the lead generation campaign.

It's quick and easy to set up conversion tracking. You copy a few lines of code from Google, you paste this into your web site's thank-you page, and Google AdWords will report on the conversions. Here's a guide:

1. To set up conversion tracking, click on it in the AdWords toolbar.

2. You can select Basic or Customized. Basic will track a conversion. Customized tracking will let you distinguish between conversions for leads, sales, signup, or page views. Select the one you want.

3. Conversion Tracking will ask for the security level of the conversion page. If you're not certain of the page's security level, visit your thank-you page and look at the URL in the browser URL bar: It is either HTTP or HTTPS. Select the appropriate type. The page will refresh itself, and the code will be displayed in a text box.

4. Copy the conversion code. Save it in a Notepad TXT file (do not save it in Word, which may insert formatting and thus break the code).

5. Paste the code in the HTML before the </BODY> tag at the bottom of your thank-you page.

Conversion data usually shows up within three hours.

The conversion tracking is good, but it has a limit. Because the cookie expires after four weeks, it only reports if a conversion happened within four weeks of the initial visit. If your industry's purchase cycle is longer (in other words, if customers take 6–12 weeks or longer to make a purchase), then the tool will report a misleading low conversion rate. To track long cycle conversions, you'll need to use analytics tools (see Chapter 3).

Errors with Conversion Tracking

You will find the conversion tracking feature is not accurate. There can be a 10%–20% difference between conversions and actual sales. For example, you know from the warehouse that you shipped 100 products, but conversion tracking may show only 85 conversions.

Some of these errors happen because the conversion code didn't have time to be carried out. If the thank-you page appears and the customer leaves immediately, the conversion might not be counted. You can improve this by keeping the customer on the thank-you page for several seconds. One way you might do this is by providing additional information about the product, including tips and ideas.

Don't use conversion tracking for your accounting or sales reports. If your commission or bonus is based on sales, it's better to get commission on 100 actual sales, not 85 reported sales.

AdWords Reports

Although AdWords includes report tools, the analytics reports are generally more useful. Look at the AdWords reports and see if there are any you can use.

The placement report is handy. Clients often ask where their ads are showing in the Content Network. Google's placement report can show which websites are showing the ads.

To use a placement report, select Placement Report and perform the following actions:

- At View (Unit of Time), select Summary. This combines the data for each website.

- At Domain or URL, select Domain (if you select URL, you'll only get a partial URL).

- Set the Date Range to a period where you have conversion tracking.

- Select the campaign. If you click on the campaign, you can select the ad groups.

- When the report is ready, select it from the list of reports.

- Click on Cost to sort the list by cost (you'll have to click twice). You'll see the sites that cost the most. If the site did not produce conversions, you can block it in the Content Network.

- You can also sort by conversions to see which sites worked for you. Make a list of those sites and use the Placement tools to find related sites.

You can download the report to Excel, where you can go through it to find the items you need.

Additional Google Tools

Under the Campaign Management | Tools tab are a couple of useful items:

- **Ads Diagnostics Tool**   Why is an ad not showing? Enter the keyword and location and see whether or not the ad is showing.

- **My Change History**   This lets you look back and see what changes you've made to your account in the last three months. If something goes wrong, you can see who made the change. If someone is managing the account for you, you can use this to check whether they are actually working on your account.

Use the AdWords Editor to Manage Your Ads and Keywords

You can download and install the Google AdWords Editor software on your computer. You then download your AdWords account, make changes, and upload the changes to your account. You can easily copy/paste keywords and ads from one campaign to another, or from Excel into the tool. You can also upload dozens of image ads in just a few steps.

If you are managing a large account (more than two or three campaigns with more than 10 to 20 ad groups), we recommend using this tool. If you manage several accounts, you definitely should use this. It'll save you time. Download it for free at www.google.com/intl/en/adwordseditor/.

Quick Tips for Using the AdWords Editor

Here are a few tips for using AdWords Editor:

- To select all items, press CTRL-A.

- Double-click a keyword to go to its ad group.

- Create draft campaigns. You can set up a draft campaign, add and change keywords and ads, review it with your team, and upload it when it's ready.

- Use Comments to write notes and info about campaigns, ad groups, and keywords. Information can include actions, dates, budgets, goals, CPLs, and so on.

- AdWords Editor has an auto-save feature. It constantly saves your current work.

- Replace allows you to modify (or delete) a name/value pair in a tracking URL. For example, in "?source=Google&campaign= summer&keyword=swimming," the part "&campaign=summer" is a name/value pair. By searching for Name=Campaign, you can change or delete this name/value pair in the entire account or a single campaign.

- You can also copy/paste from one account into another. Copy from the source account, open the target account, and paste.

- Be careful with the Editor's statistics for your keywords. It sometimes reports the keyword status (active/inactive) and CPCs incorrectly. You must look at the account to see the real values.

The AdWords Editor is compatible with Excel. You can upload keywords from and to Excel (or Word, Notepad, and so on). A common activity is to collect 1500 keywords, sort and clean them up in Excel, and move these into AdWords Editor.

AdWords Editor checks your edits before you post them. It checks for grammar, punctuation (such as too many exclamation marks), policy (you generally can't use "Best" and "Number One" or a call-to-action such as "Click Here Now"), and trademarks (you can't use certain registered trademarks). It doesn't check ads for spelling, however. If you misspell a word, the ad may be eventually rejected.

You can use AdWords Editor to group keywords into clusters. If you have an ad group with dozens (or hundreds) of keywords, AdWords Editor can use its grouper tool to cluster the ad group's keywords into themes and create new ad groups for you. You can create dozens of new ad groups in a few minutes. Here are the steps to follow:

1. Open AdWords Editor and navigate to the ad group.

2. Select Tools | Keyword Grouper.

3. Click on Generate Common Terms. This produces a long list of keywords.

4. In the right panel, add the following keywords: *of, for, free, to,* and *the.* This removes them from the left panel.

5. The keywords in the left panel will become the titles of new ad groups. Go through the list and delete keywords that don't make sense as ad groups. You'll have to experiment with this. Delete a bunch of keywords, add new keywords (that would make good ad group titles), and click Next.

6. This shows you the new ad groups with their keywords. All the keywords from the original ad group have been sorted into the new ad groups.

7. Be sure to check mark "Yes, copy ad texts into the new ad groups." This duplicates the original ads.

8. Click Finish. The new ad groups are created. You can make changes and upload these new ad groups into the account.

This works best on an ad group with several hundred keywords. If the keywords are too similar, it won't do much. You'll have to try and see what it does with your keywords.

The MCC: One Login for All of Your Accounts

If you manage several AdWords accounts, you can use an MCC account to go from one to the other without logging in and out of accounts. You log into the MCC (My Client Center, or Master Client Center) and all of your accounts are available in a clickable list.

This is useful for agencies and consultants who manage multiple accounts. You can also add MCCs to your MCC to create sub-MCCs, so account managers can have their own personal MCCs. To set up an MCC, sign up for the Google Advertising Professionals program.

PPC Blogs

The PPC services are constantly evolving. All three have blogs, where they announce news and changes:

- **Google** http://adwords.blogspot.com
- **Yahoo! Search Marketing** http://www.ysmblog.com/
- **Microsoft adCenter** http://blogs.msdn.com/adcenter/

Other Forms of Advertising in Google

For the first five years, Google's advertising services were only for the Web. There was ad distribution only in the Search Network and Content Network.

In 2007, Google began to enter other ad channels. Using the Google AdWords platform, you can now advertise inexpensively in radio, TV, newspapers, and mobile devices.

By using the Web, you can turn offline advertising into a trackable channel. You can place your ads in radio, TV, and newspapers. The ads point to unique URLs (such as Koi-Christmas-Sale.com) where you have landing pages. You add analytics tracking code to both the landing page and the goals. This lets you track the results of the channel campaign. Alternatively, you use a unique URL that points to a page that uses a 301-redirect. The redirect includes an analytics tracking URL, which sends the visitor to your website. That also lets you track the results. This means you can track radio, TV, and newspapers just like PPC campaigns. You can set a budget, carry out the campaign, measure the results, and if it is profitable, you can increase the campaigns.

You can use PPC together with radio, TV, and newspapers. Create a PPC campaign that uses a unique keyword, such as "seattle koi," and a strong ad. Tell people to Google for "Seattle Koi" and they'll see your PPC ad. We recommend you set up PPC campaigns in Google, Yahoo!, and Microsoft so they can find you, regardless of the search engine.

Why use radio, TV, newspapers, or mobile devices? There are several good reasons:

- Your advertising can max out on the Web. At some point, you may find that you increase your ad budget, but you don't get any more customers or sales. You can add other media to reach additional audiences.

- Search engine marketing lets you capture demand. People are searching for products and services. In contrast, radio/TV/print lets you create demand. You let your audience know about your product or service. Offline channels create awareness of your products. You attract that traffic to your website, where you use analytics to track it.

- Traditional ad placement in offline channels often involved several agencies, complex negotiations, up to six weeks to get verification that the ads actually ran, and months of account reconciliation to finalize the bills. With Google, you manage all your ads via one tool, place ads in dozens of markets and channels, and deal with one monthly invoice. If you are already using offline channels, it may be easier to do this via Google.

- You can test other channels and see if you can get leads and sales within your maximum CPA. You should use a multi-channel strategy to get as many leads and sales as possible. If you can increase your sales, you can lower your CPA to increase your profits.

- Google includes free call reporting. You give Google a telephone number, such as your business line or a sales line. Google gives you a new free telephone number that you place in your ads. When people call that number, they are automatically sent to your business line. Google gives you a report on the number of calls, length of call, the caller's city, date, and time. Google does not report the caller's phone number.

- Google Analytics reports your radio, TV, and print campaigns. For each, it shows the number of impressions, the number of ads displayed, the cost, and the CPM. The trends are compared to web traffic so you can see if the offline campaigns resulted in website traffic spikes.

- There are no long-term contracts. You can test a few ads and see if the channel works for you.

Think about your audience and see if you can reach them via radio, TV, newspapers, or mobile devices. Through Google, it is so inexpensive that you can carry out test campaigns, track the results, and see if it works. Google's bid auctions include a tool that shows you the range of accepted bids. In general, you should set your bids at the upper end of the price range.

In general, TV, radio, and newspapers are local channels. You can target by outlets (radio stations, TV stations, or newspapers) or demographics. You set your audience's demographics (for example, women 35-45 earning $25,000 to $50,000) and the tools will show you suitable TV channels, radio stations, or newspapers. Google's TV advertising is currently only nationwide (your ad is shown to the entire U.S.), but they will eventually allow you to advertise on local TV. We recommend you select the outlets, not the demographics. It's more expensive to target by demographic.

These offline channels have been around for decades, so there are many services and tools. By using Nielsen or Scarborough, you can get extensive demographics information. Google's media planners will help you to create media plans (such as lists of radio stations, TV channels, or newspapers).

You also have to think about day parting. Consider when your audience is listening to radio and place the ads accordingly. If they listen while commuting to and from work, then place ads in those times. You also need to plan ahead. Many advertisers will place ads for the major holidays and sports events many months in advance.

Use Google to Advertise on AM/FM Radio

You can use Google AdWords to place audio ads on radio. This is ordinary AM/FM radio, just like in your car. You can place ads on over 1700 AM/FM radio stations in the top 100 U.S. cities (more than half of all radio stations), which reaches 94% of the U.S. You can create and launch a radio campaign for less than $200. We've done radio ads for clients for as little as $2.16 per ad play on the radio.

Google offers a list of people who are professional voice actors and have experience in production of radio ads. You contact them and negotiate a price. Typical fees start at $100–$250. They produce the ad for you, including music and sound effects. In our experience, it's better to suggest the general idea and let them create the ad. For ideas, you can listen to 75+ examples of radio ads at www.google.com/adwords/audioads/ads.html. You upload the ad into Google AdWords, pick the city and the radio stations, and set the bids. If you have the highest bid for a time slot, your ad plays.

When setting up the radio campaigns, you can set the following:

- You pick the days of the week and the hours of the day. You can select timeslots, such as 6 to 10 A.M, 10 A.M. to 3 P.M., and so on.

- You can select states, cities, or DMAs (DMAs are marketing regions, such as the San Francisco Bay Area). You can also select by demographics (for example, women, age 18–20, 21–24, and so on).

- You can select radio stations by genre (for example, News, Rock, Easy Listening, and so on). This can be subdivided into smaller groups. For example, Oldies includes Classic Hits, Nostalgia, and Rhythmic Oldies.

- You can use event triggers. For example, your ads for backyard swimming pools will be played if there is hot weather.

Google sends you a report on the ad plays. This includes the radio station's call letters, the city, the DMA name, the time of play (for example, 8:32 A.M., Oct. 28), and the size of the audience. The report also includes an air check: you can listen to five-to-ten seconds before and after the ad, along with the ad, so you know how your ad was presented on the radio, along with whatever was playing before and after your ad.

Here is an example of a radio report:

Campaign	Call Letters	Station	Genre	Market	Play Time	Air Check	Listeners
Koi Ad	KAAR-FM	92.9 FM	Country	SF	Sep 23, 2008 3:43 P.M. PDT	www.dmarc.net/ db/15047658.wma	5900
Koi Ad	KSAC-AM	1590 AM	News	SF	Sep 23, 2008 4:16 P.M. PDT	www.dmarc.net/ db/15048936.wma	1000
Koi Ad	KMXG-FM	97.7 FM	Rock	SF	Sep 23, 2008 6:37 P.M. PDT	www.dmarc.net/ db/15047450.wma	2100
Koi Ad	KJJY-FM	101.7 FM	Rock	SF	Sep 23, 2008 8:46 P.M. PDT	www.dmarc.net/ db/15046108.wma	2000
						Totals	11,000

In the preceding report, an ad played in September. It played on KAAR, KSAC, and so on. The dial number (92.9 FM and so on) is given, along with the genre (Country, News, Rock) and the time. The URL (which has been shortened for this example) is clickable and lets you listen to your ad. Finally, you see the estimated number of listeners.

Each radio station sets their fee per CPM. (CPM is Cost-per-Thousand, which means an audience of 1000 people.) For example, if the station has 5000 listeners in the time slot you selected, then that's 5 CPMs × $1.32, or $6.60 for the ad play.

In your ad, you use unique URLs that are easy to say, spell, and remember, such as MacysEaster.com or NikeShoes.com.

It's a good idea to work with a Google media planner. They use media planning tools to recommend the optimal stations to reach your audience. Start with two or three cities, test the campaigns, and then increase the campaign. You can also use Google Analytics' map to see where your customers are.

You should plan for at least four weeks of ads. Two weeks is too short. Eight weeks is better. Expect about $1000 per week for a small market, $2000–$3000 per week for a mid-size market, and $4000 per week for a large market. In general, plan your ads four to six months ahead.

Google Analytics lets you track your radio campaigns. You can see the number of impressions (potential listening audience), the number of ad plays, the cost, and the CPM. With unique URLs and tracking URLs, you can compare the radio campaign against other campaigns. If you find that Sports produces few results, you can drop that category. If you find Oldies does well, you can increase the ad plays in that category.

tip *You can stop a radio ad. However, the ads may still run for up to 36 hours after cancellation. You'll still be responsible for any charges accrued.*

Use Google to Advertise on TV

Just as with radio, you can use Google to place TV ads on cable and satellite TV. Similar to Google's radio service, Google offers a list of people who will write, direct, shoot, and produce the TV ad for you. Prices for video production are as low as $200. Also, pre-made TV ads (like stock photos) are available where you simply paste your logo at the end. You upload the TV ad into Google AdWords, pick TV channels, shows, time of day (day parting), day of week, and demographics. Bids start at $1 per CPM for 30 seconds.

Your TV ads show on CNN, MTV, ESPN, MSNBC, Cartoon Network, Animal Planet, CNBC, Comedy Central, Discovery Channel, and over a hundred other TV cable networks. Google's TV advertising reaches over 13 million U.S. households.

When consumers saw a TV commercial, 44% followed up with an online search (iProspect study, 2007), which makes TV as effective as word-of-mouth referrals. TV ads increase brand awareness by 63% (ThinkBox report, 2007).

Nationwide TV advertising takes about four weeks of ads at about $10,000 per week to be effective. There has to be repetition of the ads to get results.

TV ads tend to lose effectiveness after a few weeks. Track the results and see when your ads begin to fade. Launch new ads to refresh your campaigns.

We expect TV advertising may become the largest service at Google. Google has maxed out its market share and revenues in web advertising (they've reached *Stephanie's Limit*). AdWords brings in $20 billion per year. TV advertising is nearly $200 billion worldwide, of which $70 billion is in the U.S., where 98% of the population watches TV. Google may soon allow you to place TV ads worldwide through a simple tool.

Google's tools undercut the costs of traditional TV advertising production and placement. This will also lower the revenues for TV broadcasters. Ironically, when Google takes over the $70 billion TV market, it will deflate.

Use Google to Advertise in Newspapers

You can also use Google to place your ads in newspapers. You can design and lay out your ad with Google's tools, or you can upload a PDF in black-and-white or color. You can reach 40 million people via 790 U.S. newspapers, such as the *New York Times*, the *Los Angeles Times*, and hundreds of additional college newspapers, free dailies, Spanish-language papers, and alternative weeklies. You can select the day of the week (such as Mondays or weekends) or the section of the paper (such as sports or home and garden). Ads in the Sunday papers reach 52% of U.S. adults.

44% of newspaper readers follow up on products they see in the newspaper. Of those 44%, 67% use a search engine; 48% visit a store, and 23% call a store (Clark, Martire & Bartolomeo Inc. survey, 2007).

In contrast to the other tools, Google Print Ads doesn't use auctions. You propose the price you're willing to pay and the newspapers accept or reject the offer.

In general, the larger the ad, the more attention it will get. Quarter-page ads are better than small ads. You should also consider longer campaigns. A six-month campaign will get better rates than a short 2-month campaign. A campaign should run at least two weeks with three ads per week. Newspapers don't have the space limitation of radio/TV; if there are more ads, they print more pages.

Newspaper ads are similar to web landing pages: you should use a strong headline, a good image, and a strong call-to-action. It's a good idea to offer coupons or discount codes. Include telephone numbers, URL, e-mail address, SMS code, store locations, and store hours.

This will also become a large service at Google. Through a single tool, you can place an ad in hundreds of newspapers. Google will eventually expand this to other countries and offer a one-stop service for global newspaper advertising.

The Yellow Pages business telephone directory in the U.S. is collapsing. Companies have paid for Yellow Pages advertising for decades, but there was no way to track the results. People under 35 simply don't use the Yellow Pages anymore. We met with a company that spent $600,000 per year on Yellow Pages. They cut that to $300,000 and moved the remainder to online advertising.

Google's ad platform, based on the QS system and their analytics, allows you to manage your advertising to business goals. Analytics lets you compare all your campaigns by CPA, profits, and return on investment (ROI). You know what works and what doesn't. Advertisers are beginning to demand accountability from their ad agencies. Because you have other options, the expensive media will have to lower their prices to compete, just as newspapers have to adapt to CraigsList.com.

The Other Leading Brands: Yahoo! and Microsoft

Although Google's PPC gets most of the attention, there are two other major PPC services. Yahoo! and Microsoft have PPC ad services that let you place your ads into their search engines. Yahoo! APEX (Advertising Public Exchange) is a platform for integrated marketing across all of Yahoo!'s services and properties.

All three use the same basic principles for bidding and ranking. When you know one, you can easily pick up the other two.

People often assume Yahoo! is for "consumers," and Google is somehow more "technical." This isn't true. Yahoo!'s finance and business services are the standard in the business community. But as you've learned by now, massive unfocused traffic doesn't matter. It doesn't matter which search engine has 500 million users. You want to be findable by your target audience.

What's the practical difference? Because Yahoo! and Microsoft have fewer advertisers, in general the clicks are cheaper and conversion rates are better. They also have stricter editorial policies on keywords, which reduces competition. If Microsoft adCenter rejects a keyword but you think it fits in the campaign, send them an e-mail and they'll usually approve it.

We recommend you try all three. Set up campaigns at the following sites, see which one produces the best results, and then allocate your budgets accordingly:

- **Yahoo! Search Marketing**   http://searchmarketing.yahoo.com/

- **Microsoft adCenter**   https://adcenter.msn.com

You can also advertise in Facebook.com. Their PPC service is simple compared to the others. Use tracking URLs and try a few campaigns to see if it works for you.

Selling in China with Baidu.com

If your products or services can be sold in China, you can try Baidu.com. One of the ten largest sites in the world, Baidu is the search engine of China. Baidu.com has 62% market share in China, mainly because it works well with many features of the Chinese writing system.

Baidu is the largest marketing platform for Chinese. There are 1.3 billion people in China. About four million live in the U.S., and another 40 million are in other countries around the world. The Chinese online population is larger than the U.S. online population. In several more years, the Chinese online population will exceed the entire U.S. population.

Baidu's PPC is similar to the three major U.S. search engines. However, it is entirely in Chinese. You'll need someone who can read and write Simplified (Mainland) Chinese.

In contrast to other PPC services, Baidu allows an unlimited number of keywords. Advertisers can promote as many products as they want. Of course, we're talking about keywords in Chinese.

Baidu currently requires that you pay the setup fee in person in China. You're assigned a personal Baidu representative in the city where you register. Wouldn't that be an interesting idea at Google?

If your products or services can be sold worldwide, we recommend you keep Baidu in mind. It is currently only in Chinese, but just as Google works in other languages, Baidu will eventually be available in other languages. With 62% market share in the world's largest potential market, Baidu will let you advertise to a large audience.

Global Market Share

Here's an overview of market share in other countries, ranked by the number of online users. Look at your analytics. For most of our U.S. clients, Google produces 90% of their traffic. Numbers for other countries are from *Search Marketing Standard* (Fall 2007).

Country	Search Engines and Market Share	Population	Online Population	Percentage
USA	Google 89%, Yahoo! 6%, Microsoft 3%, Other 2%	303 million	211 million	70%
China	Baidu 62%, Google 20%, Yahoo! 13%, Other 5%	1.3 billion	253 million	19%
Russia	Yandex 49%, Google 23%, Rambler 17%, Search.Mail.RU 5%, Microsoft 1%, Yahoo! 0.4%, Other 3%	145 million	28 million	19%
Japan	Yahoo! 63%, Google 22%, Microsoft 4%, Other 11%	127 million	86 million	68%
Germany	Google 94%, Yahoo! 3%, MSN 2%, Other 1%	100 million	50 million	50%
France	Google 90%, Yahoo! 3%, MSN 2%, Other 5%	64 million	38 million	59%
UK	Google 79%, Yahoo! 8%, Microsoft 5%, Ask 5%, Other 3%	61 million	38 million	62%
Italy	Google 54%, Alice Search 13%, Microsoft 11%, Yahoo! 10%, Libero Ricerca 9%, Other 3%	56 million	31 million	55%

PPC for Web 2.0

Web 2.0 sites are generally social networking sites, based on the idea of allowing people to connect to others within their communities.

PPC can be used to promote Web 2.0 sites. You can use image ads to place ads via placement targeting on sites to promote your site. You can also promote your site with Google's additional ad services for radio, TV, print, and cell phones. You can use PPC to make the site findable in search engines to investors, job seekers, and so on.

Should I Worry about Click Fraud?

Click fraud happens when someone clicks on your ads with the intention of using up your budget.

Yes, there is click fraud, but it is so small that it is not cost-effective to deal with it. For various mid-size clients, we estimated the amount of click fraud to be a few dollars per month. However, it can take a full day of work to identify click fraud and several more days to negotiate for a refund of several dozen dollars. This isn't cost-effective, so we ignore it.

Google has made a significant effort to reduce click fraud. When they see a user making many clicks but not spending time at the site, Google ignores those clicks and refunds the costs to you.

Be careful with the small PPC services. We had a client who placed ads in a little-known PPC company. For $1000 they guaranteed 250,000 clicks. He indeed got 250,000 clicks in one week. With analytics, we saw that not a single one of those visitors looked at other pages. Even more curious, he offered a free 30-minute telephone calling card if you filled out a request form. None of those 250,000 clicks asked for the free calling card. Quite simply, the PPC company used software to produce the clicks on the client's site. The click fraud wasn't from competitors; it was from the PPC company itself!

If you want to try a small PPC service, use analytics to track the results. In general, you can negotiate a free two-week trial. Use URL tagging in your analytics tool so you identify the traffic from the service. If the service produces clicks that convert within an acceptable CPA, then you can expand your campaign with them.

Is PPC for You?

PPC doesn't work for everyone. Over the years, we've looked at PPC campaigns for several hundred companies. In some cases, PPC is not an appropriate solution.

Companies sell their products in one of two ways: sales or marketing. Which method they use depends on their relation to their customers and how well they know their customers:

- **Sales**   A sales-driven company knows its customers personally. It has a sales team. A salesperson may have a territory and visits their customers on a regular basis. There are only a few hundred customers, and the salespeople know each of them. These are generally repeat customers who buy substantial amounts. These companies rely on word of mouth, referrals, and personal connections to get their customers. Sales-driven companies include companies that build large industrial machines, advertising agencies, consultants, architects, lawyers, and so on. Many B2B companies depend on a sales team, not marketing.

- **Marketing**   A marketing-driven company knows their type of customer, but they don't know these customers personally. The target audience can be a fairly broad definition (such as men 35–45 who play golf). The company advertises in mass media to reach their target audience. Their marketing material tends to be impersonal and one-way: catalog orders via telephone, online shopping, or in chain stores.

Boeing is an example of a sales-driven company. There are perhaps only 100 buyers worldwide for Boeing airline jets. Boeing's sales team knows those buyers personally and they are courted with Bermuda golf trips, Wyoming ski trips, and so on. There is no point in using PPC; the buyers know the vendors and don't search the Web to find them. The vendors don't advertise in mass media (radio, TV, and so on).

In contrast, Callaway is a marketing-driven company that sells golf clubs to a customer base that includes millions of people. Callaway knows only the general demographic characteristics for their target audience. To reach golfers, they advertise in mass media, such as golf and sports magazines, the Web, newspapers, TV, and radio. For marketing-driven companies, PPC works well.

A sales-driven company can use SEO and PPC to increase awareness about the company within their market space. The company and their principals should be easily findable on the Web. However, the company should not expect to get many (or any) sales via the Web.

Sales-driven companies sometimes evolve into marketing-driven companies. They start off as a small group of experts and eventually turn their products into an offering that can be offered to a mass market.

How Do I Get an Account Rep?

This is an interesting question. It's not clear how Google decides to give you an account rep. It's not based on the amount of ad spend. We met a company that spent $50,000 per month at Google and Google wouldn't answer their calls. When they finally got someone at Google on the phone, they were told, "Spend more money!"

We've found it's much easier to get an assigned support person at Yahoo! and Microsoft. Just ask them. In fact, Microsoft's team is very friendly and casual. Ask them whatever you want, and they'll answer.

If you are a marketing agency and you manage a significant cumulative ad spend, there are agency support teams at The Big Three.

However, account reps won't solve your problems. At best, they can answer general questions, but they can't develop a strategy or implement it for you. They generally lack business experience. Account reps handle dozens of accounts. We know an account rep at one of The Big Three who juggles 600 accounts.

Your best solution is to either hire someone with experience or outsource your PPC to an agency. Don't hire someone who only manages your bids. PPC isn't a technical issue or something for the accountant. PPC is mostly a business issue. You need someone who understands your business goals, develops strategies, and carries out campaigns. They should have a working familiarity with websites and spreadsheets. They should also have a marketing sales background.

How to Get Help with PPC

If PPC is essential to your company, consider outsourcing it. In many cases, it's cheaper to hire an agency. A PPC agency may offer a team of five or six people that includes a PPC manager, SEO manager, copywriter, graphics person, link building, and so on, all for the about the same you would pay to hire one staff person.

The PPC agency shouldn't just manage your bids; they should work with you to manage the advertising as a business project. They should be proactive with recommendations and suggestions for new strategies. Google adds new tools nearly every month. Your agency should advise you if there are new services that are appropriate to your project. Here are some tips for selecting a PPC agency:

- Look up the company or consultant in LinkedIn.com and VendorRate.com. Talk with your business network and see if they are working with a reliable service. Ask for several references and call those references.

- Make sure your project isn't assigned to an intern. Ask the agency for the resume of the person who will do the work and then interview that person. Ask them to explain the process. They should describe how they use analytics as part of the PPC. They should have a sense of your business, your market, and your goals. If you're not satisfied, ask the company to provide another person.

- If the agency doesn't include analytics, strike them from the list.

How to Tell If Your PPC Agency Is Doing a Good Job

We're often asked to evaluate PPC accounts that are managed by other companies. Here's a checklist:

- The agency should identify the KPIs and develop a strategy to reach those goals. They should discuss CPL and CPA with you. Also, they should focus on conversions, not clicks.

- They should give explanations and make recommendations that include strategies to increase conversions, improve landing pages, and use multivariate testing. There should be recommendations at least on a quarterly schedule.

- They should install and configure analytics for you.

- They should configure the PPC accounts. The agency should be able to explain why they have selected the various settings (budget, location, language, and so on).

Here are several ways for you to check that they are doing work:

- Look at the QS for keywords. It should be OK, Good, or Great. There should not be keywords with a QS of Poor.

- Every ad group should have several ads. The agency should be using A/B split testing of the ads. There should not be any weak ads with unprofitable CPL/CPA. Turn on the display of deleted ads to see if they have been testing ads.

- They should work with you to develop landing pages. They should use multivariate or A/B testing to test the landing pages.

- You can see if they are actually doing work by reviewing the Change History (see Campaign Management | Tools tab). It shows the changes that have been made for the last 90 days.

The Future of AdWords

There is a lot of opportunity to improve AdWords. It was quickly built in 2002 by Google's engineers. It reflects an engineer's preference for numbers. The AdWords interface resembles the web stats reporting tools of that time (it shows the number of impressions, number of clicks, and so on). Most of that information is useless for advertisers. Because impressions and clicks are shown, some advertisers focus on the wrong numbers—and they try to get more impressions or clicks. For years, the AdWords tool showed only the conversion rate, but not the number of conversions. It now includes the cost-per-conversion and the number of conversions, but it doesn't show the amount of profit.

The worst number on the screen is costs on the bottom line of the table. This puts advertisers in the idea of controlling (and lowering) costs ("Costs are climbing, we must reduce them"). Instead, it should show the profit, so advertisers concentrate on increasing profits. If you saw a profit (and a chart with the profit trend), you would work on getting higher profits.

The ad groups report the bid, but advertisers generally don't notice that the CPC is much lower. They manage keywords according to bids, not the CPC. AdWords doesn't show the QS (aside from a cryptic Poor, OK, Good, or Great), so advertisers don't appreciate the significance of the QS. If Google showed the numeric value of the QS (and a trend), advertisers would have feedback to improve that number.

Google is tying the advertising tools and analytics closer together. Online advertising is merging with offline advertising. Google's quantification is turning advertising into a result-based process. This brings marketing to the attention of people with a business and finance background. They can apply their methods to maximize the value of marketing. This also means the use of BI tools to manage advertising.

PPC tools could include wizards to help people determine the profits, lifetime value (LTV), cost-per-lead, and cost-per-acquisition. The KPIs could be displayed as numbers and graphs on a BI dashboard. The PPC tools can be tied to various BI tools (such as Business Objects, Cognos, and so on).

The classical AdWords interface is outstaying its usefulness. It is a tool for managing PPC on the Web, but that is just one part of the palette of advertising services that now include radio, TV, newspapers, and mobile devices. Too many advertisers think Google PPC is just for web ads. The PPC interface has to evolve to encourage the advertiser to use all of the media ads, not just web ads. It should also include tools for managing the profits in SEO. The advertiser should be able to manage all forms of advertising according to their business goals.

Books on Advertising and Sales

We've found the following books useful (listed alphabetically by author):

- *Tested Advertising Methods, Fifth Edition,* by John Caples (Prentice Hall, 1998). This is a standard handbook for advertising.

- *How to Master the Art of Selling,* by Tom Hopkins (Business Plus, 2005). Excellent book on how to sell.

- *Phrases That Sell,* by Werz and Germain (McGraw-Hill, 1998). Over 5000 phrases divided into some 80 categories that have worked for decades in many forms of advertising. The book also includes two chapters on how to write ads.

- *Ziglar on Selling: The Ultimate Handbook for the Complete Sales Professional,* by Zig Ziglar (Thomas Nelson, 2007). It's much cheaper to close the leads you have than to get more leads. E-commerce is just a modern form of sales, and the basics haven't changed. For a handbook on closing sales, see *Secrets of Closing the Sale,* by Zig Ziglar (Revell Press, 2003).

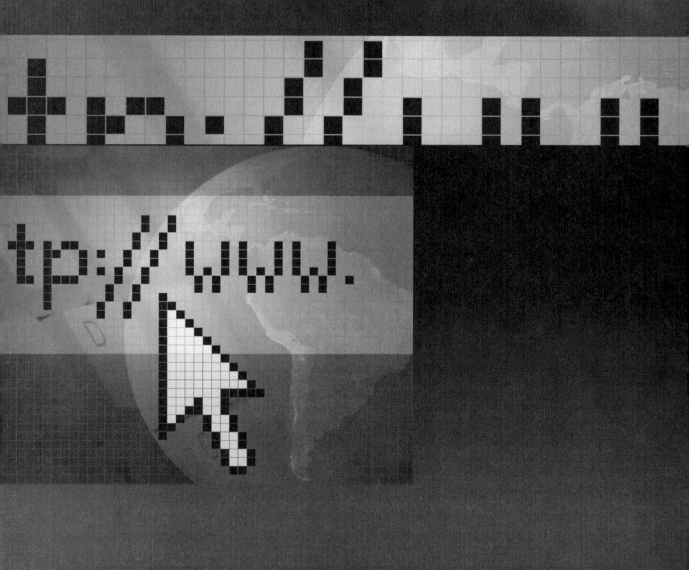

Glossary

Because integrated marketing cuts across so many areas (business, marketing, sales, analytics, SEO, PPC, and so on), we've collected some of the most common terms here.

Term	Context	Definition
A/B Split Testing	Marketing	Testing method used in marketing to find which ad performs better. Test two (or more) ads on the same audience and see which ad produces more conversions.
Action	Business	A lead converts into a buyer when he performs a defined action. Actions include register an account, subscribe to a newsletter, buy a product, download a PDF, and so on. The landing page should have a clear action for the visitor. See *Conversion*.
Analytics	Analytics	Tools that analyze and compare customer activity in order to make business decisions and increase sales. Analytics tools can report the number of conversions, the keywords that brought conversions, the sites that sent converting traffic, conversion by campaign, and so on. Analytics tools include Unica, Omniture, CoreMetrics, Google Analytics, and Microsoft Analytics. See also *Business Intelligence*.
Anchor Text	SEO	The text in the clickable part of a URL. For example, in the link <a href=http://www.Koi-Planet.com>Visit Koi Planet </a>, the "Visit Koi Planet" part is the anchor text.
Application Service Provider (ASP)	Analytics	Software services can be offered via an ASP model. The software is hosted on the developer's website and the clients often pay a license fee to use the software. For example, Google Analytics is ASP software. In contrast, some software is sold as installable software (on a disk).
Business Intelligence (BI)	Business	Software tools that gather, store, and analyze business data to help companies make business decisions. BI tools include Business Objects, Cognos, and Hyperion.
Business Rules	Analytics	Enterprise-level analytics tools allow you to create rules that automatically manage actions in the analytics. If a condition is met, a rule is triggered. This turns the analytics tool into automated decision-making. Omniture and Unica include business rules.
Call-to-Action	Marketing	In a landing page, clearly state to your visitor what you want him to do, such as buy a product, download a PDF, and so on.
Channels	Marketing	You promote your products via distribution channels. Channels include radio, PPC, TV, newspapers, bulk e-mail, podcasting, SEO, blogs, and so on.
Click Stream	Analytics	A visitor's path on your website as they move from page to page.

Term	Context	Definition
Click-Through Rate (CTR)	PPC	If an ad is displayed 100 times and 20 people click on it, that's a 20% CTR.
Close	Marketing	When you make a sale, you "close" a customer.
Close Rate (CR)	KPI	The ratio of how many leads turn into customers. If you have 100 leads and 25 turn into customers, your close rate is 25%. Also called the *conversion rate*.
Commodity	Business	A commodity is a product that is available from multiple suppliers. Table salt is a commodity. In a commodity market, producers and vendors generally compete on price. If you have many competitors, you either sell at the lowest price, launch a marketing campaign to develop a brand (an identity), or add a unique value, such as extended warranties. By using a USP (see *Unique Selling Proposition*), you can decommodify the product and increase the price. See *Differentiation* and *Disintermediation*.
Confirmation Page	PPC	When a visitor makes a successful conversion (he fills out a form, he buys a product), a confirmation page appears. It says "Your order was successful." You place conversion-tracking code on that page so you can track conversions. This is often called a thank-you page.
Conversion	Analytics	A conversion is a successful action by a visitor. If a visitor buys a product, he converts from visitor to customer. See *Action*.
Cookie	Analytics	Cookies are small files a website puts on your computer to store information about your actions that can be accessed in later sessions.
Cost-per-Action (CPA)	KPI	The cost for an action (or conversion). Divide the campaign costs by the number of actions to get the CPA.
Cost-per-Click (CPC)	KPI	The cost for a click. Divide the campaign costs by the number of clicks to get the CPC.
Cost-per-Lead (CPL)	KPI	The cost for a lead. Divide the campaign costs by the number of leads to get the CPL.
Cost-per-Thousand (CPM)	PPC	(CPM, where M is *thousand* in Latin) The cost of an ad measured by blocks of 1000 impressions. For example, if a newspaper ad is shown to 80,000 readers, that's 80 blocks of 1000 readers. CPMs are priced in dollars, such as $2 per CPM.
Cross-Channel Marketing	Integrated SEM	The ability to distribute a unified campaign across multiple channels. Instead of just using PPC, you use PPC, radio, bulk e-mail, newspapers, TV, and similar.
Customer Relations Management (CRM)	Marketing	Use CRM tools to manage customers to maximize profitability and service. A CRM system contains customer information, such as customer actions, purchase history, and customer preferences. Ideally, a company can tie together the analytics, BI, and CRM.

Term	Context	Definition
Data Mining	Analytics	Data mining is the art of identifying and extracting useful information from large collections of data in order to make business decisions. Analytics tools are capable of delivering hundreds (and thousands) of reports, but only a handful of these really matter. See also *Analytics* and *Business Intelligence*.
Data Warehouse	Analytics	Used in BI, a data warehouse is the collection of business data. It can include customer databases, inventory, and point-of-sale data. See *Business Intelligence*.
Day Parting	PPC	Displaying the ads only during certain days and hours, such as Tuesday to Thursday, 9 A.M. to 3 P.M. If your analytics shows that you get conversions only during those hours, you can save your ad budget by shutting down any advertising outside of those hours.
Designated Market Area (DMA)	Marketing	A country is divided into DMA markets, such as Los Angeles, Chicago, and New York City. Instead of using states or cities, you can use DMAs as advertising targets. Marketing people generally use DMAs, not cities.
Differentiation	Business	Making your offer unique from competitors. If you are in a commodity market (your product is the same as your competitors), you can compete either on price (offer a lower price) or differentiate by adding extra value, such as free shipping or an extended warranty. With a USP, you can differentiate yourself from competitors. See *Commodity* and *Unique Selling Proposition (USP)*.
Disintermediation	Business	This means "to remove the middleman." For example, MP3 players allow people to listen to their favorite 5000 songs without commercials. This cuts the radio stations out of the music, which ends their ability to sell advertising. The Web creates disintermediation because customers can connect directly to manufacturers.
DMOZ	SEO	Directory at Mozilla (DMOZ, pronounced *DEE-moss*), also called the Open Directory Project (ODP), is a volunteer project to create a human-edited directory of the Web. Many search engines used the DMOZ directory as part of their index. DMOZ has fallen in value in the last few years. Visit DMOZ.org.
Event-based Tagging	Analytics	Used in Web 2.0, event-tagging lets you track visitors as they click in a web page. It can track clicks, mouseovers, videos, and so on.
Funnels	Analytics	Used to track how many people enter a website and then drop out or continue at each step of the conversion process. This is also called *scenario analysis* or *path analysis*.

Term	Context	Definition
Goals	Analytics	A goal is a desired action at a website, such as a registration, subscription to a newsletter, purchase of a product, download of a PDF, and so on. See *Conversion.*
Hit	SEO	When a web page is viewed, each item on that page counts as a hit. If there are five images, there are six hits (the five images plus the web page). This means hits can be misleading when counting activity. What matters is the number of conversions.
Impression	PPC	An impression is when someone has the opportunity to see your ad. It doesn't mean they actually saw your ad. When you browse through a magazine, each ad gets an impression. Impressions don't indicate much.
Informational Content	SEO	Search engines prefer pages with information, such as articles, FAQs, help pages, and so on. Informational pages will rank higher than relevant pages (pages where the keywords are included). See also *Official Pages* and *Relevance.*
Integrated Analytics	Integrated SEM	Using analytics to measure multiple channels. See *Integrated Marketing.*
Integrated Marketing	Integrated SEM	The ability to distribute and manage a campaign across multiple channels. You measure the channels according to results and reallocate budgets to increase profitability. Similar to *Cross-Channel Marketing.*
Internal Search	SEO	A search box within a website. This lets visitors search within the web site.
IP Address	Analytics	Internet Protocol Address. The numeric address for a URL, such as 204.332.104.57. To find your IP address, use WhatIsMyIPAddress.com. See *URL.*
Key Performance Indicator (KPI)	KPI	The numbers that matter for your business. The top KPIs include Close Rate, CPL, and CPA See Chapter 2.
Keyword (KW) or Keyword Phrase (KWP)	PPC	This is the search term that someone enters in a search engine to search for something.
KPI	KPI	See *Key Performance Indicator.*
Landing Page (LP)	PPC	The visitor clicks on a link or ad and is brought to a landing page. The landing page is relevant to the visitor's search and offers a clear path to action (lead or purchase).
Latent Conversion	Marketing	A latent conversion is a visitor who visits a website but doesn't immediately complete an action. The visitor may take several weeks to return and buy. During that time, they are considered a "not-yet-completed conversion."
Lead	Marketing	Also known as a *prospect,* a lead is a potential customer.

Term	Context	Definition
Lifetime Value	Business	The lifetime value (LTV) is the total value of a customer's purchases over the lifetime of the customer. For many types of products and services, a customer returns again and again to buy more products. Instead of measuring customers by the value of a single sale, consider the total value from all sales.
Log File	Analytics	A web server records every action into a file: which file was requested, the time of request, any errors that occurred, and so on. Raw log files are a long list of numbers and are indecipherable to humans. Web stats software converts these numbers into tables and graphs. Log file tools evolved into analytics tools.
LP	PPC	See *Landing Page (LP).*
LTV	Business	See *Lifetime Value.*
Metrics	Analytics	An early name for analytics. See *Analytics.*
Microsite	PPC	A microsite is a small collections of pages which are focused on a product or a service.
Multivariate Testing (MVT)	Analytics	Multivariate testing tools let you create permutations of a page and then test all the versions to find which version performs better. MVT tools are either brute force (they test all versions) or they use Taguchi Method, which tests a subset. Google Site Optimizer is a free MVT tool. Offermatica is an enterprise MVT tool.
MVT	Analytics	See *Multivariate Testing.*
Natural Search	SEO	The unpaid results on the left side in search engines. On the right side are the PPC ads (paid placement). Unpaid listings are called *organic results, natural results,* or *algorithmic results.*
ODP	SEO	Open Directory Project. An open-source project by volunteer editors to create a human-edited directory of the Web. See *DMOZ.*
Official Pages	SEO	Search engines give the highest preference to the official page for a government office, university, company, organization, city, or person. If your site is the official site for your issue, be sure to state this clearly at your site. See also *Informational Content* and *Relevance.*
Optimization	SEO/PPC	Modifying the website or the PPC account to improve the results. You reduce costs that don't produce results and you improve the items that produce results.
Organic Search	SEO	See *Natural Search.*
Page Views	Analytics	How many times a web page has been viewed. A page may be viewed 200 times, but you don't know how many people saw it, because one person could have seen it 50 times. Unique visitors is a better number, but that doesn't really matter. What matters is the business goal, such as the number of conversions.

Term	Context	Definition
Path Analysis	Analytics	See *Funnels*.
Pay-per-Click (PPC)	PPC	This is an online advertising model in which you pay for each click on your ad. The three main PPC services are Google AdWords, Yahoo! Search Marketing, and Microsoft adCenter.
Persistent Cookie	Analytics	Also called a *permanent* or *stored cookie*. Persistent cookies are stored on a user's computer until they reach the cookies' expiration dates or the user deletes the cookies. Persistent cookies store information about the user's actions, such as settings, activity, and so on. See also *Session Cookie*.
PPC	PPC	See *Pay per Click*.
Referer	Analytics	When someone clicks a link on a web page to get to another web page, the first web page is the referer. Although the correct spelling is *referrer,* the variable is spelled *referer.*
Regular Expression (RegEx)	Analytics	A regular expression (regex) is a method for describing strings of text or numbers. This allows manipulation of the string. Regular expressions are used by programmers and database administrators. You use them to create filters in analytics. For more, visit www.regular-expressions.info.
Relevance	SEO	When someone searches for a term and the term appears on a web page, the search engine notes the page as *relevant*. This only means the keyword appears on the page. Search engines give preference to official pages and informational content. Both of those will rank higher than relevant pages. See also *Official Pages* and *Informational Content.*
Return on Investment (ROI)	KPI	ROI shows the effectiveness of your investment. Calculate ROI by subtracting costs from revenues, divide by costs, and multiply by 100. $[(\text{Revenue} - \text{Cost}) / \text{Cost}] \times 100 = \text{ROI}\%$ Remember that ROI is a number about a number. In situations with small numbers, ROI can be misleading. It's better to use CR and CPA.
Returning Visitor	Analytics	A visitor who returns to a website. Compare one-time visitors against returning visitors and see if there are differences in conversion rates. First-time visitors and one-time visitors are often looking for information. Returning visitors often look for product details and will buy.
Revenue	Business	The income that you get from sales or services.
Search Engine Marketing (SEM)	SEO	A set of sales and marketing strategies to position a web page or website for visibility online. This includes a combination of SEO and PPC. Due to Google's expansion into other media channels, SEM is evolving into integrated marketing.

Term	Context	Definition
Search Engine Optimization (SEO)	SEO	Improving a web page so your target audience can easily find it on the Web. Among SEO people, this is a verb ("We SEOed the website") and a person ("She is our SEOer").
Search Engine Results Page (SERP)	SEO	This is the position your web page gets in a search engine. For example, if your web page is at position seven, your page is number seven in the SERPs. This number is meaningless. What matters is the number of conversions.
Session Cookie	Analytics	Also called a *transient cookie.* A session cookie is erased when the user closes the web browser. Session cookies are used to hold settings during a session as you move from page to page. For example, shopping carts remember your selections as you move from the order page to the payment page. See *Persistent Cookie.*
Site Search	SEO	A search box in a website. See also *Internal Search.*
Spamming a Search Engine	SEO	Trying to mislead a search engine to rank your website higher. Don't do this. You'll rank higher for a few days and then you'll be banned.
Spider	SEO	An automated robot that crawls the Web via links on website pages.
Tagging	Analytics	See *URL Tagging.*
Thank-you Page	PPC	The common name for the confirmation page. See *Confirmation Page.*
Tracking Pixel	Analytics	Placing a blank 1 × 1-pixel image on a web page or an e-mail. When the page is viewed, the image is retrieved from the website's server, thus allowing the server to track the request via the log file. This is used for tracking views of pages and e-mails. Also called a *web bug.*
Traffic Analysis	Analytics	Another name for analytics. See *Analytics.*
Traffic Segmentation	Analytics	Using analytics to distinguish and compare different audiences. For example, you can segment your web traffic by Google users vs. Yahoo! users and see that Yahoo! users result in 22% more sales.
Unique Selling Proposition (USP)	Business	The unique selling proposition is a short statement that explains why a customer should buy from you instead of your competitors. It states the unique value that you offer, such as an extended warranty, certified service, and so on. Also called Point of Difference.
Unique Value Proposition	Business	Another term for USP. See *USP.*
Unique Visitors	SEO	The number of unique visitors who view a web page. A web page may have 100 visitors, but many of them may see the same page several times, so there may be only 60 unique visitors. This doesn't matter very much. Concentrate on conversions.

Term	Context	Definition
URI	SEO	Unique Resource Identifier. The name of the item requested by the user. This is usually a file (for example, index.html).
URL	SEO	Universal Resource Locator. The address for a website (for example, www.Koi-Planet.com).
URL Tagging	Analytics	Add a tracking tag to the URL to track activity. For example, in the URL http://www.koi-planet.com/koromo-koi.html/ ?source=google& medium=ppc& term=koromo, the URL tag starts after the "/?" and tells us the source is Google, the medium is PPC, and the keyword is koromo. This information is used by analytics.
USP	Business	See *Unique Selling Proposition.*
UVP	Business	See *Unique Selling Proposition.*
Web Analytics	Analytics	An early name for analytics. See *Analytics.*
Web Metrics	Analytics	An early name for analytics. See *Analytics.*
Web Page	SEO	A web page is a single document usually written in HTML, ASP, or PHP. A large website such as the BBC website could have millions of pages, whereas a personal website could have a few dozen pages.
Website	SEO	A website is a collection of web pages. See *Web Page.*

Index